SMITH COLLEGE STUDIES IN
MODERN LANGUAGES

Vol. XX, Nos. 3-4

Dostoevsky's English Reputation
(1881-1936)

by

Helen Muchnic

1969

OCTAGON BOOKS

New York

Originally published 1938-1939

Reprinted 1969
by permission of The Trustees of Smith College

OCTAGON BOOKS
A DIVISION OF FARRAR, STRAUS & GIROUX, INC.
19 Union Square West
New York, N. Y. 10003

LIBRARY OF CONGRESS CATALOG CARD NUMBER: 77-86281

Printed in U.S.A. by
TAYLOR PUBLISHING COMPANY
DALLAS, TEXAS

TABLE OF CONTENTS

PREFACE

IN THE preparation of a study even so restricted in scope as the present, one's indebtedness is too great to be fully acknowledged. Many kindnesses of friends and the stimulus of many books must remain unregistered. It is, therefore, in the face of an unavoidable sense of inadequacy and incompleteness that one lists with special pleasure those obligations which it is possible to record.

In slightly different form this book was submitted to the Faculty of Bryn Mawr College as a dissertation in partial fulfilment of the requirements for the degree of Doctor of Philosophy; and it is to Bryn Mawr College that my thanks are most particularly due. To Professor Samuel C. Chew of Bryn Mawr my debt is greatest. His work on Byron's fame* suggested to me the theme of this essay, and his patient and sympathetic guidance assisted me in bringing it to completion. To Professors Lily Ross Taylor, S. J. Herben, A. C. Sprague, to whom this study was first submitted, and to Professors Edna A. Shearer and Margaret L. Rooke of Smith College, who were good enough to read it in manuscript, I am also very grateful, for invaluable corrections and suggestions. To Mr. Avrahm Yarmolinsky of the New York Public Library I owe several important references which without his kind assistance I might well have missed. Finally, it was the award to me by Bryn Mawr College of the Helene and Cecil Rubel Fellowship that gave me the opportunity, in 1928, of reading at the School of Slavonic Studies of the University of London, under the direction of Sir Bernard Pares and D. S. Mirsky.

For those to whom the subject of this investigation may seem curious, I should like to say a word in explanation of its choice. The interaction between the cultures of different nationalities and its expression in art has been a problem of absorbing interest to me for many years. The extremely limited study presented in the following pages is but a fraction of an originally ambitious scheme, formed by me long ago and not yet wholly abandoned: to trace the influence of Russian literature on that of England. Dostoevsky's reputation, in other words, is to me a facet only of a large and complex whole, important not so much in itself as for what it implies with reference to that whole. However, as I hope the sequel may show, it is not, even as a fragment, devoid of independent meaning and interest.

* *Byron in England,* London, 1924.

v

The transliteration of Russian words presents some difficulties. Dostoevsky's name, for example, is spelled in a variety of ways: Dostoyevsky, Dostoievski, Dostojewski, etc. I have adopted in every case those forms which seem to be most generally accepted: Dostoevsky, Tolstoy, Turgenev, Raskolnikov, Karamazov, and so on. "English" I have interpreted broadly, including much American comment as well as that of Continental authors whose works have been translated.

I. INTRODUCTION

THE STORY of a great writer's fame has a twofold interest: it serves to gratify the curiosity which naturally attaches to important artists; and it illustrates, in a concentrated form, the progress of thought within a given time. The intellectual development of an age is often visible in the reputation of a single author, of an author, that is, whose work is deep enough to rouse judgments of such metaphysical and æsthetic implications as the merely superficial estimates of fashion cannot touch. Dostoevsky is such an artist. And what vital changes in thought and taste have occurred in Europe within the last half century are clearly traceable through the fortunes of his reputation. It is remarkable that although most of his novels were written in the 1840's and the 1860's,[1] they belong outside of Russia, to a later age and are properly classed in the twentieth century[2] and the late nineteenth. Especially is this true of England, for she has lagged far behind the Continent in knowing and appreciating him. In Germany *Poor Folk* appeared as early as 1850, *The House of the Dead* in 1864, and by 1890 nearly all of Dostoevsky had been translated.[3] In France also nearly all his works were known by 1890.[4] To England he came late, after 1880. He was not widely read there until after the publication of *The Brothers Karamazov* in 1912, and the first full English translation of his novels was completed only in 1921. But interest in him although tardy and fluctuating has been lasting, and his effect on modern literature is alleged to have been enormous. One of his recent biographers, and most sober critics, for example E. H. Carr, declared in 1931 that "nearly all the important novelists who [had] arisen in England, France and Germany during the past twenty years"[5] had been under his sway. Yet, although freely and constantly referred to, the nature and extent of this influence have never been fully analyzed. Brief studies of his relation to special authors have appeared from time to time.[6] There have been also summary discussions by recent biographers and journalists[7] and a doctoral thesis dealing with his influence on the English novel was presented a few years ago at the University of Heidelberg.[8] But that is all. This extremely complex and interesting subject demands fuller study than it has received. For such a study the present essay, however, strictly limited to critical opinion, stands only in the nature of an introduction.

Dostoevsky's fame, a less complicated theme than his influence, has

already tempted more than one student. As early as 1911 the Ukranian
University of Odessa granted a silver medal to Moisei Seidman for
an essay on Dostoevsky in the literature of the West.[9] This short work
is the first on the subject and is interesting for that reason; in other
respects, it is hardly satisfactory. Its bibliography is scanty, only the
most obvious German and French criticisms having been considered—
the English are not mentioned at all—and its conclusions are superficial and of debatable accuracy. A much fuller and more original work
is the Dutch study by Dr. J. M. Romein, *Dostojewskij in de Westersche Kritiek*.[10] Unlike Seidman's it is, if anything, too broad in
scope. Its survey includes not only Germany and France, but also
Spain and Italy, Scandinavia and England; and, covering so much,
is perforce schematic. Still, it is the most valuable work on the subject
and it has been spoken of highly by a recent Russian critic, F. P.
Schiller,[11] who confirms and elaborates its thesis that in spite of the
enormous amount of critical material about Dostoevsky in Western
Europe, he exists there but as a legendary figure. The significance of
this thesis, Schiller points out, rests on the assumption that "literary
fame is a social function, often used by one or another social group or
class to express its own objectives and ideas by means of literary
'critics', who frequently have nothing in common with the ideas of
the author 'criticized.' " In the clear statement of this view, according to Schiller, lies the merit of Romein's book; its weakness is that
although the legendary Dostoevsky emerges vividly from its pages,
the real Dostoevsky does not. Special studies have also been made of
Dostoevsky's reputation in Germany, by Theodorich Kampmann,[12]
and in France, by H. F. Minssen[13]—both of these, thorough and
well-documented monographs. Less complete but more penetrating,
have been certain articles by recent critics: that by Schiller; two by
Fatima Riza-Zade on Dostoevsky in recent French literature and on
Dostoevsky in Western criticism;[14] and a brief but meaty essay
on Dostoevsky in England and France, contributed to the *Slavische
Rundschau*[15] by D. S. Mirsky who, also, in his book *The Intelligentsia of Great Britain*, has devoted to the "Dostoevsky cult" in
England a brilliant, if caustic, page or two.[16]

Dostoevsky's introduction to England marked the culmination of
British interest in Russian culture, an interest which had been growing since the beginning of the nineteenth century. Up to 1821 nothing
of Russian literature was known in England. Then, Sir John Bowring
with his articles in *The Foreign Quarterly Review* and his *Specimens*

of the Russian Poets "made people in England conscious that there was such a thing as Russian literature."[17] Other translations and articles on Russian literature followed.[18] In 1827 in *The Foreign Quarterly Review* appeared specimens of Pushkin's verse,[19] and in 1845, translations of twelve of his lyrics by T. B. Shaw in *Blackwood's Magazine*.[20] There were other translations of Pushkin: of his verse, in 1835, and of his prose, in 1859. The first wave of interest seems to have died out in the 40's,[21] to be renewed again in the 60's and 70's when the poetic renderings of W. R. Morfill and Ralston's translations of Russian folk literature[22] were published. Of Gogol, apart from a short sketch, *The Portrait*, 1847, there was nothing until 1860 when *The Cossack Tales* were translated; and his more significant works did not appear in English until the 80's and 90's. Lermontov's *A Hero of our Times* was translated in 1854, and Krylov's *Fables*, twice in 1869.

Magazine articles in the 70's reflected this growing interest. "Perhaps no country in the world claims more attention at the present time than the empire of Russia," one reads in a journal of 1871,[23]

Impelled by the dictates of the spirit of Panslavism . . . she has been gradually stretching her conquering arms in every direction, and adding to her territory the countries of diverse peoples, until now she presents a threatening attitude towards her powerful neighbors on both her eastern and her western borders.

The article that began in this fashion maintained that too little was known about the history and the literature of "this mighty people" whom it was a mistake to look on as "barbarians" and whose literature it was wrong to imagine "as of too rude a nature to merit the consideration of scholars." The Russians, it was true, had "as yet produced neither a Shakespeare, a Corneille, nor a Gœthe, yet for more than a hundred years" they had been "steadily advancing towards this point, which by reason of their remarkable application and ability" it was "by no means certain" they would not attain. And the *Review* proceeded to give a brief sketch of Russian literature which, however, stopped short of the modern period. In 1876, *The Academy*[24] announced the publication by "Count George Tolstoy, the translator of Gogol's *Cossack Tales*" of "a highly important collection of documents relating to (and under the title of) *The First Forty Years of Intercourse between England and Russia, 1553-1593*." The following year, there appeared in *The Westminster Review*[25] a long and very well informed article on Russian literature, which began with a brief history of British interest in it. "The appearance

within a short time of each other of two histories of Russian literature," was its comment,

must be considered as a sign that an interest has been aroused among the
nations of Western Europe in the progress and development of their
Slavonic neighbors. A great change has come over the country since Mme.
de Staël sarcastically said of Russia that some gentlemen has amused
themselves with literature there.

It was since the Crimean War, in which Russia had "exhibited to the
rest of Europe a figure by no means contemptible," that Europe had
grown curious about its literature. In the detailed account of Russian
literature which followed, Turgenev alone of modern novelists was
mentioned, although Courrière, on whom the article in part relied,
had spoken at some length also of Dostoevsky.

These comments indicate the nature of the early interest in Russian
letters. It came in the wake of closer economic relations and of an
enforced political concern. A series of wars: the Napoleonic, the
Crimean, and the Russo-Turkish had brought Russia to the attention
of the West. It was not until she began to be feared that Russia
came to be known. In the 1880's, when Dostoevsky was first introduced, she seemed to England an increasingly powerful rival, and,
potentially, either a dangerous enemy or a valuable ally. The two
countries were competitors for markets in the Balkans, in the Far
East, in Afghanistan. Memories of the Crimean War and of the
Russo-Turkish War were still fresh. Russia had raised a high tariff
against English goods, and trade had fallen off. The reactionary
policy of Alexander III made Russia appear a backward, autocratic
power. Periodicals now contained numerous articles about Russia,
the titles of which alone are indicative of the nature of British in-
terest: "Russia before and after the War," "England and Russia in
Central Asia," "The Russians on the Amur," "Russian Development
and our Naval and Military Position in the Pacific," "Social and
Political Aspects of Russia," "The Army of Russia," "The Russian
Frontiers of the Austro-Hungarian Empire," "The Strength and
Weakness of Russia" and so forth. During the weak rule of Nicholas
II occurred the workingmen's strike in 1896, the formation of the
Social Democratic Labor party two years later, agrarian and
student riots in 1900. Then came the Russo-Japanese War, 1904-5,
and the first revolution, 1905. All these were violent movements that
disturbed and interested Europe. Friendly relations existed for the
short period of alliance during the World War, nullified, however, by

the treaty of Brest-Litovsk. The distrust and fear of Bolshevism, somewhat reduced during the period of the New Economic Policy, were revived again in 1927, as a result of Russian policy in China and her assistance in the British coal miners' strike. In short, for the last hundred and twenty-five years, Russia has, in friendship or enmity, stood constantly before the eyes of England.

But political interest and economic relations alone are not sufficient to make the art of a nation acceptable to a foreign people. Early trading with Russia in the seventeenth century, for example, had no artistic repercussions in England. The British traders, whether too proudly insular to appreciate a wholly foreign people or whether they found the discrepancy between the two cultures too great, had benefitted little by their contact with Russian language, religion, or folk art. It was Russia that had gained culturally from that early exchange,[26] but not England. The nineteenth century, however, presented a different picture. Russia had become Westernized. Her art was not so strange but that it could be appreciated. It possessed indeed, certain qualities of which European literature felt, at the moment, the need. Turgenev first captured the imgination of the West, and after him, Tolstoy, and finally, Dostoevsky.

Dostoevsky was brought to England as a "realist" when "realism," as applied to letters, was a comparatively new term and very inadequately defined. He roused at first a certain amount of curiosity as a new exponent of Russia and as a new "realist"; he was neglected in the 1890's when "realism" had given place in critical discussion to problems of "æstheticism'; he was idolized during the World War and the decade following; and since then he has been subjected to admiring but more scholarly criticism.

That the period of Dostoevsky's greatest popularity should have coincided with the World War is partly but not entirely due to accident. It so happened that the best translation of his work appeared between 1912 and 1921 so that only then was the way opened to a real appreciation. Furthermore, wartime propaganda in favor of Russia must be held in large part accountable.[27] But these circumstances do not explain the rhapsodies with which Dostoevsky was then received. The World War had intensified rather than changed the dominant ways of thought of the years immediately preceding, and the Dostoevsky cult embodied the heightened nationalism and individualism of an earlier period. It was a complex intellectual phenomenon, composed partly of war-time sympathies, partly of mysticism, partly of a new interest in abnormal psychology and in the revelations of psychoanalysis, partly of an absorbed concern with artistic experimentation. Dostoevsky represented an ally, a mystic, a psychologist of the unconscious, a designer of a new fictional form. The cult has not endured. But the Russian Revolution, which it would be natural to assume all important in operating the change, had, as a matter of fact, very little to do with it. It did not alter opinion of Dostoevsky, although it somewhat changed the emphasis of the admiration. The Revolution might be a calamity and Lenin, Anti-Christ; Dostoevsky remained Dostoevsky, the prophet of the Revolution just as before he had been considered the "voice" of the Russian nation. It was partly natural weariness with uncritical enthusiasm, partly the new knowledge brought by the publication of much biographical material, but mostly the spirit of the age, that served to effect the change. For, since the war, criticism has tended to interest itself not so much in adulation as in attempts to account for creative activity, as much as possible, in terms of understandable experience.

How it happened, then, that from mere curiosity and indifference Dostoevsky's reputation in England reached a stage of extravagant praise and finally subsided to a more sober appraisal, to the almost tacit neglect reserved for the "classics" of art, is the main concern of the present inquiry, undertaken in an attempt to discover what Dostoevsky has meant to England since he first became known there fifty years ago, and to suggest why interpretation of him has changed as it has. My essay makes no claim to exhaustiveness; but its conclusions are based, I believe, on sufficiently representative material.

II. FIRST YEARS—1881-1888

DOSTOEVSKY was heard of in England before he was actually introduced there. On December 25, 1875, *The Athenæum's* Russian correspondent, Eugene Schyler, mentioned[1] a story by him, "A Young Man," the subject of which, he said, was "the power of wealth in modern society." It might have been "an excellent book," he thought, for Dostoevsky's talent was "really great" and his "power of character analysis" remarkable. But he had "fallen into the habit of allowing himself too much importance to episodes, to confuse the main subject, and to draw out his reasoning to inordinate lengths," and had therefore become "simply wearisome." This is the earliest reference to Dostoevsky I have found in the English press, and the only one until 1880.

In that year a letter in *The Contemporary Review*,[2] dated St. Petersburg, Dec. 15, 1879, spoke of "a very interesting novel of Dostoevsky, *The Brothers Karamazov*" then "in course of publication." But the correspondent deemed it wiser to postpone discussion of it until after it had been completed. The same year Dostoevsky was mentioned again in *The Quarterly Review*[3] in an article of political import, "The Slavonic Menace to Europe" wherein he was classed with those Russian "imaginative writers" in whom one could "study Nihilism." His works were "yet more sombre and repulsive" than those of Chernyshevsky and Pisemsky. He was capable of putting into the mouth of "one of his hearers" (*sic*) a passage such as the following:

'Down with instruction and science; we have already enough to last us for a thousand years; the thirst for knowledge is an aristocratic thirst . . . ,' etc.

The *Review* could not "bring itself" to "transcribe" the passage in full.

But these are isolated and casual references. It was Dostoevsky's death, bringing reports of an elaborate funeral, that placed him more forcibly before the eyes of Englishmen. He died in 1881, and both *The Academy*[4] and *The Athenæum*[5] honored him in obituaries. *The Academy* described his work as preëminent in "the analysis of feeling . . . but nearly always feeling of a morbid tinge," which reached "full scope" in *Crime and Punishment* and "a still greater height" in *The Brothers Karamazov;* and compared the sombre effect of his stories, "the spell with which he [enthralled] his reader" to that of Edgar

7

Allan Poe. *The Athenæum* also mentioned Dostoevsky's "depth of psychological analysis" and his similarity to Poe, and spoke of "the mystic element" in his work which had gradually "assumed a more and more dangerous tendency" and had "threatened to ruin his genius." In England, according to *The Academy,* Dostoevsky was best known by his "Memoirs from the House of the Dead" which had been translated.

The translation to which reference was here made was Marie von Thilo's rather free rendering of Dostoevsky's Siberian memoirs. It was entitled *Buried Alive or Ten Years of Penal Servitude in Siberia,*[6] and was published in the year of his death. The comments which it received in several journals were highly favorable. The critic of *The Westminster Review*[7] was pleased that "this translation of his principal work," which was "as simple, as powerful, as *credible* in every detail as *Robinson Crusoe,*" would enable the English "to judge of the powers of one who was so highly esteemed by his countrymen." In *The Athenæum*[8] it was considered "a valuable aid towards the formation of correct ideas about penal servitude in Siberia." The book would be "widely read,"—was the prophecy of its reviewer—despite the "depressing effect" produced by "the melancholy nature of its theme." In *The Academy,*[9] W. R. S. Ralston, the Russian scholar and translator, thought it "a useful corrective to the sensational accounts of Siberian horrors which certain French writers of fiction" delighted to produce, noting as its "principal drawback" that it was "impossible to say what part of it [was] fact and what [was] fiction." In *Blackwood's Magazine*[10] the anonymous author of an article on prison life spoke of having dipped "into a book called *Buried Alive, or Ten Years' Penal Servitude in Siberia*" and of having found it "utterly antagonistic to all experiences of convict life in Britain." He quoted a portion of the book, "My First Impressions," to show that the laxity therein described would have been entirely unthinkable in the prisons of his own land, a point that had also been made by both *The Athenæum* and *The Academy.*

But the interest aroused by *Buried Alive,* was not sufficient to call forth other translations. None appeared until 1886, and in the meanwhile Dostoevsky was but rarely, and with one exception, only briefly mentioned. In October 1881, *The Fortnightly Review*[11] published an article which referred to him, for it dealt with his friend Nekrasov. Next year this article appeared again as the concluding chapter of a history of Russian literature,[12] the first such history in English. This was *Studies in Russian Literature* by C. E. Turner, lector in the University of St. Petersburg. It was an unpretentious little chronicle, historical in approach; in substance, a pleasantly readable account of the lives, works, and significance of the chief Russian authors from the seventeenth century to the nineteenth. Professor Turner made no claim to a profound understanding of his subject. His modest hope was "that an honest desire to comprehend and appreciate the character and aims of a people among whom [he had] lived for years" might save him from "glaring errors." He wished "to make the English reader acquainted with the tendencies of modern Russian literature," but he stopped with Lermontov and Nekrasov, and promised "a future volume to treat of [their] successors." The great novelists after Gogol were therefore barely mentioned. Dostoevsky figured as the friend of Nekrasov and as "the noble-hearted champion of the suffering and poor"; but his work was not discussed. Only the famous page from the *Diary of an Author* relating the "discovery" of *Poor Folk,* in which, as is well known, Nekrasov played a decisive part, was quoted at length.[13]

Greater interest in Dostoevsky was evidenced in reviews of the book than had been shown in the book itself. In *The Spectator,*[14] for instance, Turner was blamed for having insufficiently valued the place of the novel in Russian literature, whose greatest contemporary figures were "all novelists . . . Dostoevsky, Tolstoy, and Turgenev." And in *The Academy*[15] he was taken to task for having left "entirely unrepresented" certain important "phases of modern Russian thought": Dostoevsky, for example, as a champion of Panslavism as well as "an author of great talent, even genius . . . might well have found a niche in these 'Studies.' "

In another number of *The Academy*[16] the same year, a letter reprinted from a French journal, listed Dostoevsky together with two other Russian novelists, Goncharov and Ostrovsky, as an author whose works would "ever remain . . . a living witness to the memory of the time which gave them birth"; and in 1883 in *The Athenæum's* obituary of Turgenev,[17] Dostoevsky was declared to have surpassed his great contemporary "in delicacy of psychological analysis," but, unlike him, to have "succumbed to Panslavist tendencies." In 1884, Prince Kropotkin[18] referred all those who wished "to study the moral influence of Russian prisons on their inmates" to the "remarkable psychological studies" by Dostoevsky.

Then, in 1885, the first English article wholly devoted to Dostoevsky came out in *The Academy*.[19] It was a letter by H. Schütz Wilson, who related that when during a recent visit to Germany he had inquired of his "literary friends, what new books were receiving the attention of the reading public," he was told of "the great Russian writer, Dostoevsky . . . now exceedingly popular in Germany." He "found that two novels by this [to him] unknown writer, *Raskolnikov* and *Die Brüder Karamazov*, had acquired with extraordinary rapidity, a very high reputation in Germany." He was shown certain German criticisms of Dostoevsky, one of which, by Necker in the *Grentzboden*, concluded that Dostoevsky, "in some respects—particularly as regards ideal intensity—[was] the superior even of Turgenev." "Neither of his novels" was known in England, Wilson believed; and having sketched Dostoevsky's life, told something of his style and philosophy, and outlined *The Brothers Karamazov*, he translated a passage from *The Legend of the Grand Inquisitor*, and concluded that a work which could "yield such an extract" was "surely worthy to be made known to the English public."

The year 1886 saw translations of two of Dostoevsky's works, *Crime and Punishment*[20] and *Injury and Insult*,[21] and of two French studies of the Russian novel, Dupuy's *Les grands maîtres de la littérature russe*[22] and Melchior de Vogüé's *Le roman russe*,[23] all of which, but especially the last, served to establish Dostoevsky's fame.

In the critical notices of 1886, *Crime and Punishment* was, on the one hand, greeted as a work of extraordinary excellence, as a novel of a hitherto unknown, stirring realism; and, on the other, was condemned as incoherent and inartistic. In *The Athenæum*[24] Dostoevsky was declared to be, although little known, "one of the most remarkable modern writers"; and his newly translated work was hailed as "one of the most moving of modern novels." It was "realism, but such realism as M. Zola and his followers" did not "dream of." It was "more poignant and devouring" than the most stirring pages of Dickens. Every incident in it was "worthy of comment; every character . . . would furnish the matter of a long discourse." It was a book that compelled the reader to lead the lives of its characters, "suffer their tortures . . . breathe the very breath of their nostrils," a book of "strange completeness . . . as a work of art," which, in spite of a "sordid subject" and a "sense of grinding misery . . . [was] in the main ennobling and good." Similarly in *The Spectator*[25] Dostoevsky was said to be "in the opinion of some not indifferent critics . . .

superior to all other novelists of this generation," Turgenev and Tolstoy included; and was there estimated as "the one with the most
marked individuality of character, probably the most highly gifted,"
who while describing "sin in its most hideous shapes" was, yet, "full
of tenderness and loving-kindness" and showed us "that even the
most abandoned [were] not entirely bad, and that for all there [was]
hope . . . of redemption and regeneration." No one who knew the
"difference between good and evil would be the worse for reading it;
most people would probably be much better." Dostoevsky "sounded
the lowest depths of human nature, and wrote with the power of a
master. None but a Russian and a genius could draw such a character
as Rodion Raskolnikov . . . the 'Hamlet of the madhouse.' " According to *The Literary World*[26] there was "some wonderfully effective
writing" in Dostoevsky's "strange and startling novel, *Crime and
Punishment.*" "Even the minor characters" were "well described."
It spoke well for the "author's skill in narration" that although one
had "not much sympathy with any individual in the tale" one felt
"compelled to read on to the end." In the American *Literary World*[27]
the work was acclaimed a "masterpiece of one of the Russian masters
of fiction," the translation of which opened "the gates still wider"
on the "revelation of humanity" which Russian literature had already
brought. But to the critic in *The Westminster Review*[28] this "so-
called 'Russian realistic novel' " seemed "rather to be phantasma-
goric." "Hardly one of the characters" in it acted or spoke "like a
sane person." If it should be taken as "a realistic presentation of
Russian life and character, human nature in Russia must be strangely
unlike human nature everywhere else." There were, to be sure, "many
natural touches scattered here and there throughout the story" and
the whole was "powerful, and not without a certain weird fascination," but "a general want of intelligible relation between action and
motive, and an imperfect adaptation of means to ends" gave it "a
strange air of unreality, even to the verge of incoherency." It was
not "like real life either in Russia or anywhere else"; it resembled
a "wild, feverish dream." In like manner, the reviewer in *The
Academy*[29] considered that, although "not devoid" of certain desirable qualities: "literary force" and humour, an "almost Juvenilian
satire upon the present condition of society in Russia," the book was
"absurdly bepraised, extravagant, incoherent, and even tedious." Ignorant of the fact that Dostoevsky was dead, this writer declared that he

must "learn the art of condensation" if he wished to "become a successful novelist, of the realistic, or of any other order"; he should study Zola, who, whatever his faults, was "never wearisome"!

The same praise and blame held also for *Injury and Insult*. It would awaken much less interest, "whether of affirmation or denial" than *Crime and Punishment* thought a critic in *The Saturday Review*,[30] because it was "infinitely less morbid and dreadful, the style not nearly so excited and intense." But it was "typical" of Dostoevsky's "whole achievement"; and its merits, as with *Crime and Punishment*, were those of "character and emotion." Between the two views of Dostoevsky according to one of which his *Crime and Punishment* was "only tedious and unpleasant" but according to the other, a work of "unexampled vigour and directness," it was too venturesome to choose. Certainly, however, his novels established him as a "writer altogether apart" of whose talent there could be "no question," whose "view of life" though "mournful exceedingly" was "never ignoble." In *The Athenœum*[31] the qualities of understanding and sympathy which characterized *Injury and Insult* were emphasized. Although it was "a sad and depressing book to read" no one who read it carefully was "likely to deny the immense power shown by the author, his extraordinary skill in psychological analysis" and his " 'savage indignation,' " his "almost morbid sympathy" in the face of "the sorrows and sufferings of the needy and the oppressed." It was a book which deserved "much of the high praise" which had already been bestowed on *Crime and Punishment*. But William Sharp in *The Academy*[32] dwelt on Dostoevsky's stylistic deficiencies. Although he was reputed by "the Russians themselves" to be "the greatest of the celebrated trinity of writers," he lacked "a certain gracious air of intellectual refinement" which both Turgenev and Tolstoy possessed. The faults of *Injury and Insult* were "the same as those which characterized *Crime and Punishment:* too marked diffuseness, too intent a scrutiny of every physical and moral symptom, too microscopic a record of minor details." But the personages in it, he thought, were "drawn with even greater skill than those in *Crime and Punishment*." At any rate, "all lovers of the higher kind of fiction" would be "grateful to the publishers" if they carried out "their declared intention of publishing the complete number of Dostoevsky's sombre romances."

For the sake of completeness, one should mention also in this year the notice in the *Saturday Review's*[33] list of current French publications, of *Krotkaia* and of *Les possédés*. *Krotkaia*, "not, like *Crime and Punishment*, a long melodrama, but a collection of short stories of various kinds . . . all well worth reading" was capable indeed of giving "some people a higher idea of the Russian romancer than his supposed masterpiece." And *Les possédés*, together with Tolstoy's *Deux générations*, continued "the development of the Russian novel in Western tongues." There was constantly "more Tolstoy and Dostoevsky, Dostoevsky and Tolstoy," but "the 'pocket' of Russian fiction" would "no doubt, be worked out some day . . . even the Chincha Islands did not prove inexhaustible of guano."

Of the two studies of the Russian novel which came out this year, Dupuy's is the less important; Vogüé's, as will be shown presently, was of incalculable significance. Dupuy's *Les grands maîtres de la littérature russe*, translated in America by Nathan Haskell Dole, consisted of three clear, graceful, but neither very searching nor very learned essays on Gogol, Turgenev, and Tolstoy. Dostoevsky,—and this is indicative of the taste of the time,—was not included. He was, however, twice mentioned in the course of the essay on Turgenev: once, among those "superficial critics" who denied Turgenev "all capacity, all enlightenment, on the question of social order . . . certain fanatics, young or old, the Pisarevs, the Dostoevskys";[34] and then again, as the object of Turgenev's criticism, in a brief account of the relationship between the two novelists.[35] Turgenev's praise of *The Recollections of a Dead House* was mentioned, with its view that "the picture of the *banya* (bath)" episode was "worthy of Dante"; and his subsequently altered opinion of Dostoevsky's work was quoted: " 'God, what a sour smell! What a vile hospital odor! What idle scandal! What a psychological mole-hole!' " Dupuy's sympathies were entirely with Turgenev. It was, he said, when Dostoevsky's faults had grown "more pronounced" and his qualities became "mannerisms"; when his "keenness, once so fine and delicate [lost] itself in subtleties" and his sensitiveness changed to "supersensitiveness"; when his imagination came to gloat "over the pursuit of the horrible," it was only then that Turgenev's admiration changed to scorn and disgust. The original study contained no further consideration of Dostoevsky's work and no account of his life. But the translator evinced a special interest in Dostoevsky. He added to Dupuy's brief allusions a biographical sketch,[36] a translation of the *banya* passage,[37] and an elaborate footnote which cited the opinion of "a brilliant Russian lady, now in this country" concerning *Crime and Punishment*.[38] The Russian lady had written Dole as follows:

I am glad indeed that you escaped the translation of *Crime and Punishment*. You would never find readers for such a book in this country. I could never read any of Dostoevsky's books through. It made me sick. My nerves could not stand the strain on them. I don't believe in pathology in literature. And yet another of my American acquaintances, who is thoroughly versed in Russian, . . . tried to translate *Crime and Punishment*, but had no time to do it. He says he never read in any language anything so powerful as *Prestuplenie i Nakazanie*. Generally speaking, your countrymen have too healthy a constitution to appreciate such a novel. Let it turn heads among the pessimists of France and Russia, the natives of effete Europe.

The book was, on the whole, favorably reviewed. "The English people," according to *The Athenæum*,[39] had "only just discovered, as it were, this vein of gold, this strange thing called Russian literature," and a readable work about it was very welcome. It was true, M. Dupuy had not "attempted to bore very deeply into the mine, but . . . he awakened the reader's curiosity . . . and stimulated his interest." The reviewer in the American *Literary World*[40] expressed enthusiasm, with perhaps a slight touch of irony directed against the reading public. "As now constituted," he wrote, the work formed so admirable an introduction to "the study of the chief productions of the writers considered" that it might even render "that task unnecessary to the generality who find Russian Literature in *puris naturalibus* too strong a pabulum for enervated mental digestions."

The great charm, the great power of Russian Literature [he continued] is its ingenuousness, its apparent artlessness, absolute lack of selfconsciousness. Here are no traditions as to what subjects are or are not fit themes for literary treatment; here are no set methods for the management of given situations. . . . The descriptions are daring, even audacious; but the most delicate topics are touched upon with an innocent refinement of thought almost childlike in its simplicity. Compared with such realism the brutality of Zola is forever intolerable. The difference is that in the most realistic of the Russian novels from Gogol to Dostoevsky, the characters are men and women however degraded . . . they are human and not animated embodiments of the cardinal sins.

The review closed with the hope that the incipient realism in English and American fiction would follow "the poetic realism of Turgenev and Tolstoy rather than the brutalizing naturalism of Zola"—in M. Dupuy's words, the " 'natural and generally passionate' " observa-

tion of the Russians instead of the " 'systematic and cold' " variety
of the French. A critic in the American *Nation*,[41] on the other hand,
had not much to say for the book, "reared," he thought, "like an
inverted pyramid, on the microscopical incident that the author had
a speaking acquaintance with Turgenev." He took Dupuy to task for
depending upon "mutilated" French versions of the authors of whom
he wrote, and for credulously accepting absurd stories about Turgenev;
and pedantically held up to scorn certain mistranslations in the English version.

Vogüé's work, *Le roman russe*, marked an epoch in the history of
Dostoevsky's fame. To it, much more than to Frederic Whishaw's
translation of *Crime and Punishment*, was due the English readers'
acquaintance with the Russian novelist; and it must, therefore, receive
a fuller analysis than Dupuy's book. The Vicomte E. Melchior de
Vogüé, as is well known, was a French nobleman, a diplomat, and
a man of letters.[42] In 1877 he had been appointed secretary to the
French Embassy at St. Petersburg, and in the course of his stay there
had grown enamoured of Russia and all things Russian. He studied
Russian history and was enthusiastic about Russian literature; he
married a Russian lady, and met several Russian authors, Dostoevsky
among them. What he might say about Russia, therefore, would bear,
the public had a right to feel, the stamp of authenticity, so that it is
not at all surprising that the articles on Russian literature which he
published in the *Revue des Deux Mondes* from 1882 to 1885 should
have been enthusiastically acclaimed, and should have achieved, when
they were presently revised and collected in book form, great popularity in all western Europe. The book, *Le roman russe*, became a
"classic," the "main landmark in the history of the penetration of
Russian literature into western Europe."[43] An English translation
was immediately made, and Vogüé's importance straightway recognized: "It is to his articles," according to *The Nation*,[44] "that French
and English readers [were] indebted for a knowledge of Tolstoy and
of Dostoevsky and even of Gogol."

Dostoevsky emerged from Vogüé's pages a being of another world,
"an abnormal and mighty monster," a unique colossus, a barbarian,
the primitive Russian, the "true Scythian," in whom cruelty and
tenderness, love of the actual and love of the abstract were extraordinarily blended in a kind of "mystic realism." Dostoevsky was the
most Russian of the Russians; not the greatest of their novelists, for
his vision was circumscribed, limited to darkness—he was a far travel-

ler who had admirably recorded his observations but had travelled only by night[45]—but the one who had best expressed the religious beliefs and aspirations of the Russian people, their feeling of compassion for the oppressed, their "fundamental conception of Christianity": that suffering is good "in and for itself." With Dostoevsky the humanitarianism of the 40's had risen to a "desperate pity." He himself had suffered. A man acutely sensitive to the misery of the humble, nervous, epileptic, he was condemned to death, reprieved at the last moment, sent to Siberia, where he had to live in the company of vulgar scoundrels.

To appreciate his work, "the superb and cruel" *Memoirs of the Dead House*, his masterpiece, *Crime and Punishment*, one must understand all this. For, Dostoevsky's books, filled with horror, were painful reading, not recommended to women and to "impressionable natures," nor to those who look for pleasure in the novels they read. All the classics of the "genre inquiétant," Hoffman, Poe, Baudelaire, paled before these terrifying productions; and the Naturalists themselves did not surpass him in minute analyses of the commonplace and the ugly. To read *Crime and Punishment* was to make oneself voluntarily ill, of an illness from which one never completely recovered. Yet, Dostoevsky's realism was not that of the "scientists" nor of the horror-mongers. He did not revel in painful experiences, although he did not shrink from them. There was nothing of detached artistic enjoyment in his pictures of the horrible: he was himself as terrified by them as his readers. If he made one suffer it was for a good end: he was a surgeon who inflicted pain only of necessity, he wrote in order to heal.[46] " 'Une pointe de sadisme' " one did perhaps encounter here and there, Vogüé admitted, but Dostoevsky's "pious dream" transcended all painful actuality; the quality which made him great was his "sympathy of intelligence illuminated by love."[47]

Other qualities also Vogüé allowed him: profound psychological insight—*Crime and Punishment* was the best study of criminal mentality since *Macbeth*;[48] a simple, unostentatious style, characteristic indeed of all Russian realists, a style which "mounts drop by drop until one finds oneself suddenly lost in a deep lake, submerged under a rising melancholy";[49] the power of suggestiveness—Dostoevsky's pages, as well as Turgenev's "awakened resonances," like the sound of an organ,—they were great through what they left unsaid;[50] and, in a few instances, in *Poor Folk* and *Crime and Punishment*, the ability to construct a work so solidly as to make even quotation from it impossible—they were like Greek temples: a passage from them was a stone removed from a perfect edifice, without beauty or significance apart from its assigned place.[51] But Dostoevsky was the author of only three great books:[52] *Poor Folk, Memoirs from the Dead House,* and *Crime and Punishment.* With *Crime and Punishment* "le talent avait fini de monter," and after it, in spite of magnificent attempts, he was never again successful. *The Idiot, The Possessed,* and *The Brothers Karamazov* were all of impossible *longuers,* all of them failures.

One did not know, wrote André Gide years later,[53] whether to be grateful to Vogüé for his introduction of Dostoevsky to a large reading public or to be irritated by the narrowness of his appreciation. Certainly the book was very influential. Over and over again in the Dostoevsky criticism of the following decades one hears Vogüé's ecstatic tone adopted as the proper method of comment on "the Russians" and his judgments echoed down to minutest reverberations of detail: Dostoevsky as the typically Russian barbarian, as the surgeon, as the sympathetic realist, as the literary Millet, as the writer of an unanalyzable style, etc., etc.; and fifteen years passed before an English critic had courage and originality enough to speak highly of *The Brothers Karamazov,* while the phrase "the religion of suffering" has clung to Dostoevsky to this day.

What novelists themselves, rather than critics, have thought of Dostoevsky is, naturally, a matter of special interest; and, as will appear in the course of this study, English novelists have frequently expressed their opinion of him. It is in 1886 that we are given the first record of these views, that of Robert Louis Stevenson who, having read *Crime and Punishment* in French translation, wrote of it as follows to John Addington Symonds:[54]

Raskolnikov is easily the greatest book I have read in ten years; I am glad you took to it. Many find it dull; Henry James could not finish it: all I can say is, it nearly finished me. It was like having an illness. James did not care for it because the character of Raskolnikov was not objective; and at that I divined a great gulf between us, and, on further reflection, the existence of a certain impotence in many minds of to-day, which prevents them from living *in* a book or a character, and keeps them standing afar off, spectators of a puppet show. To such I suppose the book may seem empty in the centre; to others it is a room, a house of life, into which they themselves enter, and are tortured and purified. The Juge d'Instruction I thought a wonderful, weird, touching, ingenious creation:

the drunken father, and Sonia, and the student friend, and the uncircum-
scribed, protoplasmic humanity of Raskolnikov, all upon a level that
filled me with wonder: the execution also, superb in places. Another has
been translated—*Humiliés et Offensés*. It is even more incoherent than
Le Crime et le Châtiment, but breathes much of the same lovely goodness,
and has passages of power. Dostoevsky is a devil of a swell, to be sure.
Have you heard that he became a stout, imperialist conservative? It is
interesting to know. To something of that side the balance leans with
me also in view of the incoherency and incapacity of all.

It has been thought that Stevenson was to some extent influenced by
Dostoevsky,[55] but whatever may be judged of this possibility Stevenson's admiration of the Russian author cannot be doubted; and the
distaste of Henry James, which his letter mentions, is as significant
in a study of literary predilections as his own enthusiasm. There will
be occasion to quote both authors again.

A brief and almost incidental mention of Dostoevsky in 1887 gives
evidence of his increasing popularity. In *The Saturday Review*,[56]
again in its list of French publications, occurred the remark that "the
admirers" of Dostoevsky would "rally round" his most recently
published work, *L'ésprit souterrain*, "as a matter of course," and that
therefore, there was "no more to be said" about the book. Other,
and perhaps better evidence is the continued publication of his work
in English translations and their reception. Four translations came out
this year: a new version of the Siberian recollections, entitled *Prison
Life in Siberia*,[57] *The Friend of the Family* and *The Gambler*,[58]
published in one volume, and *The Idiot*.[59]

Reviews of *Prison Life in Siberia* show a growing awareness of
Dostoevsky's peculiar qualities: they tend to point to what is characteristically Russian in his work, to what is *echt* Dostoevsky, em-
phasizing especially his "realistic" effects. "Prison Life in Siberia,"
according to *The Critic*,[60] for example,

is a detailed description of such horrors as one is ready to expect from
such a theme, treated with the vigor and power by which Fedor Dostoevsky gives intense vividness to any subject he chooses to handle. There is
little attempt at a story, and none at all at fine writing. The bare facts
are sufficient to rely on for startling incident; and human nature can be
twisted to feel the sympathy desirable to rouse, without the aid of any
magnetic rhetoric.

In *The Saturday Review*[61] it was recalled that an earlier version of
the book had appeared "some six or eight years back" when Dostoevsky "was practically unknown." The new translation, read "well

enough" and conveyed "that quality of strange and dreadful life" to impart which was Dostoevsky's "peculiar gift." The substance of the book was "poignantly interesting," but its effect, of course, was that of all Russian fiction, "mostly wretchedness": "merely to peruse" it was "to take on a fine gentlemanlike melancholy" and to "study [it] deeply" was "to be miserable for the rest of one's days," whether the author were Tolstoy or Gogol or Dostoevsky or Turgenev. In the present case, the process of going through the whole work might "be by no means to [the reader's] liking," but the book was a masterpiece nevertheless. *The Athenæum's*[62] reviewer also thought it "difficult to read through." Had it been "a work of imagination," it might have been more palatable, but as it stood, it would be read "a few pages here and there." Just the same, it would produce "the effect intended by its author," for one was "struck" in it "by the matter-of-fact character of the prisoner's impressions." In *The Academy*[63] it was mentioned by E. A. Brayley Hodgetts in a review of Kropotkin's *In Russian and French Prisons.* "The student of the Siberian convict system," he said, "should read also the reminiscences of another victim of Russian autocracy, Dostoevsky, now dead." He took the "opportunity of complimenting" Mr. Sutherland Edwards on his "elegant and faithful rendering" of "one of the masterpieces of Russian literature"; and declared that nothing could be "more powerful in style and more realistic than these ghastly experiences, told in simple language."

Comments on *The Friend of the Family* and *The Gambler* show a baffled willingness to appreciate. Taken as photographic reproductions of Russian *mores,* the stories proved puzzling indeed, and their glaring similarities to Dickens served only to throw into relief what seemed to be fundamental differences between British and Russian ways of looking at things. *The Friend of the Family* it was noted, for example, in *The Scottish Review,*[64] was "thoroughly Russian" and those who were "in quest of a new sensation" would find it there:

The country, society, feeling, and habits of thought are altogether different from anything to be met with amongst ourselves. The friend of the family is a strange being, a kind of Russian Pecksniff and though probably impossible in English society, quite possible, we would say, in Russian.

The principal characters were "all powerfully drawn" and the "very simple plot [was] admirably worked out." According to *The Athenæum*[65] it was "difficult to believe that *Crime and Punishment* and *The Friend of the Family* [were] by the same hand, and were con-

tained in the same brain." The hero of the latter, "a kind of Russian
Pecksniff" was "a capital creation" and the other characters also were
good; but the whole was a "rather truculent essay in what may be
called the satirical farce of character." There was more of "the true"
Dostoevsky in *The Gambler,* which was "very powerful." The principal characters were "rendered in a fashion nothing less than masterly"; it was a story that fixed "the attention at once, and to begin
it [was] to be constrained to read on to the bitter end." But the
translation, although "lively enough" was "so full of slang as to
produce an effect of real vulgarity." In *The Spectator*[66] also the work
was thought to have suffered in translation, for it was "characterized
by that farcical kind of humour," not unlike "the trial scene in Pick-
wick" which would "not bear without almost entire loss of its essential quality, reproduction in an alien tongue." Indeed, Dostoevsky's
humour, one could imagine, was much like Dickens', the friend of
the family being a "Muscovite Mr. Pecksniff" who, however, "done
into English" seemed "so utterly incredible that it [was] impossible
to laugh at him as we laugh at the Salisbury architect." *The Gambler*
was "more satisfactory" but it was "straggling"; one had to "wade
half way through it" to "understand the relations of the characters
to each other." According to *The Literary World,*[67] *The Friend of
the Family* was "a lively farce, admirably concocted and full of
clever touches" whose plot "would readily lend itself to stage effects."
In *The Gambler* there was "humour of a saturnine sort"—but both
stories were marked by an "extravagance of expression and uncon-
trolled style of action" which might be "accurate as portraying Russian fashions, but [would] strike the English rather unpleasantly."
In *The Saturday Review*[68] neither story was considered capable of
supporting "the very high reputation of Dostoevsky." The tales
were written "in an old-fashioned manner" that reminded one of
Smollett, "the characters being excessively high-coloured, the senti-
ments elaborately ironical, the bustle of incidents extreme." But it
must be admitted that "to judge a work of fiction by a translation
alone" was "excessively unfair," and Dostoevsky's reputation "in his
own country" was such as "only work of an exceedingly high order"
could have created. The critic would not "profess to say" therefore
how much of what left him "languid" in *The Friend of the Family*
was due to Mr. Whishaw. William Sharp, once again in *The Academy,*[69] wrote that Dostoevsky was "likely to become as familiar to
French and English readers as Turgenev himself"; but that the

"radical difference between Eastern and Western ways of looking at life" became "more and more manifest" in his work, so that the two stories which had just been published could "hardly attain popularity" in England. Dostoevsky was "absolutely Russian, the un-Westernized Russian"; and this, although it added to the interest with which his "sombre tales" were read, stood in the way "of their popular appreciation." Furthermore, *The Friend of the Family* was "terribly diffuse" and *The Gambler,* although "more interesting," was also too verbose; "one [wearied] for the analyser to become the romancist." A reviewer in the American *Public Opinion,*[70] was also overwhelmed by the strangeness of *The Friend of the Family:*

Russia to most of us is such a *terra incognita* [he wrote] and the social conditions of the people in remote districts so different to any aspect of Western life with which we are acquainted, that we have, as it were, no unit of measure to test the truth and realism of the character-drawing in this interesting but very singular work.

The Gambler he thought "less amusing" but both stories were "very valuable as pictures of a society and a people with whom we are imperfectly acquainted, but who deserve the closest study." Dostoevsky, he said, was "one of the keenest observers of humanity amongst modern novelists."

The reception accorded *The Idiot* was much like that which *Crime and Punishment* received: vociferous in both praise and blame, and on the same grounds. It might be "considered tedious by ordinary readers," according to *The Athenaeum,*[71] but "upon those minds to which its author's other writings appeal with irresistible force" it would "exercise a weird fascination." It was as "unconventional" as *Crime and Punishment* and *Injury and Insult,* and as "rich as they . . . in minute studies of moral disease." But why, even so, one wondered, was Dostoevsky popular in England? It was "easy to understand the immense charm which such works" could have for Russian readers who were "terribly in earnest in their study of vexed social problems" and found "only in fiction the free discussion of questions of that nature." It was "more difficult to explain the remarkable influence they [had] recently exercised in France and, to a certain extent" in England. *The Spectator*[72] reviewer declared that "the appearance of a well-defined and original figure in fiction" was "an event of too rare occurrence to be passed over in silence." He therefore wished "to make known" that Prince Myshkin was such a figure. But in spite of this *The Idiot* was "tedious reading on the whole": without plot, "composed chiefly of a series of scenes strung together on a slender thread of story," inadequately translated, furthermore, and thus suffering from "a good deal of disjointedness and want of smoothness." Some of its incidents were probably not "taken from real life" although they were not "absolutely impossible" and there was "not a single pleasant [scene] to be found in the whole series." Perhaps that was "only what might be expected in a novel which [professed] itself 'realistic,' " since the term seemed to imply necessarily an interest in the "ugly and disagreeable." And yet, this critic reminded aspiring authors, the world contained much that was "fair and beautiful" and those among them who were "desirous of popularity" should "bear in mind that the so-called realism which [consisted] in a display of deformities, more or less hideous, dragged forth and paraded for the public to gloat over . . . [was] unquestionably unpleasant." In *The Literary World*,[13] *The Idiot* was considered "the best of the batch" of four recent realistic novels. The other three were "decidedly nasty"; Dostoevsky's was "peculiar rather than nice," but, at least, it abounded "in striking dramatic situations" and had "an estimable, though weakly, character to its hero." According to *The Saturday Review*[14] "the new Dostoevsky —*The Idiot,* as it [was] called—[was] not particularly good." It was confusing, disappointing, and tedious. One seemed, when one had read it, "to have been living in a madhouse"; the personages in it were "violent and uncommon"; the incidents, "fantastic" and "strange." The "idiot himself" was "the only sane thing in the book" and when one last heard of him he had "lost his wits for ever" and was "the maddest of them all." The book was "harder reading than it ought to be"; it was impossible "to keep the wits abreast of the author's intention." Of course, being Dostoevsky's it was bound to contain "a number of striking conceptions, with not a little excellent dialogue, and more of the better sort of description than the average novelist [was] ever able to command." His "results" indeed were "plain enough" but not the process by which they were reached. To understand that, was "a joy reserved for readers whose state of mind [was] more or less abnormal." Similarly, for the critic in *The Westminster Review*[15] there was no merit in the work:

No one person in it seems really sane. Indeed the so called 'Idiot' is throughout the greater part of the work quite the sanest of the party. . . . Every one seems to act, speak, think, feel, as no man or woman ever did, out of a Russian novel.

Apart from these reviews, two longer studies of Dostoevsky appeared in the course of this year. In an article on Russian novels in *Scribner's Magazine*,[76] Thomas Sergeant Perry wrote of him at some length; and in *Macmillan's Magazine*,[77] a long article by John Lomas was devoted entirely to him.

Perry's article was designed to show in what respects and why Russian fiction was superior to English. The difference lay, he said, in the seriousness, the honesty, and the artistic independence of the former as against the superficiality and the conventionality of the latter. And the reason for this was a social one. The English novel was "the mirror of a calm conservatism." If it looked at all "at the storms of life" it looked at them "only through the windows of a comfortably warmed and charmingly furnished room." Its "monotonous record of tennis and dinner parties, its tepid love-making, its judicious distribution of moderate wealth, its exalted aristocrats, worthy clergy, and strictly subordinate peasantry and working people" reflected a life where "the ghosts of the past [lived] long in secure entrenchments," a life that was not "eager and impetuous." "Clouded by a host of literary conventions" which were mistaken "for real things and confounded with facts," it lacked that quality of fresh vision which made the Russian novel what it was. Whereas in England, readers had "all become accomplices of the writers," were "perfectly familiar with the working of the machinery," and knew precisely to which page to turn, "toward the end of the book," where the hero, having tumbled down a well or been supposedly lost at sea, returned "dripping with fresh or salt water, as the case [might] be and [married] the constant heroine," in Russia, it was possible to treat the most hackneyed subject in an entirely new way. Dostoevsky, for example, had used the theme of a "murderer's heart" as no one else had used it: "not with any design of playing an amusing game with the reader, hiding a secret, as children hide a handkerchief, leaving the work of guessing to be done for a discreet time, and then making the mystery clear by bringing out the missing object from beneath the hearth-rug or from behind the clock. Nothing of the sort." He forced one to stay with the murderer from the moment he thought of the crime, "through his subsequent sufferings, and up to his absolution." One's mouth grew "dry with terror" at the recital "of his agony and fear of detection." Such was the effect of "realism" when writers "set their foot on the earth, not in an imaginary region" and described what they saw. Raskolnikov, to be sure, was a Nihilist; but realism might be considered the literary expression of Nihilism, for its "whole meaning" was the "denial of conventionalities." It was "not merely" that Nihilists such as Raskolnikov were written about; "that, if done only from the outside, would be of comparatively slight importance." It was rather that in the very "appearance" of "realism" one recognized "the voice of Nihilism." One perceived it "in the whole list of Russian novels."

John Lomas found much the same distinction as Perry between the English and the Russian novel. Fiction in England, he said, had come to depend for its success on academic rules—all of which in Russian work were "ignored with the most direct and evidently untutored simplicity." One met there with a man who had "a tale to tell" which he "poured out" in "his own intensely thoughtful fashion, quite regardless of any set of guiding principles save those of his own intuitive genius." And of these story tellers, the most interesting was Dostoevsky. His "materials were more solidly arranged, his purpose and plea more direct, and his analysis of human nature more searching, subtle and true" than those of "his great rivals," although "his range of conception and expression" was "more limited" than theirs. For the rest, Lomas echoed Vogüé. He told again the well known dramatic episodes of Dostoevsky's life; remarked upon the unostentatious quality of his style—"there is no striving after effect, no mere fine writing for the sake of display . . . no *striving* after anything . . . the whole thing hangs together naturally, page by page and scene by scene"; spoke of the humanitarian implications of his work: "if poor burdened humanity is staggering thus secretly at our side under anything like this load—one ought truly to spend one's life in some great and definite labour of helpfulness"; discussed *Poor Folk, The House of the Dead, Crime and Punishment;* and dismissed *The Insulted and Injured* as unsatisfactory. Raskolnikov he thought too Russian to be understandable:

An impossible figure, it may be urged. I can only say . . . that we are constantly bound to confess that we are in the presence of types which our English prejudices will not allow us to comprehend among people so strange to us, from whom we can but expect strange things.

And *Crime and Punishment* was for him, as it had been for Vogüé, the last of Dostoevsky's great novels. After it, "his writings became more and more the vehicle of a set of narrow opinions." These later books Lomas laid aside "willingly enough."

Edmund Gosse, although he was later to change his mind about

Dostoevsky, this year wrote enthusiastically to an American friend about *Crime and Punishment*,[78] which he had read in French. He said it was "a masterpiece of psychological study," the "most successfully daring, domestic novel" that he had "ever read." The subject was "distressing enough, but most thrilling and entrancing in its carrying out."

In America, it seems, the Russian novel had by now achieved a certain vogue. A "witty correspondent," said Harriet Waters Preston in *The Atlantic Monthly*,[79] had written her that most people at the time were "consumed by one of two passions—for the German opera, or the Russian romance." "Both of the new and rather portentous developments of art here indicated," Miss Preston commented, "in their solemn intensity and merciless complexity, their scorn of old-fashioned laws and symmetries, their desperate grasp after the expression of the unutterable, [appealed] to the same dark and disillusioned yet restless and expectant temper in the modern mind." Dostoevsky, "the prophet of . . . a return" from Nihilism, she thought had been unfortunate "in the order in which his productions [had] been given to the western world"; *The House of the Dead* should be known before *Crime and Punishment* and his personal history before either. Of her own experience she wrote that she had been "beaten" by *Crime and Punishment* when she had "first attempted to read it." She had not had "nerve enough to finish it." But afterwards when she had read *The House of the Dead* from "beginning to end" she became "reconciled" to the later work. She found a similarity between *Crime and Punishment* and "Hawthorne's latest, and in some respects profoundest romance," *The Marble Faun,* and wondered "that no one should yet have noted" their identity of plot: "a horrible crime committed under overwhelming temptation, a long evasion of justice, followed by a voluntary surrender and a course of unflinching expiation." The "mystic element," she wrote, predominated "in the American fiction, the realistic in the Russian; and both elements [were] present in both works, combined in previously untried proportions."

In November and December of this year a series of six lectures on Russian literature was delivered in various parts of the United States by Ivan Panin.[80] A correspondent in *The Boston Home Journal*[81] wrote of him that he was "one of the most interesting men" that he had heard that season; and that "in the present craze for Russian literature he [deserved] hearty support." The subjects of Panin's

lectures were Pushkin, Gogol, Turgenev, and Tolstoy. Dostoevsky was
not included.

In an article on Tolstoy, however, in *Public Opinion*,[82] Dostoevsky
was mentioned as one of the authors whose popularity was increasing: "no amount of dreariness apparently" stood in the way of "the
growing popularity of Turgenev, Tolstoy, Gogol, and Dostoevsky."
He was mentioned again in a review by John Heard, Jr., of Isaac
Pavlowski's *Souvenirs sur Tourgueneff*,[83] wherein Turgenev's opinion
of him was cited: "an epileptic maniac, a Russian Marquis de Sade,
whose life was spent in writing against the cause of progress." "Thus
we see," said the reviewer, "that in literature, as in life, Nihilists do
not seem to live harmoniously with one another," for all three great
Russian novelists might be called Nihilists, since "Dostoevsky sav-
agely defies, Tolstoy sternly denies, and Turgenev sadly despairs."

The last of the Whishaw translations, published by Vizetelly, came
out in 1888, *The Uncle's Dream* and *The Permanent Husband*, included in one volume. This was the year of the publisher's arrest and
imprisonment; and nothing more by Dostoevsky appeared for six
years.

Of this last publication *The Literary World*[84] thought that "except
as a study of method" the two stories were "not specially attractive."
Of course, since *Crime and Punishment* had become known in England, "any work" by Dostoevsky was "certain to be read with interest" but his books were "decidedly unequal." *The Uncle's Dream*
was "conventional" and "commonplace," its plot, "too artificial and
improbable to produce the required effect"; and *The Permanent Husband*, although "far more powerful" was "also repulsive." It was, in
fact, "a study in morbid psychology" and could not be recommended
to any one who was "not obliged to read it by necessity." In *The
Saturday Review*[85] the stories were called "powerful," the second of
them, "almost delirious," and "a word of warning" was added that
The Permanent Husband was not "amusing reading," its "grotesque
passages" being "the least amusing of all." In *The Academy*,[86] William Sharp was surprised that Dostoevsky, "that sombre Russian
romancist," all of whose tales he thought he had read, was capable
of humour. But *The Uncle's Dream* was "comedy of a very original
and effective kind," which might do well on the stage. It formed,
with *The Permanent Husband*, a "more exciting" but "not more
entertaining" story, a volume that could, at any rate, be read "with-

out a prolonged fit of 'the blues'—a rare event with this author."
Whishaw's version was excellent—one could "well believe" what one
heard, that Dostoevsky's novels were "more literary in English than
in Russian."

The London Quarterly Review[87] this year published a comparative
study of Dostoevsky and Tolstoy, both of whom, the anonymous
author thought, represented better than Turgenev, who was too "familiar with French models," that "passionless realism of a faultless
photographing camera" which was peculiarly Russian. The article
was of the impressionistic variety. Of Dostoevsky one read that "when
we open Crime and Punishment, The Idiot, Injury and Insult . . .
a sense of bewilderment, almost of loathing comes over us," but that
"by degrees a certain order discloses itself . . . the characters . . .
take on an air of reality, and reveal themselves . . . our brothers and
our sisters"; and that his special merit lay in making us "recognize
that the miserable criminal" was "still our brother." Indeed, the
author seemed torn between a desire to admire and the inability so to
do. He paid Dostoevsky the dubious compliment of excusing his
faults by sympathizing with his misfortunes, appealing to the public,
with well-meant condescension, not to "blame fastidiously the strange
hue of the letters" where "every page" was "written with his heart's
blood." "We must remember," he wrote "that the artist drew life
as he had been compelled to see it. . . . His faults are pardonable
when we recall the long years of torture that shook the health both
of his mind and body."

An article in The Contemporary Review[88] mentioned Dostoevsky's
"orthodox fanaticism" as an indication of "an unhealthy society";
and in The Saturday Review,[89] in the periodical report of French
literature, The Brothers Karamazov was said to have "the same
undisciplined and desultory fluency, the same incoherence and horror,
as of a bad dream, the same flashes of talent, and the same (to some
persons attractive) unfamiliarity of manners, sentiment and setting"
which distinguished most of Dostoevsky's "long romances," when
they were not "simply dull." This book had the "advantage," the
reviewer continued, "that one character (we regret to say that she
is a kind of Improperia)" was "human and striking . . . 'Grouschegnka'
for love and euphony, 'Agrafena Alexandrovna' when a brief but
ceremonious appellation is desired."

In this year also we have the comment of a second British novelist on Dostoevsky. This time it was George Gissing who recorded in his diary[90] his impressions of a stage version of *Crime and Punishment* which he had seen in Paris:

Evening to see adaptation of Dostoevsky's *Crime et Châtiment* at the Odéon. Effective here and there, but on the whole poor play—inevitably so and poorly acted. Paul Mounet played Rodion; made him too much a melodramatic Hamlet. One of the two murders is cut out; alas! how much else also, from Dostoevsky's marvellous book! Sonia very poor.

Two years earlier[91] he had written to his sister Margaret: "The writers who help me most are French and Russian; I have not much sympathy with English points of view." And presently he was to elaborate, in his study of Dickens, a comparison between Dostoevsky and the English novelist.[92]

In America the same year, Nathan Haskell Dole, in *The Chautauquan*,[93] giving a short sketch of Russian literature designed as a help for those wanting to make a study of it, wrote that Dostoevsky's influence was "still extremely powerful" and that "his most famous novels . . . *Crime and Punishment, Injury and Insult,* and *The Idiot*" were "unfortunately . . . wretchedly translated into English from a wretched French translation." In *American Notes and Queries*,[94] *Crime and Punishment* was called an imitation of Bulwer Lytton's *Eugene Aram.* In answer to the query "What was the true story of *Eugene Aram?,*" an account of it was given with a sketch of Bulwer's novel, and the comment:

Bulwer's story has been imitated by the Russian Dostoviesky (*sic*) in his novel *Crime and Punishment,* where a young student kills a miserly old hag with the intention of using her money for praiseworthy objects.

But there could be no clearer proof that at this time Dostoevsky was widely read in the United States than the type of charge brought against him in a volume such as that on the novel by Maurice Francis Egan.[95] This author, having "humbly offered himself" as a guide "to his young friends—wandering in gardens of romance" to "warn them against the weeds growing among the flowers of the fictive art," raised his hands in special horror upon Dostoevsky. His "masterpiece," he wrote of *Crime and Punishment,* "one of the gloomiest of the gloomy works of a writer persistently puffed by certain critics . . . is a book no careful mother could give her daughters, no prudent father advise his son to read." One could understand, he said, that "the Russians oppressed and overridden by administrative power" would "be tempted to despair." But one need not admire them for it.

Look at the Irish. They were "a people as horribly oppressed as the Russians had ever been," but their literature was none the less brightened with "flashes of wit and humor." Your Russian was a godless being. Torn away from "the church" there seemed to be "no consolation" for him "in his schism." If he cast aside "the forms and ceremonies of his enslaved religion" he became "materialistic and superstitiously atheistical"; if he accepted The New Testament he adapted the "teaching of our Lord to his communistic theories, Count Tolstoy, for instance." "We must protest against the further introduction of Russian novels," wrote Egan. "The novel-reading public ought by this time to be weary of Russians—the Russians depicted in the fashionable translations," and especially ought they to be weary of Dostoevsky, who was the most popular of them all, having replaced Turgenev and Tolstoy in general favor. He was now "the leading man" and "not to know him well" was "as fatal to the literary *fât* as not to know who Schopenhauer was a few months ago, or not to have an opinion on the Nirvana" was now. And what kind of writer was Dostoevsky?

. . . a realist—that is [one who] looks carefully for the gloomy, criminal, mean impulses and acts in life. He drags up the dregs of human nature and muddies his stream with them. The stream may be placid, limpid, or sparkling, and graceful shadows of green trees may pass over it; but Dostoevsky never sees these things. Above all, he never sees anything that brings humanity nearer God. God, if he exists, according to Dostoevsky is a being who laughs at the inexpressible vileness of the man he has created vile: therefore he is a "realist"; he draws things as they are; he is Great, and Mr. Howells is his prophet!

Howells, of course, was not his prophet; but, to Egan, a realist was a realist.

In these introductory years, then, during which seven of his works were made available to English speaking readers, Dostoevsky came to be recognized as a novelist of first rate importance, although enthusiasm for him was mingled with distaste for his morbidity and his lack of artistry. He was brought to England on a wave of interest in all that concerned Russia, and was therefore looked to for illuminating commentary on that little known country. His books seemed, on the whole, more valuable as pictures of Russian life and Russian thought than as imaginative productions, although, as such, they often seemed puzzling, demanding for appreciation, credulity rather than understanding. They were often appraised on the basis of what was held to be Russia's peculiar contribution to European thought, Nihilism; Dostoevsky was spoken of as a greater or lesser Nihilist than Turgenev, or he was said to mark a departure from Nihilism altogether. And this view of his work as valuable not only in its own right but also as representing a nation, called forth comparisons between the thought of England and of Russia, and of their relative achievements in fiction, in which comparisons Russia was generously given the palm. Artistically, Dostoevsky seemed classifiable as a realist and as such, to be estimated in comparison with Zola. But it was also seen that he did not really fit this category, for, his gloomy tales, impregnated with a humanitarian sympathy, had nothing in common with Zola's documentary sordidness. It was this difference which was emphasized by Melchior de Vogüé, the most influential critic of Russian literature at this time.

III. INTERVAL—1889-1911

O N THE whole, then, although he was by no means unanimously praised, Dostoevsky received from the beginning an enthusiastic reception in England and America. After Vizetelly had published the last of Whishaw's versions, however, came a long period of comparative neglect. Dostoevsky's books were soon out of print, and during the next two and a half decades, only one new work was translated. It would be wrong to say, however, that Dostoevsky was entirely forgotten, for much was done at this time, as the present chapter will show, to prepare the way for a new and a deeper understanding of him.

There was, to begin with, the essay about him by Georg Brandes in his *Impressions of Russia*,[1] originally published in 1888 and translated into English the following year. Brandes was interested in the philosophic and the psychological implications of Dostoevsky's works. What he saw in him was "the typical Christian" philosopher, the embodiment of Nietzsche's "slave morality"; a masterful dialectician with whom dialogue was "a kind of inquisition," a "continued contest between men who seek to wrest their secrets from each other"; a neurotic genius, whose love of suffering and torture sometimes conflicted with his religious idea of pity; and "a poet . . . visionary enough to proclaim the presence of a 'divine spark' even among the wretched." His "inclination to describe bodily sufferings, the dwelling greatly on cruelties" were "suggestive of unnatural desires"; he liked "to take his stand on the dividing line which separates rational trains of thought from the exalted, and proper modes of action from the criminal," for he knew better than any one "the irresistible attraction of gulfs." But his work had both religious and political meaning. In his "thoroughly democratic stamp" he was comparable to Rousseau, but was unlike him in his primitive Christianity with his favorite types "of paupers . . . poor fellows," etc., who were "just the same types as prevailed centuries ago." The "religious problem, as it appeared to him," he developed "with a very extraordinary sublimity and greatness . . . in the ingenious poem, 'The Chief Inquisitor' . . . for whose sake alone," wrote Brandes, as H. S. Wilson had previously written,[2] *The Brothers Karamazov* ought to be translated. In *Crime and Punishment*, to which the essay was mainly devoted, Dostoevsky "plainly intended to give a picture of the times." Its central problem was "the two apparently contradictory estimates which society places upon the value of human life," the independent and sufficient value of each individual and his value as a social being. Raskolnikov's problem was not the purely personal one of the right of individual transgression, but the more general one of the justification of means by ends. Raskolnikov's murder of the pawn-broker was not in essence different from the assasination of the Czar, and it was of crimes such as this, committed from noble motives, that Dostoevsky thought in writing of the pawnbroker. Dostoevsky did "not particularly deny the justice of Raskolnikov's reasoning," but showed that Raskolnikov was "confused as to his end," "uncertain about his end and uncertain about his inward authority to pursue the indefinite end, which, according to his own theory, only the elect are at liberty to use all means to attain." When for a whole day he had "tortured himself with the question whether Napoleon would have done such an act, he already felt dimly that he was not a Napoleon." The problem therefore remained unresolved, but the inference was that to Napoleons certain acts might be permitted which were impossible for lesser men.

As an artist, Brandes held, Dostoevsky was very great. *Recollections of a Dead House* was "one of the greatest masterpieces descriptively and psychologically, which any literature [had] to show." But he was essentially a dramatic artist: his narrative style was not equal to his dialogue. "As soon as the author himself [began] to talk" art ceased. Dostoevsky was "the autochtonic author, 'the true Scythian' [in Vogüé's phrase], the legitimate barbarian without a drop of classic blood in his veins." He was a "national optimist" in contrast to Turgenev who was a "national pessimist." The "great sceptic Turgenev, who believed in so little, believed in the culture of Western Europe. Dostoevsky despised the Occident and believed in Russia."

Brandes's book was praised in *The Spectator*[3] for its "intensity and concentration"; "in depth of insight, range of knowledge, and vividness of presentation" it was said to have surpassed all other work on Russia known in England. Its "brief but sufficient and most admirable studies" of Herzen, Turgenev, Dostoevsky and Tolstoy would "well repay perusal." W. R. Morfill, on the other hand, in *The Academy*,[4] took the trouble to point out a host of minor inaccuracies, described the work as a compilation of other writers' views on Russia, and declared that although Dr. Brandes wrote "throughout with the facile pen of a practised littérateur" and although what he said of

Pushkin, Tolstoy, Dostoevsky, and other Russian authors made "very pleasant reading," one never felt "quite sure" whether he had used "original sources." The essay on Dostoevsky was presently translated into German[5] and into Russian,[6] acquiring thus something of a European reputation.

In America, the lectures delivered by Panin in 1887 were now published as a book.[7] The omission of Dostoevsky from it is significant, for, in the preface Panin explained that he had chosen his authors not because they were "the greatest names of Russian literature" but because they best illustrated his central theme: that "what Nature is to God . . . Literature is to the soul," that "God ever strives to reveal himself in Nature. . . . And the human soul strives to reveal itself in Literature." By implication Dostoevsky was neither one of the greatest Russian authors nor one in whose work the human soul was revealed. The book was none too favorably reviewed, but in dealing with it a writer in *The Literary World*[8] commented eloquently on Russian literature:

Complex, conflicting, painful as are these Russian presentations of life, they have an overwhelming force in that they are intensely earnest and sincere. The art, even when imperfect, and it often is, is large in that it forgets itself. It is, indeed, so sincere, so wholehearted, as to be to some extent incomprehensible to Western civilization. We are too practical to comprehend that which is wholly opposed to the motive of self-interest. Yet, in so far as this is true, our civilization is a failure.

A casual, unflattering mention of Dostoevsky occurred in *The Fortnightly Review*[9] in 1889, in one of a series of four articles on "Russian Characteristics" which developed the general thesis that "the theory of right conduct universally accepted in Russia" was "void of ideals." In the second instalment of the series Dostoevsky was cited to illustrate the specific charge that "a Russian changes his point of view . . . with amazing suddenness":

The picture of Dostoevsky, the great psychological novelist, solemnly offering up his heartfelt gratitude to the Emperor of Russia for having banished him to Siberia . . . cannot be matched in Christendom, outside the walls of a lunatic asylum.

C. E. Turner's promised sequel[10] to *Studies in Russian Literature* came out in 1890,[11] and in the same year there was a translation of a popular Spanish work on Russia by Emilia Pardo Bazán.[12] So far as Dostoevsky was concerned, both books were collections of what were by now current estimates of his work. Señora Pardo Bazán, in her enthusiasm, adhered largely to Vogüé's judgments, "the intelligent French critic whose work on the Russian novel has been so useful to me in these studies."[13] Dostoevsky was "really the barbarian, the primitive type"; "like his student hero, he [prostrated] himself before human suffering"; "no one [had] carried realism so far, but his may be called mystic realism"; it was impossible to select from *The Dead House* any one passage to illustrate its excellence, for its excellence depended on the whole; his books made one ill;[14] and so on. Turner approached Dostoevsky from the angle of traditional British common sense which found the Russian difficult to understand and thought his work good because it displayed a kind heart. Dostoevsky's novels were a protest against social injustice, and the sum of his philosophy was a broad sympathy which showed that "even in natures the most crushed and humiliated, the presence of the heavenly, common to us all, may be found."[15] Turner concluded that Dostoevsky's was "the gospel of hope, the creed of progress, that not only lends us encouragement to advance, but points out the way we should go, and puts into our hands the staff of religious faith by which we may support and guide our steps."[16]

An article in *Temple Bar*[17] concerning characteristics of Russian literature presented Dostoevsky as having shared Turgenev's "ardent desire to regenerate Russia" as also his "hopeless and helpless undercurrent of negation," although in other respects no two authors could be "more opposite." He was spoken of admiringly as a writer with whom "all social conventions" were "set at nought," his most prominent characters being murderers, prostitutes, and epileptics; and as a penetrating observer who saw that there was "no abrupt demarcation between health and disease, between physiology and pathology, between right and wrong."

The following year the same journal printed an enthusiastic essay on Dostoevsky,[18] the only essay given over entirely to him in the five years between 1889, when Brandes's book appeared, and 1894, when *Poor Folk* was published with a preface by George Moore. It was "perhaps difficult for English readers to understand the admiration entertained by Russians for Dostoevsky and his writings," this essay began. Most people were willing "to acknowledge the genius of Turgenev and Tolstoy; but Dostoevsky with his wild extravagance, his lack of humour, the gloomy and often repulsive character of his subjects, and his wearisome diffuseness, who [could] abide?" But it then pointed out that "truth and delicacy" of psychological analysis, "quickest, keenest powers of observation," "so intense an aim of realism that . . . wildest fictions read like truth," and a "warm heart that never [ceased] to bleed for every act of cruelty, injustice and oppression" were Dostoevsky's distinguishing merits. There was an echo of Vogüé in all this, and especially in the judgment that after *Crime and Punishment* Dostoevsky wrote nothing equal to it "in conception and execution."

One of the most important factors in a changing view of Dostoevsky was the development and popularization of abnormal psychology. Among the principal contributions in this province were Lombroso's now superseded researches. In his study of genius, translated into English in 1891, he spoke of Dostoevsky[19] as among those geniuses who together with Socrates, Rembrandt, Darwin, and others possessed a cretin-like physiognomy, and as one of those also, such as Whitman, Rousseau, and Musset who, "much preoccupied with their own *Ego*," know and proclaimed their disease, "as though they wished by confessing it, to get relief from its inexorable attacks." Thus could be explained Dostoevsky's habitual introduction of "semi-insane characters, and especially epileptics . . . and moral lunatics." The descriptions of epileptic seizures in *The Possessed* and *The Idiot* were quoted at length to illustrate the resemblance between inspiration and epilepsy.

Comment of this kind gave a novel view of Dostoevsky by suggesting a personal basis for his realistic observations. This "psychological" approach was furthered by such thinkers as Havelock Ellis, who now became one of those most interested in the Russian novel. In his collection of essays, *The New Spirit*, published the same year as Lombroso's *Man of Genius*, there was one on Tolstoy which spoke also of Dostoevsky,[20] of his "profound science of the human heart" which "could never get near enough to its primitive and instinctive element." Of the great Russian novelists, said Ellis, Dostoevsky was the "most intensely Russian," "throughout penetrated by the passion of pity" which seemed to be "deeply rooted in the national character," "sympathy and the need of comradeship" being "the characteristics of Russian religion." The "democratic element" in him was "more fundamental" than in either Turgenev or Tolstoy; there were "two or three scenes in *Recollections of the Dead House*, of Dantesque awfulness" which brought "nearer to us than anything else the very flesh and spirit of humanity." In all his books, indeed, one was "constantly irritated and fascinated by this same strange penetrating odor of humanity." Dostoevsky was "so faithful in his studies that he sometimes" forgot how great an artist he was; and Ellis quoted the following passage in which Dostoevsky had "justified" his artistic procedure:

"What is the good of prescribing to art the roads that it must follow? To do so is to doubt art, which develops normally, according to the law of nature, and must be exclusively occupied in responding to human needs. Art has always shown itself faithful to nature, and has marched with social progress. The ideal of beauty cannot perish in a healthy society; we must then give liberty to art, and leave her to herself. Have confidence in her; she will reach her end, and if she strays from the way she will soon reach it again; society itself will be the guide. No single artist, not Shakespeare himself, can prescribe to art her roads and aims."

Although the new psychology tended to be tolerant of "morbidity" in literature, this tolerance was slow in taking possession. In America, for instance, William Dean Howells, in 1892, pointed out with some complacency,[21] that to write novels of suffering might be all right for Russians but not for Americans. After all, "whatever their deserts, very few American novelists [had] been led out to be shot, or finally exiled to the rigors of a winter in Duluth." And "in a land where journeymen carpenters and plumbers [went on strike] for four dollars a day the sum of hunger and cold [was] comparatively small." That was why in this land novelists concerned themselves "with the more smiling aspects of life, which [were] the more American." Whoever, in American fiction, "struck a note so profoundly tragic," as for example Dostoevsky's, "would do a false and mistaken thing— as false and as mistaken in its way as dealing in American fiction with certain nudities which the Latin peoples seem to find edifying."[22]

In 1893 the fourth edition of *Crime and Punishment* came out.

In 1894 Elkin Mathews and John Lane published a translation of *Poor Folk*,[23] with an introduction by George Moore and a frontispiece by Aubrey Beardsley. Moore declared himself won over to Dostoevsky by the stylistic excellence of this story. He confessed to having once written of *Crime and Punishment* that it was "Gaboriau with psychological sauce"; and he now professed to regret, without wholly repudiating, his epigram. "The desire to be witty," he said, had "led men into phrases which they afterwards" regretted. Still this phrase[24] did not seem to him "to be wholly unwarranted," for he remained of the opinion that "notwithstanding some magnificent passages" *Crime and Punishment* "lumbered along luggage-train fashion." He thought that perhaps when he had read the second volume, his opinion would change. *Poor Folk*, however, was so good that one asked oneself, was it "as perfect as Turgenev"; that it was not, of course went "without saying," for was not Turgenev "the greatest artist since antiquity?" But the book showed genius. The "theme of the story [deepened] as it proceeded and [would] be found deepest in the last pages. And to maintain a sensation in vibration to the last page [was] surely genius." It was a realistic novel whose realism, however, depended on its intensity of passion, not on a precise accumulation of detail. It was like the *Letters of a Portuguese Nun*, "written two centuries ago," through which it seemed to Moore that one could know "the unfortunate Marianna and the balcony on which she stood" although one was "not told the colour of that balcony, nor of Marianna's hair and eyes." Similarly, with *Poor Folk* "the least critical" could not "fail to perceive that these letters were unlike real letters, that they bore no kind of resemblance to the letters that might have passed between a half-witted clerk and a poor girl living over the way; nevertheless we realized the character of the old man far better than we should from the publication of the actual correspondence of two such people." The story was very moving. The love of the poor clerk Makar for the little seamstress across the way was like that of a prisoner for the mouse that visits his cell. And the account of Pokrovsky's funeral was such that "no whole year" of his life, said Moore, would pass without his seeing "that old man running through the mud after his son's coffin."

This last episode was quoted at length by *The Literary World*.[25] "Could anything," its reviewer commented, "be more supremely pathetic? We recommend *Poor Folk* with all the emphasis of which we are capable." It was "indubitably a masterpiece"; the picture of Makar was "one to draw tears," was "one to make the righteous thank God for those finer ingredients that are prominent in the composition of human nature." *The Westminster Review*[26] found in it "to an unusual degree, that strange saddening quality that so often attaches to Russian literature"; the narrative "vibrated with feeling" and conveyed "a cry from the depths of a famished human soul." In *The Academy*[27] W. R. Morfill was "glad," in his habitually chilly way, that an English translation had appeared of "the first fruits" of Dostoevsky's genius; and according to the American *Nation*[28] everything in it was "perfect." The least sympathetic review came from *The Spectator*[29] in which Dostoevsky was compared to a student dissecting and studying "the limb of some small creature under a microscope";

the limb appeared to him "magnified enormously" and assumed in his perceptions, "a space . . . out of all proportion with its real size and importance." One forgot in reading the book that there were "lights as well as shadows in the great panorama of life." As for George Moore's introduction, it was in *The Spectator's* opinion "in itself an excellent piece of writing," although its praise of the book's construction was excessive. But in both *The Academy* and *The Literary World* there were objections to the preface. "Good wine needs no bush," was the comment of W. R. Morfill. And the critic of *The Literary World* thought that "in some instances" the introduction was "not conspicuous by reason of its wisdom." There was indeed no service in prefacing "Dostoevsky's novel by any remarks whatever, and an introduction which [claimed] to be critical should be more careful." Had Mr. Moore's characteristically daring comments been "printed at the end of the book as a note," his action would have been "more defensible." In short, his preface was *de trop*, nor did Mr. Beardsley "improve the title-page."

There now began to be heard more frequently than heretofore lamentations that Englishmen and Americans were ignorant of Dostoevsky. Such was the tenor of an article by Arthur Salmon in the American *Poet Lore*,[30] 1894. With Turgenev and Tolstoy readers were "tolerably familiar," but Dostoevsky was "still to a great extent unknown." This ignorance was partly due, Salmon thought, to the inadequacy of translations but more to the "morbid" character of Dostoevsky's work, which "the censor of the British press . . . a near relation of Mrs. Grundy, if not that lady herself" was perhaps right in condemning. Furthermore, he pointed out, Dostoevsky's genius was essentially foreign. He was more Russian in his allegiance and philosophy than Turgenev, for instance—"a thorough Russian, a Slavophile, a foe to modern ideas of liberty and broad thought," "not quite such a pietist as Gogol," but still distant enough from Western thought to render him strange reading. And yet, in spite of his strangeness and morbidity, in spite of the fact that but a "narrow gulf . . . separated his genius from insanity," Dostoevsky was a "most forcible writer—a writer whom no student of literature [could] afford to ignore," whose writings "must be a revelation" to "persons unfamiliar with the Slav character and literature." "We ought," he said, "to become more cosmopolitan in our literary taste; and happily signs of the times are already pointing that way."

In 1895, *The Westminster Review*[31] published an "Appreciation of

Russian Fictional Literature" by R. G. Burton, Captain, Indian Staff Corps, who thought that Mrs. Grundy need have no fear of Dostoevsky. Captain Burton admired Russian realists, and Dostoevsky among them, precisely because, even if they were occasionally morbid, they were always decent. In their works "there could be found scarcely a line which could offend the most sensitive reader," wherein they differed from the "unhealthy imagination of the New Woman and the vapid vapourings of the fin-de-siècle young man." Dostoevsky's mind, to be sure, had been "unhinged by what he went through," but his *Crime and Punishment* was, just the same, "one of the most remarkable books ever published."

Nordau, whose extremely popular *Entartung*[32] (dedicated to Lombroso) was translated in this year, considered that Dostoevsky, although he had certain affinities with degenerates—his "mystic fright," for instance—was yet distinguishable from them through the excellence of his work. *Crime and Punishment* stood as an example of how it was "possible for that which is most ugly and vicious in artistic portrayal to operate in the direction of the morally beautiful," when the "moral purpose" and the "sympathetic emotion" of the author are betrayed in his work. The confession scene in *The Wild Duck* Nordau described as "a tame imitation" of that in *Crime and Punishment* "where the assassin and the prostitute . . . unite their soiled and broken lives." Ibsen's scene was "stripped" of the "sombre grandeur" of Dostoevsky's and "lowered to the ridiculous and vulgar."

On the whole, America more than England displayed an interest in Russian literature during these years. In 1896, *The Chautauquan* published a translation of an Italian article on the Russian novel;[33] in Warner's *Library of the World's Best Literature* appeared translations from *Poor Folk* and *Crime and Punishment* and an essay on Dostoevsky by Isabel Hapgood;[34] and the Lowell Lectures[35] the same year were delivered by Prince Serge Wolkonsky.

Isabel Hapgood gave a biographical sketch of Dostoevsky, called him "in certain respects . . . the most characteristically national of Russian writers," which was the reason, she said, for his lack of popularity abroad. He dealt with "a sort of Russian Society" which it was "hard for non-Russians to grasp"; he had "no skill whatever in presenting aristocratic people or society," and he did not write of peasants. His "special domain" was that which Turgenev and Tolstoy "did not understand." This was but "one reason the more why he should be studied."

Wolkonsky spoke of the "sudden interest in Russian writers which [had] broken out in these last twenty years"; but which, he said, was "too recent to compensate for many years of indifference." Even now the Russian novel had for Western readers "a sort of exotic charm: snow and wolves and police agents, with the threatening prospect of Siberia in the background." He remembered an American girl "who frankly confessed that she did not like Russian novels representing Russian life," because she thought they lacked "local color"; "she much preferred English novels about Russia, they were so much more 'Russian' "; and he quoted a friend of his, Prince Viazemsky: " 'If you want an intelligent Englishman or Frenchman to talk nonsense, let him emit an opinion on Russia: it is a subject which intoxicates him and at once clouds his intellect.' " Wolkonsky's remarks, therefore, addressed to what he considered an interested but ignorant public, were elementary but eloquent, and somewhat tinged with princely hauteur. Dostoevsky he characterized as "the sombre epileptic, disenchanted with 'civilization,' disgusted with the upper classes and all that comes from Europe";[36] he went "to the outcasts of society" among whom he discovered "jewels of moral beauty, and, in an act of mystic veneration, ... [knelt] down before the collective soul of the Russian lower people." One "experienced and paid with the torment" of one's soul the "terrifying fascination exercised by that crowd of lunatics, criminals, epileptics, suicides, and all the 'Humiliated and Offended' outcasts of society" which people his works. Dostoevsky "the artist was almost screened by the thinker and novelist," just as Turgenev "the thinker disappeared under the artist." But "in spite of the somewhat clumsy shape of his overcrowded novels" he was "a unique figure in universal literature." Nothing frightened him. "No obstacle" was "powerful enough to arrest this Livingstone of darkest misery."[37]

According to *The Athenæum*[38] Wolkonsky's book "retained the essential features" of its origin: it was "rhetorical," as lectures were, and it appealed to "Transatlantic views." The information which it gave would "seem to Englishmen a little rudimentary"; it used sources indiscriminately, without distinguishing between the good and the bad; and a "visible over-straining for epigrammatic effect" had led it occasionally to "extravagant writing." For example: "Turgenev the thinker, over-weighted by the artist; Dostoevsky, the artist over-weighted by the thinker; and finally, Leo Tolstoy, the artist and the

thinker in rivalry" seemed "a little fanciful." Still, the book was
"interesting"; and the reviewer hoped, would be successful.

In 1898 Gissing's biography of Dickens[39] was published. Comparisons with Dickens had been forced on the attention of readers before
now: *Injury and Insult, The Friend of the Family, The Gambler,*
had all suggested obvious analogies.[40] But Gissing's comparison was
the most elaborate of all.[41] Dickens, Gissing said, "would have found
much to like and admire" in "the great Russian novelist," who often
reminded one of him, even to his "peculiarities in humour." It was
"not impossible," in fact, in *Injury and Insult* in the opening especially, that "Dickens's direct influence worked with the writer." And
Dostoevsky's "masterpiece, *Crime and Punishment*" abounded "in
Dickens-like touches in its lighter passages." Dickens might have
written the "long scene at the beginning of the book, where Sonia's
father, the eccentric drunkard, makes himself known to us in his
extraordinary monologue." "For that matter" had he been a Russian
and poor "he might well have written the whole book." As it was, he
had been "obliged to ignore or to hint . . . with sighing timidity" facts
which Dostoevsky could frankly acknowledge. Sonia "could not have
been used by the Englishman as a heroine at all," while "as a subordinate figure" she would have been turned to his "most stagey pur-
poses": and "the crucial chapter" of Dostoevsky's story, "the magnificent scene in which Raskolnikov makes confession to Sonia" was
"beyond Dickens, as we know him." Yet, "it would not have been
so but for the defects of education and the social prejudices which
forbade his tragic gift to develop." Such a character as Raskolnikov,
Dickens "never attempted to portray; his motives, his reasonings
could not be comprehended by an Englishman of the lower-middle
class. And the murder itself—Bill Sikes, Jonas Chuzzlewit [showed]
but feebly after we [had] watched that lank student, with the hatchet
under his coat, stealing up the stairs; when we [had] seen him do
his deed of blood, and heard the sound of that awful bell tinkling in
the still chamber." Dostoevsky's work was "indescribably powerful
and finely tragic; the murders in Dickens [were] too vulgar of motive greatly to impress us, and [lacked] the touch of high imagina-
tiveness."

Brander Matthews in reviewing Gissing's book[42] indicated that in
his opinion it was Dickens who had been complimented in the comparison with the Russian writer. "Mr. Gissing," he wrote, "even ven-

tures to compare Dickens with Balzac, with Victor Hugo, with Dostoevsky, and with Daudet."

In 1900 there appeared in America a thoroughly unsympathetic study of Russian literature, *A History of Russian Literature* by K. Waliszewski, which, according to Christian Brinton, in *The Critic*,[43] was "written in French by a Pole" and "clandestinely translated with scrupulous inaccuracy." Nowhere was Waliszewski's lack of sympathy more obvious than in his treatment of Dostoevsky.[44] There was in his discussion of him an attitude of wilful misunderstanding which gave it the tone of a polemic. He seemed to take pleasure in crying down the author who had received extravagant praise on the very grounds on which that praise was given. Thus, for example, the originality of Dostoevsky's genius he explained away with sly insinuations of borrowings: *The Insulted and Injured* smacked of Eugene Sue, *The Dead House* of Victor Hugo, *Crime and Punishment* of Bulwer Lytton; Stavrogin, in *The Possessed,* was "strongly tinged with Romantic features, which the author seems to have borrowed from every quarter—from Byron's *Corsair,* from Victor Hugo's *Hernani,* and from the aristocratic demagogues of Georges Sand, Eugene Sue, Charles Gutzkow, and Spielhagen." His realism and his interest in suffering and pity stemmed from that deplorable Russian morality wherein "the moral law and the political law" were held "on one and the same conventional level" and on the basis of which punishment for crime was meted out like forfeits "in a round game." "The idea that crime is not a fault, but a misfortune, and the idea of the sovereign power of expiation, [were] the basis of this method of thought and feeling. They pervaded the whole of Dostoevsky's work." On Dostoevsky's lack of constructive skill, Waliszewski dwelt at some length, accounting for it, not as others had done, sympathetically, by the pressure under which Dostoevsky was obliged to write, but by "his urgent desire to keep up constant communication with the public, and his ambition to preserve his influence over it." Waliszewski's conclusion, that "for all his prolixity and incoherence, Dostoevsky was a very great writer" and that "in the whole field of contemporary literature there was only one man, Tolstoy, who [stood] a step above him," remained naturally unconvincing after the unattractive picture of the man which he had drawn.

The Spectator,[45] none the less, thought that Waliszewski's book "put all students of literature under a very considerable obligation," for it introduced them to a world which unless they were "exceptionally well informed" would be "mostly new" to them. *The Literary World*[46] "cordially paid tribute" to the "learning and brilliancy" of the book, but warned readers of its bias: it was not "a model book to put into the hands of those" still unfamiliar with Russian literature. It was "more fitted to be a secondary than an elementary course." But in America, in the pages of *The Bookman*,[47] the volume occasioned a sharp skirmish. Waliszewski was there denounced as "a well-bred Pole" who "saw Russia from the window of his carriage, or, still worse, of his train"; and was accused of plagiarism. To this Waliszewski replied weakly and petulantly and was answered with parallel-column substantiation of the charge. In *The Critic*, Christian Brinton, cited above, called the work "brilliant, biassed, full of luminous exposition and ludicrous error . . . all that a history of literature should be and all that it should not be." And he used the occasion for taking England and America to task for "lagging farthest behind" in appreciation of Russian letters. The Russian novel, he wrote, was "the heroic literary phenomenon of modern times." And yet, "occidental interest" in it was "mainly accidental. Much was known of Russian authors, little about Russian letters."

Another article on Russian literature by Havelock Ellis appeared in *The Contemporary Review*,[48] in 1901. It was called "The Genius of Russia" and dealt with the by now familiar subject of the differences between Russian and English fiction. According to Ellis, however much the great Russian novelists might differ from each other in other respects, they had this in common: "a certain convincing sincerity, an appealing sympathetic personal quality" which had never been attained by English novelists. "Our English novelists," he wrote, had "never been simply and frankly personal. They may have been individual, even eccentric; they may have written their books to discharge their exuberant energies, but certainly not from any overmastering impulse to reveal the secrets of their own souls. Indeed the word 'soul' never [occurred] to us" with reference to their work. The novels, for example, of Bulwer Lytton, Thackeray, Dickens, might reveal "personal qualities," but they were not "revelations of personality." With the Russians, on the other hand, there was an "instinctive craving for orgiastic moments of self-forgetfulness" to which perhaps was due "that strange proclivity to unconscious impulsions and outbursts which Dostoevsky noted among Russian convicts, in that volume of Siberian reminiscences . . . one of the most fascinating and illuminative books ever written about criminals." *The Idiot* also was one of "the most impressive and significant" of the Russian novels.

Arnold Bennett, to whom there will be occasion to refer again, is to be counted among the most enthusiastic admirers of Dostoevsky. At this time, in a book entitled *Fame and Fiction* which examined certain literary popularities, he gave "three reasons why Turgenev, despite the unaffected and zealous support everywhere extended to him by men of letters, should have failed to grip the public as Tolstoy and even Dostoevsky" had "gripped it."[49] These reasons were that "as an artist" always "restrained and refined," without "the least inclination to either flamboyance or vulgarity," Turgenev had "hardly a fault"; that his novels had "a moral basis beyond the ordinary"; and, finally, that "Oriental melancholy and other Oriental attributes" characteristic of Russia, were in him "intensified to a special degree."

In this year also a new cheap edition of *Crime and Punishment* was published.[50] In America the Lowell Lectures were delivered by Prince Kropotkin, on Russian literature in the nineteenth century, published four years later as *Ideals and Realities in Russian Literature*.[51] It was noted in *The Saturday Review*,[52] that the author of a new book on Siberian prisons, Mirolubov, was "naturally put at a disadvantage by the ever present comparison with Dostoevsky's *Notes from a Dead House*," a "great book," remarkable in its understanding of the prisoners, "their manners and inner social organization," compared with which Mirolubov's was like that of "a day-boy writing of life at a public school which had been described by a boarder." In a short textbook of Russian literature by Isabel F. Hapgood,[53] which appeared in America in 1902, Dostoevsky's work was represented as "overwhelming, even stunning and nerve-shattering," resembling Dickens in its "pictures of low life." *Crime and Punishment* deserved "to rank among the greatest and best monuments of European literary art in the nineteenth century" by virtue of "its psychical and psychological analyses," but "unfortunately, it produced a strange impression on all reasonable people" because the crime in it appeared "dependent upon the influence of new ideas, as though they justified crimes committed with good objects"; and "the manner in which the romance wound up with the moral regeneration of Raskolnikov under the influence of exile with hard labor" was "no less surprising" than the strange ethics of his crime.

Also in 1902, *The Athenæum*[54] announced in its Russian report the publication of "a lengthy critical study of Tolstoy and Dostoevsky" by Dmitri Merezhkovsky. This study had appeared from 1900 to 1901 in a Russian journal and had now come out in book form. Part of it was immediately translated into English.[55] The original consists of three long separate studies: "Tolstoy and Dostoevsky as Men"; "Tolstoy and Dostoevsky as Artists"; "Tolstoy and Dostoevsky as Religious Thinkers." The English translation was an abridgement of the first two sections, a note appended by the editor announcing that the translation of the rest would depend "upon the reception accorded" to this volume. The reception, it seems, was not sufficiently favorable to justify the undertaking, for the rest of the translation has never been made.

Merezhkovsky's study may be described as an elaborated antithesis whose purpose was to show that in every respect the two great authors were completely opposed to each other: in the circumstances of their lives and their natures; in their philosophies; their artistic methods; their literary and philosophic significance. Tolstoy was emotional but self-restrained, Dostoevsky, uncontrollably passionate; Tolstoy was at war with reason, Dostoevsky was passionately rational. "All that Tolstoy dreamed of and aimed at, serious in plan, but play in practice—forswearing property for manual labour, becoming one with the people, all this Dostoevsky had to experience under the crushing vigor of the hardest fact."[56] What one desired, the other had; what one pretended, the other lived. "All worldly advantages in Tolstoy were so to speak centripetal, in Dostoevsky centrifugal." "The sacred and demoniacal sickness of the one" should be contrasted with "the not less divine and demonic superflux of bodily carnality, strength and health" in the other. And this indeed, the preeminence of matter over spirit, a clear and sharply defined dichotomy with Tolstoy, of spirit over matter, a hardly realized distinction with Dostoevsky, was the crux of these differences between them, which embraced their whole scheme of thought, from their concepts of life and death to their literary methods. "For Tolstoy the light of death [was] thrown on life from without, operating and dulling the colors and shapes of life"; there existed for him "only the eternal antagonism of life and death; for Dostoevsky only their eternal oneness." Dostoevsky had seen as no other author had seen the containment of the supernatural in natural objects; Tolstoy had seen principally the material composition of things, and "in proportion as" he left this soil that was always "firm and fruitful under him" for "the province of independent

spirituality," his psychology became "doubtful." But Dostoevsky arrived "from the internal . . . at the external, from the mental at the
physical, from the rational and human . . . at the instinctive and ani-
mal." Dostoevsky's characters were "living souls"; Tolstoy's were
"overgrown beef." One was the artist of the spirit, the modern Leonardo; the other, the artist of the flesh, the modern Michelangelo.[57]
These fundamental attitudes were reflected in their styles: in the narrative method of the one, as against the dramatic method of the
other. The exact, sharply-noted, frequently repeated descriptive detail of Tolstoy, for instance, was almost completely absent in Dostoevsky. With Tolstoy one heard because one saw, with Dostoevsky
one saw because one heard. *War and Peace* and *Anna Karenina* were
"really novels, original epics"; but the principal works of Dostoevsky
were "in reality not novels nor epics, but tragedies." In his dialogue
was "concentrated all the artistic power of his delineations," and
what rivals he might have were not to be found among present-day
novelists but among the tragedians of antiquity, "the creators of
Orestes and Oedipus."[58] Dostoevsky was the more intellectual of the
two artists. Whereas "the resourcefulness of Tolstoy's Muse [lay]
precisely in this, that . . . with her" one sometimes forgot "the existence of the human mind," of Dostoevsky's Muse one might doubt
whatever qualities one pleased, "only not her intelligence." Dostoevsky's heroes "felt deeply because they thought deeply; they suffered
endlessly because they were endlessly deliberate; they dared to will
because they had dared to think." One learned from them "how abstract thought" might be "passionate."[59] And in this, Dostoevsky's
art was of the future. "The great poets of the past ages, in depicting
the passions of the heart, left out of consideration the passions of the
mind." Where one found the heart, the mind was lacking; and where
the mind, the heart. Thus Faust and Hamlet, "nearest to us of all
heroes," thought more but felt less than all others, acted less because
they thought more; their tragedy lay in the contradiction which they
could not solve "between the passionate heart and passionless
thought." To the future belonged the synthesis: "the tragedy of
thinking passion or passionate thought"; and Dostoevsky was "one
of the first to make an approach to it."[60]

Tolstoy and Dostoevsky, in sum, were two opposed but comple-
mentary forces. They were "two lines running in opposite directions
from a single point that at an opposite point [would] meet, completing
a circle; . . . two prophecies, seemingly contradictory, but really in

accord, of some unseen yet forseen Russian genius" who should arise
one day, "elemental and national." They were "the two great columns, standing apart in the propylæum of the temple—parts facing
each other, set over against each other in the edifice, incomplete and
still obscured by scaffolding, that temple of Russian religion" which
in the future would be the "religion of the whole world." In terms of
Hegelian dialectic, Tolstoy was thesis, Dostoevsky antithesis; the
synthesis would be some future national and universal genius.[61]

It was reported in *The Athenæum*[62] that Merezhkovsky's book
treated of "many interesting episodes in the lives of Tolstoy and
Dostoevsky," but that the English reader would find the book be-
wildering, for in spite of occasional notes, it left "the names of works
by Russian authors frequently . . . unexplained." In *The Academy*,[63]
Merezhkovsky's estimate of Dostoevsky was incidentally mentioned
in an article on *Crime and Punishment* as one about which there
could be "no question," whatever might be thought of his view of
Tolstoy.

The article in *The Academy* was, in reality, a further application
of Merezhkovsky's method of balances. Dostoevsky, it held, was the
"antithesis" not only to Tolstoy, but also to Balzac, which meant
that he was the antithesis to European fiction generally. The aim of
European fiction was "to express from the standpoint of hate or joy,
the pride of life," an aim that had "reached its zenith in the author of
La comédie humaine." But to Dostoevsky, "pride of life, the assertion of the individual will, was wholly repellent." His were "the tenets
of the old Russia, the tenets of faith, of silence, and of endurance."
His feeling for suffering—and he had "caught the under-current of
stifled suffering" in the "withering life of cities"—was very different
from Western humanitarianism, from Hugo's feeling of pity, for
example. To Hugo "an object of pity was a part of the terrible, and
he expressed it as such." But for Dostoevsky "the humble were never
Titanic figures"; he "recognized in them human beings who were
slowly learning what appeared to him to be the supreme lesson of
life—*le besoin de souffrir.*" In one book, however, *Crime and Punishment*, he gave "utterance to the protest of the individual." There,
"this Bossuet of the *détraqués* denounced the over-man who would
violate the law of the humble." For therein lay Raskolnikov's sin, in
his desire "to break away from the common life"; and his punishment as he himself knew, was not Siberia but "the severance from
his fellow man." The "inmost core of Dostoevsky's faith" as well as

"the patient, inarticulate philosophy of the old Russia" was embodied
in the sentence about Raskolnikov's regeneration: " 'La vie s'était
substituée chez lui au raisonnement.' "

Comparisons between Russian and Western fiction continued to
be popular. In 1903 *The Academy*[64] published another article on the
subject which, taking Dostoevsky's short story, *Krotkaia,* and Turgenev's *Smoke* as exemplifying what was typically Russian, contrasted
them with *Robinson Crusoe* and *The Book of Snobs,* chosen to represent what was most characteristically English. The fundamental difference between them was that "the heroes of English fiction, from
Tom Jones to Tom Tulliver" were "for the most part self-centered,
objective, strenuous towards a definite goal, relatively moral by reason of robustness of temperament . . . naturally optimistic, and . . .
governed by a sense of duty, incapable of emotional rhetoric, [but]
absolutely reliable in the hour of need . . . essentially individualistic,
non-democratic, non-sentimental." They found their "raison d'être
in doing" and were "more or less representative of what the race
tended to produce," whereas the Russian heroes belonged to "quite a
different type." For them "the dreams of la vie intérieure" were more
important than "the facts of life." They tormented themselves "with
the endless analysis of motive" and were "at once vague and self-
conscious." The Englishman was "more or less kindly towards a person whom he half despised" because he understood, "no one better,
the give and take of life." But the Russian, "democratic, even socialis-
tic in his tendencies" was "bitter towards the individual because he
expected so much from humanity." It was a mistake to draw comparisons between Russian and Western novelists: "the evanescent
aloofness of Turgenev" was "not kindred to the sustained detachment
of Flaubert" nor was "the wail of pity in Dostoevsky the same as the
modulated emotion of Alphonse Daudet." That such comparisons had
been made, that both Dostoevsky and Daudet, for example, had "been
called, respectively, the Russian and French Dickens" was due to
writers' never tiring "of juggling with great names."

An anthology of Russian literature was published this year by
Professor Leo Wiener of Harvard. It contained a translation of the
passage in *Crime and Punishment* wherein Raskolnikov confesses his
crime to Sonia, and gave a bibliography of Dostoevsky translations.[65]

In 1904, there was an article in the American *Review of Reviews*[66]
entitled "Dostoevsky Still Dominates Russian Literature." Based upon
a French review of Dostoevsky's letters, it gave a sketch of Dostoev-

sky's life, discussed his political views, and quoted at length the French critic's estimate of him.

But although these essays and reviews might be thought indicative of a certain interest in Dostoevsky, Maurice Baring recalled in reminiscences many years later that when in 1903 he "approached a publisher with the proposal of translating all Dostoevsky's novels or those of Gogol" he was told that "there would be no market for such books in England."[67] Even "as late as" 1905, he wrote, Dostoevsky "had not yet been discovered," for in that year he was spoken of "in a long and serious article" in "one of the leading literary London newspapers" as "a kind of Xavier de Montepin!" During the Russo-Japanese War, Maurice Baring was in Russia, in the capacity of war correspondent for *The Morning Post*. There he read *The Idiot* and *The Brothers Karamazov*. "I remember devouring them both," he relates, "I had only read *Crime and Punishment* up till then, and these two books were a revelation."[68] Of his continued interest in Russian letters there will be occasion to speak more fully below.

Whatever may have been the attitude of the general public, however, critics displayed a growing interest in Dostoevsky and sometimes even thought they detected his influence in current fiction. Thus, for example, in 1905, James Gibbons Huneker wrote to Edward C. March, pointing out a certain similarity to Dostoevsky (as well as to Chekhov) in a magazine story he had just read;[69] and W. L. Courtney considered a woman novelist of the time, Mrs. Voynich, more influenced by Dostoevsky than by either Zola or Tolstoy.[70] There were, furthermore, two dramatizations of Dostoevsky in New York: of *Crime and Punishment* and of *The Brothers Karamazov*,[71] translated from the French and published with synopses by Isabel Hapgood in Orleneff's *Russian Lyceum Series*.

Kropotkin's Lowell Lectures, published this year as *Ideals and Realities in Russian Literature,* received very enthusiastic reviews in both the English and the American press.[72] But with Dostoevsky Kropotkin had little sympathy. He thought "the artistic qualities of his novels . . . incomparably below those of any one of the great Russian masters: Tolstoy, Turgenev, or Goncharov" and he accorded him scantier consideration than any other of the great Russian novelists.[73] The sketch of his life was full of minor inaccuracies; even the date of his death was incorrectly given.[74] When, said Kropotkin,

some twenty years ago, his novels were first translated into French, German and English, they were received as a revelation. He was praised as one of the greatest writers of our time, and as undoubtedly the one who 'had best expressed the mystic Slavonic soul'—whatever that expression may mean! Turgenev was eclipsed by Dostoevsky and Tolstoy was forgotten for a time. There was, of course, a great deal of hysterical exaggeration in all this, and at the present time sound literary critics do not venture to indulge in such praises.[75]

For the "hysterical" enthusiasm of twenty years back, there was, of course, some reason. Certainly "in whatever Dostoevsky wrote" there was "a great deal of power." He was comparable to Hoffman in "his powers of creation"; his "sympathy with the down-trodden" was deeply impressive; and "his analysis of the most varied specimens of incipient psychical disease [was] said to be thoroughly correct." But his artistry was poor: pages of "consummate realism" were "interwoven with the most fantastical incidents worthy only of the most incorrigible romantics. Scenes of a thrilling interest" were "interrupted in order to introduce a score of pages of the most unnatural theoretical discussions." But worst of all for Kropotkin was Dostoevsky's absorption in psychical disease and moral perversion. "Not in any literature" was there "such a collection of the most repulsive types of mankind—lunatics, half-lunatics, criminals in germ and in reality, in all possible gradations" as one found in *The Brothers Karamazov*. Whatever the comments of "a certain portion of contemporary critics, fond of all sorts of morbid literature," Kropotkin could only say that he had found it "all through, so unnatural, so much fabricated for the purpose of introducing—here a bit of morals, there, some abominable character taken from a psychopathological hospital; or again, in order to analyse the feelings of some purely imaginary criminal, that a few good pages scattered here and there [did] not compensate the reader for the hard task of reading these two volumes." He confessed that he himself "had the greatest pain lately in reading through" it and that he "never could pull himself through such a novel as *The Idiot*." *Crime and Punishment* he thought psychologically unconvincing. In its "very profusion of accidental causes" Dostoevsky himself showed how difficult he had felt it "to prove that propaganda of materialistic ideas could in reality bring an honest young man to act as Raskolnikov did." Raskolnikovs did not "become murderers under the influence of such theoretical considerations," while murderers who invoked "such motives" were "not in the least of the Raskolnikov type." What had preoccupied Dostoevsky in the book was "whether he himself, or a man like him, might have been brought to act as Raskolnikov did, and what would be the psychological explanation if he had been driven to do so." With all its faults, however, the novel contained "real pictures of slum life," through which it roused in "every honest reader . . . the deepest commiseration towards even the lowest sunken inhabitants of the slums." It was this faculty of inspiring love "even for the least interesting types of mankind" which was Dostoevsky's redeeming quality. It was for that that he would continue to be read, not for the artistic finish of his writings but for the good thoughts . . . scattered through them, for their real reproduction of slum life in the great cities and for the infinite sympathy which a being like Sonia [could] inspire in the reader."

By this time, Dostoevsky's novels were out of print. So, at any rate, wrote Edward Garnett in *The Academy*,[76] September 1, 1906, declaring it was "impossible, apparently, to procure to-day any of the translations of Dostoevsky's work that the late Mr. Vizetelly issued about twenty years ago." The "present generation of English readers," he said, "knows not Dostoevsky. So much the worse for the present generation!" He explained this neglect by "the Englishman's fear of morbidity" and then proceeded to show that it was precisely in this morbid strain that lay Dostoevsky's special strength: his "peculiar and unique value" was that of the great writers he was the one who stood "furthest down the slope of that deep underworld of tortuous, diseased impulse, . . . the one who had established best the relation the abnormal bears to the normal mind, and . . . who had most fully explored the labyrinthine workings of the mind unhinged . . . while still mixing with and surrounded by the world of normal men." His peculiar achievement in the realm of the abnormal showed us "just what value [was] to be placed on 'wholesomeness,' " for Dostoevsky's underworld of suffering, Garnett declared, yielded us "insight into . . . ranges of spiritual truths for ever denied to healthy, comfortable, normal folk." He granted that there was sentimentality in *Crime and Punishment* and "a certain love of melodramatic situation"—which, however, he said, did "not seriously impair the force of his psychological genius." But in *The Brothers Karamazov*, Dostoevsky had "established his greatness beyond question." The book had a "breadth and depth of vision, a temperamental richness and sustained intensity which characterize tragedy." It was "much to be regretted" that no English translation of "this great novel" had been made, although there were two versions of it in French. Finally,

Garnett thought it "small wonder" that Nietzsche had hailed Dostoevsky as his master, "for many of the most brilliant ideas of the German philosopher [were] to be found, either crystallized or in solution, in the pages of the great Russian."

Garnett's view was not shared, however, by Professor Saintsbury who in the twelfth volume of his *Periods of European Literature*[77] (1907) deplored the "tartar invasion" of an "extraordinary group of novelists, from Turgenev to Tolstoy" and suggested that their value be taken "as Scotch judges say, to *avizandum*." They represented "a practically savage, and at any rate quite un-European race-substance, superinoculated with a civilization which had no root inside, and had not even penetrated deeply as yet from outwards." Whether the influence of such a nationality could be profitable Professor Saintsbury doubted, and "while acknowledging . . . the magnitude of the phenomenon" he was "a little inclined" to wonder whether it was "a phenomenon of beginning or of end—a promise or a warning," especially when one noted with it "the outbreak of the abnormal, the anti-normal and antinomian, the bizarre and the eccentric . . . in every literature during the last decade of the nineteenth century."

Edmund Gosse, on the other hand, in an article on Tolstoy in *The Contemporary Review*[78] of September 1908, spoke of the Russian novelists in terms of the highest praise. He paid tribute to Dostoevsky's French translator: "it would be personal ingratitude," he said, if he "forgot to acknowledge what we all owe to Dérély for his wonderful versions of Dostoevsky"; and bowed in admiration before Vogüé's "rare book . . . *Le roman russe*" in which "criticism rises to its highest function, and becomes creative art." And now one could, he said, form a juster estimate of Russian fiction than had been possible before. "In the first blush of revelation," when Russian novels had been "taken without discrimination, Western readers were embarrassed by the wealth of authors. . . . In England, Turgenev and later Tolstoy were chiefly studied. . . . The 'Russian sentiment' was intensely admired, and presently it became disconcerting to discover it more amply and poignantly expressed by Dostoevsky." But now it was clear that only two of the Russian writers were "absolutely in the first class." These were, "of course," Tolstoy and Dostoevsky. Dostoevsky first discovered "the painful morbid sensibility of the Russian nation" and it was he and not Tolstoy who was responsible for what was "most vigorous in subsequent Russian literature."

A writer in *Blackwood's Magazine*,[79] the same year, with reference

to a French translation of Dostoevsky's letters, gave a brief sketch
of their author's life; said that although he had neither "the intimate
and subtle knowledge of character which distinguished Turgenev" nor
Tolstoy's lofty view of mankind, and though there was "something
in his works of melodrama, and very much of the element which we
call macabre," he was "one of the greatest Russian novelists"; and
reflected that "his career, in its submission and in its patriotism"
proved "once more that it [was] impossible for the West to appreciate
the grandeur and simplicity of Russia." In *The Athenœum*[80] the reviewer would not agree with the French translator's reference to
Dostoevsky's letters as "la si intéressante correspondance du génial
écrivain russe." Dostoevsky, he said (obviously mistranslating the
word), "was not 'genial' " nor were his letters interesting, "except
those to ladies, beginning in 1876 . . . 'begging letters' seldom
were." Then, also this year, there was published in *The Library of
Literary History*, a translation from the German of Professor A.
Brückner's *Literary History of Russia*,[81] a book which was on the
whole favorably received, although its Polish bias was noted, as well
as the difficulty of its style, and the undistinguished quality of the
translation. In the opinion of the American *Nation's*[82] critic it could
be "recommended almost without reserve as the one thorough, com-
prehensible and scholarly account of Russian literature in any of
the languages of western Europe"; and according to *The Literary
World*[83] it was "almost as indispensable" as it was interesting.

Brückner's admiration of Dostoevsky[84] was fervent: "the dæmonic,
mystic, ecstatic visionary, satanic Dostoevsky, Nietzsche's great
teacher, his profound man"; he had anticipated the most significant
contemporary movements in thought and art:

the 'mystic dread', the dæmonic in beauty, love and woman, the decadence,
the supermanhood, the symbolism—we find it all in Dostoevsky—before
Nietzsche, Strindberg, or Mæterlinck, and you find in him also much else
of which his contemporaries never allowed people to dream, such as the
whole modern psychological pathology.

Dostoevsky's art began where that of Flaubert and Bourget ended.
He would write, for example, a "continuation to 'Madame Bovary':
how when the chemist extracts from the papers left by his wife that
his much-loved child . . . is not his but another's" he becomes a
monomaniac and is driven by hatred "to seek the acquaintance of the
other man." And as for Bourget, one need only compare *Le Disciple*
with *Crime and Punishment*. "How he lags behind the Russian! Yet the

former was written twenty years later and Bourget was proclaimed
a 'psychologist.' "

As long as metaphysical questions—questions of good and evil or of the
darker side of the human spirit—are raised, so long will Dostoevsky be
read. He is one of the few in the world's literature who can never be forgotten: he leaves behind him the profoundest impressions, which can never
be effaced . . . what most enthrals us in him is his fervent love, his respect
for man as man. . . . Not in *Faust,* but rather in *Crime and Punishment*
does 'the whole woe of mankind' take hold of us.

In 1909 *The English Review*[85] published a translation by Constance
Garnett of the short story called *An Honest Thief;* and Maurice
Baring contributed to *The Quarterly Review*[86] an essay which was to
form a chapter in his study of Russian literature, published the following year. This essay, although dealing with Tolstoy and Turgenev,
had much to say of Dostoevsky with whom the other two novelists
were constantly compared. It was indeed impossible, said Baring,
not to mention Dostoevsky "because the very existence of his work
powerfully" affected one's judgment of his contemporaries; it was as
impossible to ignore "his existence and presence and influence" as it
would be to ignore "a colossal fresco by Leonardo da Vinci in a room"
that contained "only two other religious pictures, one by Rembrandt
and one by Vandyck." Any one who had felt Dostoevsky's "tremendous influence" could not look "at the work of his contemporaries
with the same eyes as before." Turgenev was "like the moon faintly
seen in the East at the end of an autumnal day" beside the "two great
planets," Tolstoy and Dostoevsky, who shone and burned "in the
firmament of Russian literature." Beside Tolstoy's characters Turgenev's seemed "caricatures" and besides Dostoevsky's they were "conventional." Compared with Dostoevsky's Nihilists, for instance, in
The Possessed, Turgenev's Bazarov was a "book-character." Tolstoy and Dostoevsky were "two great columns" which supported "the
temple of Russian literature,"—he wrote, not unlike Merezhkovsky,—
inside which Turgenev had his "shrine and altar," possessing in "a
minor degree" qualities which they both possessed, and his own "exquisite" being, "not of the kind which [belonged] to the greatest
representatives of a nation or of a race." Russian character could be
"roughly speaking . . . divided into two types," Lucifer and Ivan
Durak, *i.e.* Ivan the Fool; and the latter was "the hero of all Dostoevsky's novels" as he was also "the aim and ideal of Tolstoy's
teaching."

Landmarks in Russian Literature, the study of which this essay formed a part, came out in 1910. It was devoted largely to Dostoevsky.[87] His life and character were sketched; six of his works, *Poor Folk, The House of the Dead, Crime and Punishment, The Idiot, The Possessed,* and *The Brothers Karamazov* were examined in it at length; and there was a summary of the nature and significance of his work. Dostoevsky's message to the world, said Baring, was "love and pity," love "so great, so beautiful, so overflowing" that it was "impossible to find a parallel to it, either in ancient or in modern literature." His greatest fault, "a want of proportion," was more than redeemed by the special quality of his genius, for what it lost in "serenity, balance, and steadiness" it gained in "intensity." His genius "soared higher and dove deeper than that of any other novelist, Russian or European." *Crime and Punishment* was "the greatest tragedy about a murderer" since *Macbeth;* it was Dostoevsky's most popular work, but *The Idiot,* "the main character of which" was "the very soul and spirit of Dostoevsky," the type of Ivan Durak, was the most characteristic. *The Possessed* revealed his "powers at their highest pitch," for nowhere "in the whole range of his work" did we find "such isolated scenes of power . . . white hot with the fire of his soul, and characters in which [was] concentrated the whole dæmonic force of his personality, and the whole blinding strength of his insight"; and *The Brothers Karamazov* was a "monumental work" which would have been Dostoevsky's masterpiece had he not died before completing it. *Poor Folk* contained "the germ of all Dostoevsky's talent and genius"; and *The Letters from a Dead House* was the "one foreign book in the whole world which [deserved] to be well known." Dostoevsky was in the true sense a realist, "exactly the contrary of those people who when they wrote particularly filthy novels in which they singled out and dwelt at length on certain revolting details of life, called themselves realists. He saw things as they really" were. He sought and found "the sanity of the insane, a healthy spot in the sorest soul, a gleam of gold in the darkest mine, a pearl in the filthiest refuse heap, a spring in the most arid desert."

The work was reviewed with exceptional enthusiasm. It was praised in *The Nation.*[88] In *The Spectator*[89] it was reported to be "a very notable piece of criticism," a book at once "brilliant and judicious." In *The Athenæum*[90] the opinion was expressed that "no other non-Russian writer [had] shown so intimate a knowledge of Russian character"; and in *The Literary World*[91] that his book would "not only send a multitude of people to study for themselves" the Russian writers of whom he spoke, but would actually "foster a deeper and wider goodwill on the part of English people for the Russian nation." It was mentioned by Edmund Gosse in an article on Vogüé:[92] "Mr. Maurice Baring has recently defined for us the elements of the realism of the Russians," and in the American *Current Literature*,[93] under a portrait of Dostoevsky, one read:

Proclaimed one of the two great Figures of Russian Literature. According to Maurice Baring, the English writer, Dostoevsky is one of the two great columns which support the temple of Russian literature. Tolstoy is the other. Turgenev is placed by Mr. Baring inside the Temple.

John Galsworthy wrote to Edward Garnett:[94]

I've been reading Baring's book on Russian Literature. He's piqued me up to a desire to read Dostoevsky's *The Idiot* and *The Brothers Karamazov* and *The Possessed,* but *what translations are there?* It's interesting too what he says about the Russian estimate of Turgenev, but that's obviously a fashion—though I agree that Tolstoy and Dostoevsky reach places which Turgenev doesn't even attempt. I saw your critique, it was not long enough.

Shortly after, he wrote to Garnett again: "I've read *The Dead House,*—splendid"; and he said he would "like awfully to read *The Brothers Karamazov* in the French." This was sent him and he gratefully acknowledged its receipt.[95]

But in *The Contemporary Review*[96] Mr. Baring was advised to "chasten his enthusiasm and his prose" and was reminded that Russian literature was not "florid." His "claims of Dostoevsky," the reviewer contended, were put so high that they "paralysed" judgment; and yet one might doubt whether *Crime and Punishment* and *The Idiot* filled though they were "with an indescribable charm" could "with their impress of a non-normal and unequilibrated personality show Russian genius at its highest point." The book, however, made one wish "that English people knew more—knew something" of Russian literature, for "to the average English reader" the great names of Russian literature, other than Tolstoy's which was "familiar, though his works in fact [were] unfamiliar," conveyed "little or nothing" and were indeed "symbols of outer barbarism." Whereby the English lost in three ways: first in their failure to establish a sympathetic understanding with a people on whose relationship with England "the future of the world must largely turn"; secondly, in not availing themselves of a much needed foreign influence: "we need now as we have always needed at the successive periods of crisis in our literary history, a powerful foreign influence. That influence will have to be Russian"; thirdly, in "the loss of the literature itself . . . a first class literature." All of which, however, did not make Baring's study all it should be.

In *The New Age*[97] the reviewer, under the pseudonym of "Jacob Tonson," was Arnold Bennett. Mr. Baring, he said, seemed to have "a greater love of literature than an understanding of it;" he wrote "like a whole-hearted amateur"; but "his chapters on Russian characteristics and on realism in Russian literature" were "genuinely valuable." He made one see that "compared with the spontaneous, unconscious realism of the Russians," "even French realism" was "artificial and feeble"; and his account of Dostoevsky was "straightforward, detailed, homely." Had he, instead of comparing Dostoevsky to Charlotte Brontë, "bracketed" him with "the lonely Emily" he could have been "credited . . . with a subtle originality." It was but a year ago, wrote Bennett, that he himself had "come across" *The Brothers Karamazov*, of which he had not heard before. He read it in French translation and thought it "contained some of the greatest scenes" he had "ever encountered in fiction." He classed it immediately with *Crime and Punishment* and *La Chartreuse de Parme* as "one of the supreme marvels of the world." But, puzzled by "certain aspects of it," he asked his friends and was told by them that "it was not a major work." He turned to Mrs. Garnett, and she said: " 'it is his masterpiece,' " but separated from her at that moment "by a ruthless host," he remained with his difficulties unsolved until he learned from Mr. Baring's book that the French translation was incomplete and the original work unfinished. Still, even in an imperfect translation, "the scene with the old monk at the beginning" of the book appeared to Bennett to be "in the very grandest heroical manner." There was "nothing in either English or French prose literature to match it, outside Dostoevsky." It ranked "with the scene towards the beginning of *Crime and Punishment* when in the inn the drunken father relates his daughter's 'shame.' " Indeed, "if an author's reputation among people of taste depended solely on his success with single scenes" Dostoévsky would outrank all other novelists, if not all poets. But that was not so; and Dostoevsky's novels had "grave faults." They were "tremendously unlevel," faults which Mr. Baring had admitted, but had not, according to Bennett, sufficiently emphasized.

In the article on Vogüé, referred to above, Gosse said the French

critic had been rightly called the "Chateaubriand of the Third Republic," for to him was "due the reappearance of mystery and illusion
in French imaginative literature"; and *Le roman russe,* his principal
work, was "perhaps the most epoch-making single volume of criticism
issued in France during our time." It had opened the eyes of his contemporaries "to the fallacies" of the French Naturalists, as his own
eyes had been opened by a comparison of their "formal and mechanical realism" with that of the Russians,—whose attitudes, especially
Tolstoy's and Dostoevsky's "included a moral inspiration which alone
could excuse the harshness of the realistic method."

There was also in this year a new edition of *Crime and Punishment*
and a stage version of it, *The Unwritten Law,* by Laurence Irving,
who acted the part of Raskolnikov. The play did not pretend to be
faithful to the original; it was advertised as only "founded" on Dostoevsky's book. Sonia was presented in it as "an innocent girl who
is threatened by the lust of her landlord" and this landlord, a "rather
melodramatic villain," not the old pawn-broker, became Raskolnikov's
victim. This "bowdlerization," according to *The Athenæum,*[98] was
necessary to make the play presentable to the English public. A story
which deals "with the redeemining love of a courtesan for a murderer"
would not be "endured by our insular sentiment" without "considerable modification." But "despite such changes," Laurence Irving had
preserved "pretty faithfully . . . the ethic of the tale," and had "compressed its incidents so skillfully as to produce a compact, vigorous,
and thrilling play."

The next year Laurence Irving wrote an introduction for the Everyman edition of *Crime and Punishment.*[99] It was a book, he said, by
the side of which "the stories of Poe [seemed] strained; Hoffman
[sank] to the level of a highly self-conscious poseur; . . . while Robert
Louis Stevenson [became] but as a melting rushlight." It was a story
that "for the deepest essence of tragedy" had no equal in fiction.
And the reason for Dostoevsky's preeminence was not "far to seek";
one had but to scan the facts of his life to see "whence, apart from
any possibly innate difference of gifts, his superiority was inevitably
bound to flow"; and he accordingly gave a brief chronological summary of his life, quoting passages from his letters and from the *Recollections* of Sonia Kovalevsky. Of his work it was not "too difficult to
convey a summary impression," for there was about them "a homo-
geneiety and a pervasive atmosphere" in keeping with the circumstances of his life. They were "a region of volcanic eruption, with

vast tracts devastated by passion and overlaid with the scoriæ of vice" but even "athwart the most stagnant places" illuminated by "a light of some heavenly region," Dostoevsky's defects needed "no critic to point them out"; they were "as large and as unescapable as his powers." His style was "cumbrous and loose; his plots . . . devious and spasmodic" and often melodramatic. But so were Shakespeare's. What did it matter, "where the insight [was] so deep, evocative power so unfailing, the flux of the emotion so sure, the analysis so keen, the idea propounded so daring and so subtle?"

Another cheap edition of *Crime and Punishment* came out in this year, and *The House of the Dead* was reprinted in the Everyman collection. William Lyon Phelps's *Essays on Russian Novelists*, containing one on Dostoevsky,[100] were published; and *The Hibbert Journal* printed an authorized translation of an essay on Dostoevsky and Nietzsche by Otto Julius Bierbaum.[101]

Professor Phelps thought that "of all the masters of fiction both in Russia and elsewhere" Dostoevsky was "the most truly spiritual." Yet he wrote that the hero of *Letters from Underground* was "the regulation weak-willed Russian," "sickly and impractical" who spent "most of his time analysing his mental states" and whose "singular adventures" had "only occasional and languid interest"; that the book was "one of the many books of Dostoevsky that one vigorously vowed never to read again." *Crime and Punishment* was "abominably diffuse, filled with extraneous and superfluous matter, and totally lacking in the principles of good construction"; the narrative was interrupted with dreams that often had "no connection with the plot" and whether they were "interjected to deceive the reader, or merely to indulge the novelist's whimsical fancy" Professor Phelps found it "hard to divine." *The Idiot* was "almost insufferably long . . . a combination of a hospital and insane asylum . . . filled with sickly, diseased, silly, and crazy folk." *The Brothers Karamazov* was "incomplete . . . badly constructed . . . very badly written." Its women could not be told apart. But into it Dostoevsky had put "all the sum of his wisdom, all the ripe fruit of his experience, all his religious aspiration," and so it was preferable to Dostoevsky's other novels. In sum, "the deficiencies and the excrescences" of Dostoevsky's art were "glaring"; he had been "surpassed in many things by other novelists," but he was the most "spiritual" of them all.

Bierbaum's praise of Dostoevsky was very high, but coupled with a warning. Dostoevsky he said was "more than a hill-top," he was a 'mountain-peak, measured by whose loftiness all other writers of our time, with one sole exception," looked "small indeed." The exception was Nietzsche who "towered" above him and "affected us in a way" that might be called "disquieting, as a finished work of art, as something constructed, beside something elemental." These two were "the only really great minds in modern literature since the days of Goethe and Byron." And their greatness derived from what they represented, for they were symbols. Nietzsche symbolized "the downfall of Western European culture, which [had] its roots in the antique"; Dostoevsky, "the rise of Russian civilization, which [was] derived from the Empire of the East." Therein lay the peril of Dostoevsky: "Our hearts [were] not with him whose ideals [had] nothing in common with our own," but there was a risk of coming "so completely under the spell of his strong personality" as to become "unconscious of all the strong and dangerous elements" in his art. His charm was seductive. That was why "the world so long overlooked the fact that this great enchanter" was "something more than a deeply interesting portrayer of Russian life, a wise and poetic interpreter of Russian character," that he was "as well the conscious apostle of the hidden forces at work among the Russian people, forces [destined] as he believed to make of Russia a mighty and consolidated power, and to turn the tide of Western culture from its present course, diverting it into channels of their own." Dostoevsky was "a great Russian prophet," and his philosophy was in every way the opposite of Nietzsche's. On one thing only were they agreed, that reconciliation of their doctrines was impossible. "What contradictions" were implied in them! There was, "in fact, little else"; and "the one in which all others were comprised" was Nietzsche's "will to power" and Dostoevsky's "will to humility." Dostoevsky was a spellbinder, an artist whose characters had a "Shakesperean wealth and fascination" which was the reason "the world [had] been conquered by [his] books." His was an art that veiled its purpose, but once this purpose had been recognized, it must be rejected: to accept it "would be to deny Goethe and to regard Nietzsche as a disease." "It is a divergent path," said Bierbaum, "that we are called to tread." And so, "paying to Dostoevsky's devotees of humility the ready tribute of our admiration," he concluded, "we rejoice with confidence to think that, if the Russian spirit be in reality one of perverse passivity . . . there is no danger that we shall be mastered by it. A train of flagellants will never conquer the world."

Another book on Russia by Maurice Baring came out in this

year.[102] Dostoevsky was frequently mentioned in it as having comprehended the "Russian soul": he was the first great Russian writer after Pushkin "who understood what the Russian people felt"; in him, "Russia found a sombre Titan, who laid bare the Russian soul in the depths of its agony, and broke a jar of myrrh, made of pity, precious beyond rubies, over its gaping wounds"; "to the student of Russia" his books were "valuable as a revelation of the Russian soul." But as yet no complete translation of his work existed in English. His "most important book, *The Brothers Karamazov*" was unknown and even its French translation was "mutilated and hopelessly inadequate." Until such an adequate and complete translation was made, "his work would not obtain recognition in England and the praise that [was] accorded him [would] doubtless seem exaggerated."[103]

In 1912, the much heralded *Brothers Karamazov* appeared in Constance Garnett's translation, and with it Dostoevsky's reputation entered a new phase.

IV. THE DOSTOEVSKY CULT—1912-1921

"IN THE thirty years which have elapsed since Dostoevsky's death," wrote *The London Times*[1] reviewer of Constance Garnett's translation, "with all the obstacles there have been to keep us at a distance from his work, we have at least learned enough to know how greatly a full English version of it is to be desired." The critic of *The Spectator*[2] declared that Mrs. Garnett's intention of publishing the whole of Dostoevsky would soon remove the "material difficulty" which had hitherto "stood in the way" of his popularity in England:

Soon there should be no valid excuse for the most insular of English readers if he refrains at least from *trying* to become acquainted with a writer who, in the opinion of his countrymen, has high claim to rank as supreme spokesman of the Russian race.

Constance Garnett's version of Dostoevsky has been recently criticized by Avrahm Yarmolinsky who has said that excellent as it is "it leaves something to be desired, particularly as regards accuracy."[3] Yet it was the first adequate translation in English and remains the most honest, close, and natural one. It reproduces better than other translations the special quality of Dostoevsky's style, an eminently "plain" style, of a plainness that is the product of two qualities: a sharp intelligence which strikes through to the ultimate simplicity of what it observes, and a democratic temper which expresses itself most easily in colloquial rather than "literary " idiom. A good translation should convey his effect of bare simplicity. But before Constance Garnett this was not achieved, as one may readily see by comparing the different versions of any given passage; of, for example, a paragraph from the well known "Dantesque" description of the prisoners' bath in *The House of the Dead*.*

In the original, the horror of the scene lies not only in its accumulation of revolting detail, but in the rhythm of the brief sentences which fall monotonously in a kind of calm hopelessness of factual statement. Its effect of compression, of undistracted observation and unspoken horror, as well as the cadence of the Russian, a translation may be powerless to convey exactly. Even Constance Garnett, who is the most successful in approximating the original, must use 286 words to Dostoevsky's 193. But her additions are either necessitated by linguistic differences—Russian, for example, has no article either definite or indefinite, and being an inflected language, may often omit

* See pp. 64, 65.

pronouns—or they are made for the sake of clarity as, for example, in the sentence beginning "some wanting to pass," the insertion of "in their chains," which is not in the original. Other modifications one might note. "The place was alive with human beings" is in the original expressed in four words: "there too people swarmed" (though *swarm* does not render the Russian exactly); "as big as the palm of your hand" stands for two Russian words which might be Englished, "a hand's breadth"; "that is their whole idea of a bath" is for a brief, colloquial "that's the whole bath." Such expansions spoil the rapidity of the original; other instances destroy its simplicity. *"Accompaniment* of chains" should be *"sound* of chains"; "clanking on the floor," although it has the merit of logical connection with "sound," loses the original's more simple observation, "dragging"; and "on all *sides"* had been more just to the colloquial Russian idiom than the Latinism of "in all *directions."* But Constance Garnett is, on the whole, faithful to the text in so far as seems consistent with clarity and the demands of another language. She is never grossly inaccurate, or purely fanciful.

So much cannot be said of the other translators. Marie von Thilo, for example, although in effect more graceful than Constance Garnett, compresses or expands the original at will, reducing in the interests of smoothness a forceful piece of writing to weak commonplace. Dostoevsky's first three sentences are in her version cut down to one, with much detail omitted; while further on, the explanation of how steam was produced, the description of "human beings swaying backwards and forwards," the tautological insertion of "dirt" before "filth," of its *actually flowing,* of the weakly intensive *perfectly wild,* of the invented *like demons,* of the *cans* of water, of the *buyers,* are all gratuitous additions. Mr. Dole's version errs on the side of awkwardness and colloquial exaggeration: "would not be sitting doubled up," "hullaballoo," "broomed themselves." "But precious little washing they got" adds a note of critical comment not intended in the original. That the men, passing by, dragged others "into the quarrel" and not actually after them, is an understandable mistranslation of the Russian, *uvlekali,* which has both a primary physical meaning and a derivative intellectual one; but a mistranslation it certainly is. H. Sutherland Edwards, in spite of the authenticity claimed for his version, follows all the mistakes of his inaccurate French original. The places *above* instead of *under* the benches (Edwards had obviously misread M. Neyroud's *audessous* for *au-dessus*); on the *floor*

Garnett

"But even the space under the benches was all filled; there, too, *the place was alive with human beings.* There was not a spot on the floor *as big as the palm of your hand* where there was not a convict squatting, splashing from his bucket. Others stood up among them and holding their buckets in their hands washed themselves standing; the dirty water trickled off them on to the shaven heads of the convicts sitting below them. On the top shelf and on all the steps leading up to it, men were crouched, huddled together washing themselves. But they did not wash themselves much. Men of the peasant class don't wash much with soap and hot water; they only steam themselves terribly and douche themselves with cold water—*that is their whole idea of a bath.* Fifty birches were rising and falling rhythmically on the shelves. They all thrashed themselves into a state of stupefaction. More steam was raised every moment. It was not heat; it was hell. All were shouting and vociferating to the *accompaniment* of a hundred chains

Few, however, of the convicts really washed themselves, as the common people care but little for soap and hot water; their idea of a bath consisting in getting up to the highest shelf, whipping themselves violently with a bundle of birch twigs, then pouring cold water down their backs. About fifty birch rods were in constant movement on the shelves, *water was being continually thrown at the hot oven to make more steam,* till the heat was almost unbearable. And all this mass of *human beings was swaying backwards and forwards,* shouting and yelling and clanking their chains on the floor. Some, in trying to cross the floor, were caught in the chains of those who were sitting down, and falling on their heads, knocked them down, cursing and swearing. *The dirt and filth actually flowed in streams everywhere. The men were perfectly wild* with excitement, and yelled and shrieked *like demons.* A dense crowd had collected round the window where the *cans* of hot water were handed in, and carried by *the buyers* to their respective places, not, however, without spilling half of

heat, it was hell let loose. It was all one uproar and *hullabaloo,* with rattling of a hundred chains dragging over the floor. . . . Some, trying to pass, entangled themselves with the chains of others, and they themselves bumped against the heads of those sitting below, and they tumbled over, and scolded, and *dragged into the quarrel* those whom they hit. The filth was streaming on every side. All were in an excited and as it were intoxicated, state of mind. Shrieks and cries were heard. At the dressing-room window, where the water was handed through, there was a tumult, a pushing, even fighting. The hot water ordered was spilt on the heads of those sitting on the floor, before it reached its destination."

Edwards

"Even the places *above* the benches were occupied, the convicts swarmed everywhere. As for the floor there was not a place as big as the palm of the hand which was not occupied by the convicts. They sent the water in spouts out of their pails. Those who were standing up washed themselves pail in hand, and the

fell dragged down the ones whose chains had become entangled in theirs. They were all in a state of intoxication of wild exultation. Cries and shrieks were heard on all sides. There was much crowding and crushing at the window of the dressing-room through which the hot water was delivered, and much of it got spilt over the heads of those who were seated on the floor before it arrived at its destination."

Neyroud

"Même les places qui se trouvaient au-dessous des banquettes étaient occupées: les forçats y grouillaient. Quant au plancher, il n'y avait pas un espace grand comme la paume de la main qui ne fut occupé par les détenus; ils faisaient jaillir l'eau de leurs baquets. Ceux qui étaient debout se lavaient en tenant à la main leur seille; l'eau sale coulait le long de leur corps et tombait sur les têtes rasées de ceux qui étaient assis. Sur la banquette et les gradins qui y conduisaient étaient entassés d'autres forçats qui se lavaient tout recroquevillés et ramassés, mais c'était le petit nombre.

clanking on the floor. . . . Some of them, wanting to pass, got entangled in other men's chains and caught in their own chains the heads of those below them; they fell down, swore, and dragged those they caught after them. Liquid filth ran *in all directions*. Every one seemed in a sort of intoxicated, over-excited condition; there were shrieks and cries. By the window of the anteroom from which the water was handed out there was swearing, crowding, and a regular scuffle. The fresh hot water was spilt over the heads of those who were sitting on the floor before it reached its destination."

Von Thilo

"Even the space under the benches was occupied; the men squatted about on the floor washing themselves, while others who had been less fortunate in obtaining a place stood upright between them, the dirty water trickling down from their backs on the cropped heads of those who sat below. The shelves were covered with convicts who tried to screw themselves into the smallest possible space.

it over the heads of the bathers who squatted on the floor."

Dole

"But the places under the benches were also taken; even there, the crowd clustered. On the whole floor, there was not a free place as large as the palm of the hand where the prisoners *would not be sitting doubled up*, washing themselves in their pails. Others stood upright among these, and, holding their pails in their hands, washed themselves as best they could. The dirty water ran down directly on the shaven heads of those who sat beneath them. On the platform, and on all the steps leading to it, were men washing themselves, bent down and doubled up. *But precious little washing they got*. Plebians wash themselves very little with hot water and soap: they only steam themselves tremendously, and then pour cold water over them, and that's their whole bath. Fifty brooms or so on the platform were rising and falling in concert: they all *broomed themselves* into a state of intoxication. Every instant steam was let in. It was not merely

dirty water ran all down their body to fall on the shaved heads of those who were sitting down. On the upper bench, and the steps which led to it, were heaped together other convicts who washed themselves more thoroughly, but these were in small number. The populace does not care to wash with soap and water, it prefers stewing in a horrible manner, and then inundating itself with cold water. That is how the common people take their bath. *On the floor* could be seen fifty bundles of rods rising and falling at the same time, the holders were whipping themselves into a state of intoxication. The steam became thicker and thicker every minute, so that what one now felt was not a warm but a burning sensation, *as from boiling pitch*. The convicts shouted and howled to the accompaniment of the hundred chains shaking on the floor. Those who wished to pass from one place to another got their chains mixed up with those of their neighbours, and knocked against the heads of the men who were lower down than they. Then there were volleys of oaths as those who

La populace ne se lave pas volontiers avec de l'eau et du savon; ils préfèrent s'étuver horriblement, et s'inonder ensuite d'eau froide; c'est ainsi qu'ils prennent leur bain. *Sur le plancher* on voyait cinquante balais de verges s'élever et s'abaisser à la fois, tous se fouettaient à en être ivres. On augmentait à chaque instant la vapeur; aussi ce que l'on ressentait n'était plus de la chaleur, mais une brûlure *comme celle de la poix bouillante*. On criait, on gloussait, au bruit de cent chaînes, traînant sur le plancher . . . Ceux qui voulaient passer d'un endroit à l'autre embarrassaient leurs fers dans d'autres chaînes et heurtaient la tête des détenus qui se trouvaient plus bas qu'eux, tombaient, juraient en entraînant dans leur chute ceux auxquels ils s'accrochaient. Tous étaient dans une espèce de griserie, d'excitation folle; des cris et des glapissements se croissaient. Il y avait un entassement, un écrasement du côté de la fenêtre du cabinet par laquelle on délivrait l'eau chaude; elle jaillissait sur les têtes de ceux qui étaient assis sur le plancher, avant qu'elle arrivât à sa destination."

instead of on the *benches,* indicate that he had not grasped the setting. And "as from boiling pitch," accurately translating the French, is not in the Russian at all.

Each of these translators, except Constance Garnett, has introduced his own feelings about the situation; and so has, to a greater or less extent, destroyed Dostoevsky's. There is no reason to suppose the passage in any way exceptional, and, taken as typical, it shows clearly that Constance Garnett's translation was the first in English to render the real flavor of Dostoevsky with any degree of accuracy.

Her translation was welcome; the reading public, as the reviews indicated, was curious about Dostoevsky. He had been proclaimed "the most distinctively Russian of writers." "Through him alone," it had been said, could one "hope to understand the Russian soul";[4] by the Russians themselves he was "esteemed . . . as one of their greatest writers . . . greater than Turgenev";[5] and of his "pictures of Russian life," *The Brothers Karamazov* was "the most detailed, vivid, and significant" that he had drawn. "The deeper one penetrated into it," to be sure, "the wider [seemed] to grow the difference between this life and that of Western Europe." This strangeness, indeed, this remoteness of Dostoevsky from the familiar concepts of the West could be held largely accountable for his lack of popularity in England, for it always took "a long time, even for the most enlightened critics, to appreciate in a foreign literature anything but those qualities which it [shared] in common with their own." That was why Turgenev, "a writer influenced far more than either of his great contemporaries by the literary traditions of Western Europe" was "for many years . . . the one Russian author really appreciated by English readers"; why he was succeeded by Tolstoy, who was somewhat more Russian, yet not completely foreign; and why Dostoevsky still remained unknown. And yet, according to *The Spectator,* "the true greatness of a foreign literature" was to be found "precisely in its peculiar and unfamiliar qualities."

Among the unfamiliar qualities of Dostoevsky "the most obviously disconcerting" was the form of his novels: "not only excessively long" but also " at any rate on a first inspection extremely disordered," an effect to be explained by the hurried method of their creation which a closer analysis, however, was bound to prove to depend on the reader's erroneous judgment, for an "underlying spirit" in each novel gave "a vital unexpected unity to the whole." But stranger than his form, and so "an even more serious stumbling-block to English readers," was the strangeness of Dostoevsky's "spirit." His books seemed "written by a man who [viewed] life from a single angle; everything in them [was] agitated, feverish, intense"; they were "screwed up above the normal pitch; they [appeared] to be always trembling on the verge of insanity, and sometimes, indeed, to plunge over into the very middle of it"; theirs was an atmosphere which offered "a peculiarly marked contrast to that of the ordinary English novel" whose "great tradition . . . with a very few exceptions"—such, for instance, as Emily Brontë—was to treat life "from the standpoint of common sense," its object, to present life "with sanity, with breadth, with humour; to throw over the vision of it the plain clear bright light of day." The habit of English novelists was "to stand on one side themselves, with the detachment of amused and benevolent spectators." And to those who had "grown accustomed" to this "body of literature remarkable for its sobriety, its humanity, and its quiet wisdom," the "extravagance and the frenzy that seethe in Dostoevsky's pages" must be perplexing and repellent.

How with its intensity of passion, could Dostoevsky's work be realistic; and how, with its nervousness, could it be anything but neurotic? "Paradoxical as it may seem," in the opinion of *The Spectator's* critic it was "yet certainly true" that Dostoevsky "with all his fondness for the abnormal and the extraordinary" was a "profoundly sane and human writer." He was in this respect "the exact opposite of Tolstoy" who "under the cloak of a strict and elaborate adherence to the commonplace" concealed "a neurotic temperament." Dostoevsky used what was "horrible, grotesque, and disgraceful in life" not because like "the French writers of the Naturalistic school" he took "a pleasure in these things"; he faced the worst only "to assert, with a fuller courage and a deeper confidence, the nobility and splendor of the human spirit." His power lay "in the sudden strange vision" that he gave to the "poignant underlying humanity" of his characters. He was a realist, according to *The Athenæum*, which was a "trite thing to say," but it was "worth while to notice that his [was] that mode of realism which works from within outwards, using the outward phenomena, however boldly, only in subservience to the discovery and explication of inward truth." There was "an ancient mystical speculation . . . according to which the soul possesses a hidden inviolable center, incapable of sin, and never implicated, howsoever distressed, by sins committed." It was "the recognition . . . of some such mystery" as this that constituted "the ultimate secret of Dostoevsky's fearful poignancy and truth. . . . The most tragic victim of the vilest criminal [was] found to be, after all, his own miserable soul." Dostoevsky's view was comparable to the Greek idea of "Ate, and again of ἀμαρτία, not μοχθηρία, as the proper subject of tragedy." Furthermore, one had been "again and again reminded" of Nietzsche's declared indebtedness to Dostoevsky; and "if there were nothing else to rouse curiosity, it would be enough to know there met in him two such widely opposed suffrages, generally speaking, as those of Nietzsche . . . and Tolstoy." *The Brothers Karamazov,* wrote its reviewer in *The Literary World,* was "full of intimate pictures of Russian life and character," but its subject, "a sustained study of heredity as represented in a family of degenerates" was not "exhilarating"; it was "fascinating" but could be "commended" only to those readers who were "of particularly robust mental and moral stamina."[6] In *The Academy*[7] the work was described in words of one syllable as follows:

This volume is a wonderful production at the price. The story has been very ably translated by Constance Garnett, who has done much good work in rendering Tolstoy and other Russian novelists familiar to English readers. The author of this very long novel writes with an intimate acquaintance of Russian life and gives striking pictures of many of its phases. Alyosha, one of the chief characters, is a monk, and shows a very Christian disposition. His two brothers are wild characters brimming over with good impulses one minute and barbaric the next, almost like children in their want of control of their emotions. In fact, the general impression the book gives is that of thunderstorm and sunshine rapidly following each other.

The evolution of Russia and its people is shown in the conversations, some of great length, and the Russian judicial procedure in all its stages is exemplified by a trial for murder. . . . The book, although so long, is quite interesting and gives us real life and men and women with primitive passions on which they act, and not dolls. . . . The preface should be carefully read, as it explains much.

For eight years after *The Brothers Karamazov* Constance Garnett published her versions of Dostoevsky's novels until she had translated them all. *The Idiot* and *The Letters from the Underground* came out in 1913, *The Possessed* and *Crime and Punishment* in 1914, *The House of the Dead* and *The Insulted and Injured* in 1915, *The Raw Youth* in 1916, and in 1917, 1918, 1919, and 1920, collections of his short stories.[8]

All were received with almost unanimous approbation. Even though *The Idiot* might be "a picture of chaos," a "mad world," full of "drunkenness and insincerity," it "gave us a deep vision of the infinite potentialities of man."[9] It was "the most characteristic and personal" of Dostoevsky's novels; one welcomed "with special pleasure a sympathetic version of it."[10] It was a work of humor, "reminiscent of the Molière of 'Le Médecin malgré lui' and 'Georges Dandin.' " Its "mood of pure comedy" had disappeared in *The Double* and *Crime and Punishment;* but here, as well as in *The Possessed,* it was again to be found, a "strange power of ridicule," the "laughter of loving-kindness" which "dominated and inspired all Dostoevsky's other qualities," a "makeweight to those intense and extreme qualities in his composition which would otherwise have carried him into mere extravagance." Prince Myshkin would be "very difficult for the readers of the western world to understand" so "alien" was he to their "ideals and desires,"[11] but, if understood, he would be seen as "a national answer to those uprooted ones in 'Demons,' "[12] the "actual embodiment of a personal and a national ideal":

Dostoevsky was the observant endurer of *The House of the Dead;* he was the sombre and self-sacrificing wooer of *Injury and Insult.* He sounded the last depths of Sonia's despairing compassion in *Crime and Punishment;* he groped with Ordinov in the dimmest lurking places and the most cob-webbed corners of *The Underground Spirit.* He suffered with the dark, self-condemning arrogance of the ape-haunted Stavrogin in *Demons;* he absorbed, while retaining his unsullied kinship with the most sinless hopes, all the swinish darkness of the hereditary curse of *The Brothers Karamazov.* But in the finished portrait of Prince Myshkin he has given us, once and forever, the projection of his long dream of the nobler, regenerated Russian to be.

The Possessed might be "the least 'sympathetic' of Dostoevsky's more important novels," a "bitter and incoherent attack on antinationalism," written to "picture an insane state of affairs," a "terrible and thrilling book," and to those who knew Dostoevsky, obviously, not one in which "his deep spirit of forgiveness and pity could show to full advantage," yet notable in that "even here" Dostoevsky, although "out of sympathy with most of the characters," made them "very different to what they appear on the surface. Verhovensky . . . a kind of monster of subtlety, callousness, and violence [was] all at once presented . . . as a mystical idealist; Stavrogin, the man without a conscience, [was] a strange dreamer; Kirillov, the madman, [was] a lofty moralist."[13] The critic for *The Athenæum*[14] wrote that "the greatest interest" of the book, as also that of *The Brothers Karamazov* was not so much its "actual events" as its "extraordinary handling of psychological abnormality," as well as the fact that this handling was "largely autobiographical," the "autobiography of one who independently came to the conclusions of Blake and Nietzsche in matters of religion—sometimes almost echoing their very words." So also the reviewer in *The Nation*,[15] who said that "the overwhelming importance of *The Possessed*" lay in the fact that it was Dostoevsky's "final refutation of those infamously stupid accusations through which he had been robbed of eight years of his creative power."

The House of the Dead, probably "the best known of its author's works among English readers," was a "vivid and terrible picture" but "above all a revelation of certain fundamental Russian qualities."[16] There was "no chatter about the ennobling power of misery" in it; Dostoevsky's "ex-convict" was left a "broken man." The "beauty" and "force" of his book lay in "his understanding of the whole, good and bad, his gentle, powerful unfolding of a secret place in infinitely various life."[17] In *The Eternal Husband* there was "a sense of terrible inevitableness." It had "all the gloom and relentlessness of Greek drama." And "hideous" as it was, "its exposure of human morbidity" bóre "the unmistakeable hall mark of truth." It was not among the best of Dostoevsky's things but it was interesting as an illustration of his unique method: proceeding "upon lines of its own," making no use "of the usual stock-in-trade of the fiction writer"; caring "not at all" for "externals,"—the work of "the novelist of the soul."[18] It was another example of Dostoevsky's unique power to reconstruct "swift and complicated states of mind," his ability "to follow not only the vivid streak of achieved thought, but to suggest the dim and populous underworld of the mind's consciousness where desires and impulses are moving blindly beneath the sod." His method was "the exact opposite" of that adopted "by most of our novelists" who reproduced all the externals of the hero but "very rarely" penetrated "to the tumult of thought" within his mind, whereas the "whole fabric" of Dostoevsky's books was "made out of such material," out of "the intricate maze" of people's emotions. And for this reason, that is, because they forced upon us a "different point of view from that to which we were accustomed," his books "bewildered" us.[19]

Dostoevsky's less important works were disappointing but not a disillusionment; their faults could not obscure the greatness of the major novels. Concerning *White Nights and Other Stories*, for example, *The Times* reviewer[20] wrote that he found them "difficult and unpleasant to read" and of interest only "as showing, not the limitations, but the perversions of a great man." Dostoevsky required for his philosophy more space than a short story allowed. That "relation between good and evil, which [was] the theme of his novels" was "not established here." Here one saw "evil alone in no relation to anything." It was "Dostoevsky not himself, yet recognizable, Dostoevsky giving way to insane moods and taking them seriously enough to write in them." *An Honest Thief* displayed its author's limitations as a humorist[21]—"the restraint and aloofness of the great comic writers [were] impossible for him." But even these limitations were a mark of his greatness. They proceeded from the "fervour of his genius." It was "sympathy" that caused "his laughter" to pass "beyond merriment into a strange violent amusement" which was "not merry at all." Dostoevsky made the "perfection" of the English *Cranford,* to which *The Uncle's Dream* bore a "superficial resemblance," "appear to be the result of leaving out all the most important things," which of course, was no reason for underrating comedy of the English sort; it was "the old unnecessary quarrel between the inch of smooth ivory and the six feet of canvas with its strong coarse grains." As for *The Raw Youth,* "for half a lifetime," complained *The Nation's*[22] critic, "the existence of a Dostoevsky novel entitled *The Raw Youth* [had] been known." It "meant as much to us and as little as the lost plays of Æschylus." One had hoped that it "might prove as rich a mine of mingled realism and romance as *Crime and Punishment* itself." But now that hope was past: "a cherished pleasure is subtracted from our expectations." None the less, he took this opportunity to write a long analysis of the differences between the usual Western novel and the Russian as exemplified by Dostoevsky. The Karamazovs, one suspected, "might all have been perfectly sane if they had been sent at an early age to an English Public School. But they would have lost with their sanity, not merely their unbridled passions, but also their theoretical curiosity about the universe. They would not have been tempted to murder their father, and they would have stopped discussing whether God exists, and whether all things are lawful." To the reviewer in *The Athenæum,*[23] *The Raw Youth,* "with all its incoherent rapidity of action" was "a novel of growth and development which could have few to resemble it," and *The Spectator's*[24] critic saw in it "the usual twilight atmosphere" but less sordidness than in Dostoevsky's other novels, and a more subtle humour. *The Times*[25] review expressed conviction that Dostoevsky "was drawing his own youth in this book," was showing "lovingly" the Nietzschean philosophy which he himself had abandoned. It proceeded then to a general discussion of Dostoevsky's style in relation to his theme. There was, of course, no coherence in his novels "except the coherence of character and even that was difficult to grasp sometimes," for those things which we expected "to be told of characters" Dostoevsky took for granted. He knew "too much about men and women to pretend" that he understood their motives, so that one could know his characters as little as one knew Hamlet. Dostoevsky, like Shakespeare, gave "the characters themselves, their minds drawn as a great artist might draw their bodies" without explaining motives of action, thought, or feeling. For this reason he was puzzling, but he was even more puzzling because his interest in people was so different from ours. He cared nothing for men's actions and he never judged them. He dealt "with those depths of the mind in which evil impulse starts before the motive has been manufactured." What he showed us was "actual good and evil deeds," and to this "life of truth and intense emotions" we were not accustomed. He was "the greatest" of all novelists but we could not "for long stay at the height of his greatness."

The Insulted and Injured, in the opinion of the critic in The Saturday Review,[26] although "the first of Dostoevsky's novels to be translated into French and made known in Western Europe," was "a comparatively poor example of his work," lacking "the psychological interest, as well as the dramatic force of Crime and Punishment" and "the awful wonder" of The House of the Dead. Natasha "not only reminded us that we did not in the least understand the Russian heart, but forcibly suggested that the Russians themselves did not understand much better." But for the reviewer in The Athenæum,[27] the story had "not merely poetry" in it, "but also a power of recalling the very smells of Petrograd"; "technically," although lacking "the overwhelming moments of Crime and Punishment" it ranked "high among Dostoevsky's works." According to The Times[28] it was not so good as The Idiot but easier to read, although Dostoevsky was "never easy to read." There were two reasons that made for the difficulty of his work. In the first place, the events which he related were "real events" in the sense that they seemed "to move us directly and not through the comment of the author." They were not "mitigated," as were, for example, those of Dickens, with sentimental commentary. For this reason one could not "go on reading him with comfort for long." One was obliged to stop as if to reappraise "a momentous actual experience," to "disburden" the mind "with thinking" as one passed from chapter to chapter. In the second place, Dostoevsky's "peculiar malease," his epilepsy, colored everything that he wrote so infectiously that one shared "his experience of life and his mental pain" as one read him; and this could not "be borne for very long." But whatever one must endure in reading him, one knew it was worth "bearing" for the sake of experiencing "his peculiar joy and faith." For his apprehension of evil was combined with his feeling for good. Good and evil exisited for him as they existed for Shakespeare "when he wrote King Lear." "Beyond all the pain and malease of Dostoevsky" was a deep "tranquility." Peace was "very far from him, but he [looked] out upon it, and all of his novels [were] long vistas of darkness and storm with a shining peace at the end of them, the more real because he [did] not pretend to reach it."

On the whole, admiration of Dostoevsky was ardent not to say excessive; within four years after the publication of *The Brothers Karamazov* it reached the proportions of a cult. There were, however, a few dissenting voices, Joseph Conrad's, for example, Henry James's, John Galsworthy's and D. H. Lawrence's.

Joseph Conrad to whom Edward Garnett had sent a copy of *The Brothers Karamazov* wrote of it as follows:

I do hope you are not too disgusted with me for not thanking you for the 'Karamazov' before. It was very good of you to remember me, and of course I was extremely interested. But it's an impossible lump of valuable matter. It's terrifically bad and impressive and exasperating. Moreover, I don't know what D. stands for or reveals, but I do know that he is too Russian for me. It sounds to me like some fierce mouthings from prehistoric ages. I understand the Russians have just 'discovered' him. I wish them joy.

Of course your wife's translation is wonderful. One almost breaks one's heart merely thinking of it. What courage! What perseverance! What talent of—interpretation let us say. The word 'translation' does not apply to your wife's achievements. But indeed the man's art does not deserve this good fortune. Turgenev (and perhaps Tolstoy) are the only two really worthy of her. Give her please my awestruck and admiring love. One can be nothing less but infinitely grateful to her whatever one may think or feel about D. himself.[29]

Similarly Henry James wrote to Hugh Walpole[30] that he did not "fully share" his "literary emotions":

At least [he said] when you ask me if I don't feel Dostoevsky's "mad jumble, that flings things down in a heap," nearer the truth than the picking and composing that you instance in Stevenson, I reply with emphasis that I feel nothing of the sort, and that the older I grow and the more I go the more sacred to me do picking and composing become. . . . Form alone *takes,* and holds and preserves substance, saves it from the welter of helpless verbiage that we swim in as in a sea of tasteless tepid pudding, and that makes one ashamed of an art capable of such degradations. Tolstoy and Dostoevsky are fluid puddings, though not tasteless, because the amount of their own minds and souls in solution in the broth gives it savour and flavour, thanks to the strong rank quality of their genius and their experience. But there are all sorts of things to be said of them, and in particular that we see how great a vice is their lack of composition, their defiance of economy and architecture directly they are emulated and imitated; *then,* as subjects of emulation, models, they quite give themselves away.

John Galsworthy wrote Edward Garnett[31] that he was reading *The Brothers Karamazov* "a second time"; "and just after *War and Peace*" was "bound to say" it didn't "wash."

Amazing in places, of course; but my God!—what incoherence and verbiage, and what starting of monsters out of holes to make you shudder. It's a mark of these cubistic, blood-bespattered-poster times that Dostoevsky should rule the roost. Tolstoy is far greater, and Turgenev too.

As for D. H. Lawrence, his relations to Dostoevsky would make a very interesting study. Dostoevsky's influence on him has been more than once alleged. When *The Brothers Karamazov* appeared, his own novel, *The Trespasser,* was reviewed with it in *The Athenæum,* the critic noting that in its "psychological intensity" his book recalled "the best Russian school"; the conclusion of the novel was "poetic realism of a Dostoevskian order." And Lawrence wrote Edward Garnett that he had enjoyed his Dostoevsky review in *The Daily News.*[32] With reference to *Sons and Lovers,* "Confound all these young fellows; how they have gloated over Dostoevsky," wrote Galsworthy.[33] But Lawrence, again and again, expressed his dislike of Dostoevsky. He could not get away from him but at the same time, it seems, could not endure him. In 1913 he wrote Garnett[34] that he did not like any of the Russian novelists:

I don't care about physiology of matter [he said]—but somehow—that which is physic—non-human, in humanity, is more interesting to me than the old-fashioned element—which causes one to conceive a character in a certain moral scheme is what I object to. In Turgenev, and in Tolstoy, and Dostoevsky, the moral scheme into which all the characters fit—and it is really the same scheme—is, whatever the extraordinariness of the characters themselves, dull, old, dead.

At another time he asked Lady Otteline Morrell, if she had "a Chap-

man's *Homer* or a *Brothers Karamazov* to lend" him.[35] And wrote
to her later:[36]

I have been reading Dostoevsky's *Idiot*. I don't like Dostoevsky. He is
again like the rat, slithering in hate, in the shadows, and, in order to
belong to the light, professing love, all love. But his nose is sharp with
hate, his running is shadowy and rat-like; he is a will fixed and gripped
like a trap. He is not nice.

And again:[37]

I send you also Petronius. . . . He is a gentleman, when all is said. I have
taken a great dislike to Dostoevsky's *The Possessed*. It seems so sensational, and such a degrading of the pure mind, somehow. It seems as
though the pure mind, the true reason, which surely is noble, were made
trampled and filthy under the hoofs of secret, perverse, undirect sensuality.
Petronius is straight and above-board. Whatever he does, he doesn't try
to degrade and dirty the pure mind in him. But Dostoevsky, mixing God
and sadism, he is foul.

On February 17, 1916 there was a long letter to John Middleton
Murry and Katherine Mansfield about Dostoevsky,[38] and another one
to Murry, August 28, 1916, on the occasion of the latter's study of
Dostoevsky.[39] In December 1916 he told Catherine Carswell[40] not to
think that he "would belittle the Russians," that they had "meant
an enormous amount" to him; "Turgenev, Tolstoy, Dostoevsky—
mattered almost more than anything"; he had once "thought them
the greatest writers of all time"; but that "now, with something of a
shock" he realized "a certain crudity and thick, uncivilized, insen-
sitive stupidity about them," he realized "how much finer and purer
and more ultimate our own stuff is." *The Spirit of Place*, an essay
published in 1925—if I may depart for the moment from the chronological bounds set by this chapter—speaks of "Dostoevsky posing
as a sort of Jesus but most truthfully revealing himself all the while
as a little horror."[41] And *Pansies*, 1930, contains a poem[42] about the
waning influence of the Russians and of Marcel Proust, which speaks
of how "strange" it would be "to think" of "the Alyoshas and Dmitris
and Myshkins and Stavrogins, the Dostoevsky lot all wiped out";
and of how "the Dostoevsky lot wallowed in the thought: let me sin
my way to Jesus!—So they sinned themselves off the face of the
earth." Also in 1930 Lawrence wrote an introduction to a special
edition of *The Grand Inquisitor*.[43]

In the letter to Middleton Murry and Katherine Mansfield he had
written:

I've just read *The Possessed*. I find I'm gone off Dostoevsky, and could write about him in very cold blood. I didn't care for *The Possessed:* nobody was possessed enough really to interest me. They bore me, these squirming sorts of people: they teem like insects.

I'll write you some notes on the Dostoevsky [he continued] you can translate them into your own language if they interest you.
  1. He has a fixed will a mania to be infinite, to be God.
  2. Within this will, his activity is two-fold:
      (a). To be selfless, a pure Christian, to live in the whole, the universal consciousness.
      (b). To be pure, absolute self, all-devouring and all-consuming.
That is the main statement about him.

Dmitri Karamazov, Rogozhin, and "not so clearly" Stavrogin were examples of the second category, representing Dostoevsky's "desire to achieve the sensual"; Prince Myshkin, Alyosha, and "partly" Stavrogin, of the first, "his desire for the spiritual, turn-the-other-cheek consummation." There was a third type, which represented "pure unemotional will . . . the third Karamazov brother, and Pyotor Stepanovitch, and the young secretary man at whose house the Idiot at first lodges—he who is going to marry the young woman, Gavril, is [that] his name?"

What Lawrence found obnoxious in Dostoevsky was that his people "squirmed" and were not real, that behind them lay Dostoevsky's "mania . . . to be God" and behind that a secret, unacknowledged, and corrupted sensuality. That was why Dostoevsky was "impure," "not nice." What Dostoevsky really desired was not the Idiot's selflessness, "becoming disseminated out into a pure, absolved consciousness," the "Christian ecstasy, when I become transcendently superconsciousness," but the urge of Dmitri Karamazov to "reach such a pitch of dark sensual ecstasy" when one's self seems to be "the universal night that has swallowed everything . . . the universal devouring darkness," the "sensual ecstasy of universality." Dostoevsky was divided between this fundamental sensuality and his feeling that "his sensual seekings" were wrong. That was why "he was cruel . . . tortured himself and others, and *goûtait* the tortures." His will "was fixed on the social virtues." The "full sensual ecstasy" was "never reached" in his work "except by Rogozhin murdering Nastasya." It was "nipped in the last stages by the will, the social will. When the police stripped Dmitri Karamazov naked, they killed in him the quick of his being, his lust for the sensual ecstasy." Lawrence, feeling that nobody was "ready to face out the old life and so transcend it," that "the mind must follow the being" and not "the being the mind" felt that Dostoevsky put "the cart before the horse"; that with the rest of "the cursed cowardly world" he had not "the courage to follow" his own being with his mind, had not "the courage to know what" his "unknown" was. The "world's trick" was when you drew "somewhere near the 'brink of the revelation,' to dig your head in the sand like the disgusting ostrich, and see the revelation there"; and Dostoevsky "like the rest" with "their head in the sand of pleasing visions and secrets and revelations" could "stick his head between the feet of Christ and waggle his behind in the air." Lawrence did not "think much even of the feet of Christ as a bluff for the cowards to hide their eyes against." What he felt, then, to be a fundamental hypocrisy, made him see Dostoevsky's novels as "only parables," "great" parables, he admitted, "but false art." "All the people" in them were "fallen angels—even the dirtiest scrubs." He could not "stomach" this, he said. People were "not fallen angels, they [were] merely people. But Dostoevsky used them all as theological or religious units . . . all terms of divinity like Christ's 'Sower went forth to sow,' and Bunyan's Pilgrim's Progress." They were "bad art, false truth."

How the long letters about Dostoevsky came to be written we learn from Middleton Murry's recent autobiography.[44] In 1915, when he and Katherine Mansfield were in Bandol, he was "made aware, in a way that penetrated even [his] obtuseness" of the "gulf" between him and Lawrence. He had told Lawrence before leaving that he "was at last going to write" his book on Dostoevsky which had been delayed, he said, "for the good reason that he found he had nothing really to say about Dostoevsky." This time, however, he was "determined either to make up [his] mind about that strange Russian who fascinated and perplexed and stimulated [him], or forever hold [his] peace." He "would not" because he "could not 'make' a book about him." He had "never been able to 'make' a book about anything, or anybody." And so Lawrence promised "to meditate his own opinions of Dostoevsky" and to write him "some notes," for which proposal Murry, in his condition of "mental indigence concerning his subject" was "more than ordinarily grateful." That winter, however, Lawrence fell ill and could not write his notes until the following spring. By that time Murry had read "all Dostoevsky's major books over three times, first with a glimmer of comprehension and finally with an altogether unprecedented flood of illumination. Suddenly the whole thing had fallen into pattern" for him; he was "for the first time, the victim of the strong sensation of being hardly more than the amanuensis of a book that wrote itself." To a person of his "peculiar composition" this experience was "an inward revolution." For the first time in his life he had "the experience of certitude":

It was no question of my opinion of Dostoevsky; I had no opinion of Dostoevsky and if I expressed any personal opinions about him in the book, they were certainly exaggerated and probably wrong. All that had happened—I speak, of course, of my sensation only—was the objective 'pattern' of Dostoevsky had declared itself, through me as an instrument.

And just at this moment, "when the book had written itself," Lawrence sent him his notes. To his "consternation" Murry "found them completely incomprehensible": he could not "translate" them into his own language, as Lawrence had enjoined; his language had "no equivalent for such ideas, and the ideas themselves were such that, by no exercise of his imagination" could he "take hold of them." Nor had he ever been able "to connect them vitally with Dostoevsky." Then, when his book came out, Lawrence "jumped" on it, and bitterly offended Murry by his undignified description of Dostoevsky between the feet of Christ:

Since there was a good deal of hero-worship of Dostoevsky in the book, he had me fairly on the raw by suggesting that posture of the man whom I admired, and have not ceased to admire, was contemptible. [*sic*]

Murry's study, published in August 1916, represents a characteristic mood of the war years and is a high water mark of Dostoevsky adulation in England. It was based on the conviction that no traditional approach could do justice to Dostoevsky, neither the biographical—for there was "not a single fact" in Dostoevsky's life that could not be "deduced from his books" and what could be deduced from them "with certainty" was "infinitely more than the most keen-eyed biographer" could discover—nor the "literary." Hitherto Dostoevsky's work had been viewed mistakenly as fiction to which ordinary standards were applicable, and for this reason all previous comment on him was false. He had been made to "conform to the tradition of the art with which his life was occupied." But Dostoevsky was not a novelist, and he could not be judged as a novelist. What he was, it was "more difficult to define," but the definition demanded "a new attitude towards his work." His books must be treated in a way in which no books before had ever been treated: "a new creation" demanded "a new criticism."[45]

The reason Dostoevsky's novels were "not novels at all" but something wholly different was that "the proportion of life, the sweet reasonableness of things human" had been "dissolved away" in them. They contained "neither night nor day," neither rising nor setting of the sun. They lacked the very element "upon which the novel itself depends . . . a sense of time," for without it "a novel is not a representation of life," and what was a novel "if not a representation of life"? The novelist's mind, said Murry, was "as it were bathed in the sense of time and succession." But in Dostoevsky there was "no sense of evolution and slow growth." His mind was "timeless" and the people of his books were "not so much men and women as disembodied spirits" who "for the moment" had "put on mortality." In reading him Murry was sometimes "seized by a suprasensual terror." He saw things "with the eyes of eternity" and had "a vision of suns grown cold" and heard "the echo of voices calling without sound across the waste and frozen universe."[46] Such moments, whose "individual terror" consisted "in the unexpected physical presentation of the timeless world" he had experienced on two notable occasions, unconnected with Dostoevsky but which illustrated his meaning so admirably that he described them at length.

Once in reading a translation of "the Egyptian sacred books" he had "stumbled upon the phrase 'The Boat of the Million Years' "— which he probably would have passed "safely," had "it not been that it was repeated several times." Then, a strange thing happened: "Suddenly each faint impression united in my brain and I saw the boat. I was cold with horror; it was as though my very spirit had frozen. I dared not move; I dared not look out of the window, for I knew that all that lay outside would be old and cold and gray." So shaken was Mr. Murry that he wept: "wept bitterly and sobbed"; then was roused by this "involuntary action" again "to physical life." The "moment was over."[47] This episode held deep meaning for Mr. Murry, for he related it again, amplified with circumstantial detail, in his autobiography.[48]

The other occasion was his second visit to "the Zoological Gardens."[49] Stopping by the cage of vultures, he saw them huddled together high up, while at the bottom of the cage there lay a bone, a "big, bloody" one with "bits of flesh . . . clinging to it." Again cold horror overwhelmed Mr. Murry. He looked closely at the bone "to see . . . what kind of marks their beaks had made upon it." Then "suddenly . . . looked up and saw the birds motionless, looking out

with blind and lidded eyes"—so that he murmured "in a kind of
delirium . . . 'obscene, obscene.'" The word "seemed to have taken
on a new sense, a profounder meaning." This then he thought, was
"the eternal and absolute obscenity"; and he ultimately reached the
conclusion that there was "an obscenity beyond the bodily world, a
metaphysical obscenity":

To conceive, to have the power to conceive, the timeless world, yet physi-
cally to be set in the world of time and to be subject to its laws—that is
the last verge of the fantastic. There is in this a grotesqueness and
obscenity which can freeze the mind which broods upon it with a palsy
of horror, which reaches its climax in the sudden vision of the timeless
world made apparent in that which is time.[50]

"Metaphysical obscenity" was "the devilish poverty of the human
thing beside the superhuman intention"; and it was known to Dostoevsky. The thought of it haunted "his great characters, as it haunted
himself." It was "in a peculiar sense the distinguishing mark of his
imaginations." Stavrogin, for example, "was strong, . . . against
terror beyond the physical . . . but before the obscenity of timeless
things he was afraid." And the dream of Ivan Karamazov was "saturated with metaphysical terror and obscenity which is the appointed
end of the human striving of the human consciousness."[51]

In this way, Mr. Murry evolved for himself a new comprehension
of Dostoevsky. Dostoevsky was for him in every way "symbolic"
rather than "real": his Christianity, "not Christianity, his realism . . .
not realism, his novels . . . not novels, his truth . . . not truth, his art
not art." He himself was a kind of symbol: "the category of life could
not contain his being which existed in another category."[52] He was
"consciousness incarnate," "rather a mind brooding on life than a
living man," for whom "life itself was in a profound sense inadequate."
"Looked at from the angle of rational human existence" he was "a
monstrosity"; he had "no life": his "outward and visible life" was
"in the nature of a clumsy symbol of that which he really was."
Even his epilepsy was "no more than a concomitant of his spiritual
torments." His novels were "a world of symbols and potentialities . . .
embodied in unlivable lives," his characters were not "human" but
"disembodied spirits." Rogozhin, for example, was "Body, as Myshkin
was Soul"; they were not men, they had "only the semblance of men,
in which the Ideas" which they were, had been "clothed." And Nastasya was "not a woman, but the embodiment of the idea of Pain."
Rogozhin was "the way of doing" and Myshkin was "the way of suf-

fering." Together they were "the restless spirits that walk up and down the earth seeking their lost unity." They were "that which is, the final word of the epoch of human consciousness in which we live, body conscious of soul, and soul conscious of body." Stavrogin was "Will incarnate"; he was not a man, but "a presence" who had "looked upon the frozen waste of eternity,"—his "expedition to the icy North," being indeed, as was also Svidrigailov's, "only a symbol, by which Dostoevsky could convey in temporal terms, the lonely and infinite distance to which their spirit had been driven."[53]

"The slow emergence" of Dostoevsky's "own essential conceptions, and their evolution to the final vision of *The Brothers Karamazov*" could be traced as follows: from the underworld of pain, evil, and despair, shown in *Poor Folk, The Insulted and Injured,* and the *Letters from the Underworld,* emerged two possible ways of escape, both of them assertions of the individual will: one, the will to act, as incarnated in Svidrigailov who, rather than Raskolnikov, was the real hero of *Crime and Punishment;* the other, the will to suffer, as exemplified in the idiot Prince Myshkin. Stavrogin, in *The Possessed,* was a further development of Svidrigailov, as Alyosha, Dostoevsky's crowning achievement, was the further development of Myshkin. Of *The Brothers Karamazov* there was the following explanation:

The pain and chaos of the mighty blind Karamazov spirit strives toward creation by paths which the human consciousness, though working in the light of its extreme incandescence, cannot discover. . . . From the womb of lust and destruction leaps forth the child of life. [That is, Alyosha]. . . . The father [Karamazov] is the blind force of life, which arose we know not how. It brooded over the face of the waters. Taking the forms of life, high and low, birds of the air and creeping things, obscene, terrible, and beautiful, it rose through slime and lust and agony to man. Old Karamazov is life under the old Dispensation. He is a force and no more; he does not know himself for what he is. He contains within himself the germ of all potentialities, for he is chaos unresolved. He is loathsome and terrible and strong, for he is life itself.

And this old life is slain by his sons, for by the death of the old Life and the breaking of the old Covenant, the new Life lives and the new Covenant is established.[54]

For those who had found Dostoevsky difficult reading and the Karamazov murder especially mystifying, Mr. Murry suggested as explanation that perhaps "there really was no Smerdyakov as there really was no Devil"; perhaps "they both had their abode in Ivan's soul. But then who did the murder? Then, of course, it may have been

Ivan himself, or, on the other hand, there may have been no murder
at all." The "trouble" was that "all the solutions" were true. "Smerdyakov murdered Fyodor Pavlovitch; Ivan murdered him; and he was
not actually murdered at all."[55]

All in all, through his "physical vision of timelessness" Dostoevsky
had entered the world of "pure spirit," where the values were no
longer the transitory, multiple ones of earth, but the unified, absolute
ones of heaven, where sufferings rose to Suffering and obscenities to
Obscenity. His art was "metaphysical, which no art could be. He
struggled to express conceptions which were truly inexpressible."[56]

When Murry looked at his completed work, he tells us in his autobiography,[57] he thought "it might be partial" but he "could see that
so far as it went, it was good." So also did the journals which mentioned it. And only much later was it to be characterized as "Pecksniffian sobstuff."[58] According to *The English Review*,[59] it was "a book
of great and permanent worth" in which the author's "devotion" to
his subject was never allowed "to mar his estimate of the man and
his work," and for *The Athenæum*,[60] it contained "a close and thoughtful analysis of the greater productions of Dostoevsky's genius." "A
very remarkable and thoughtful essay in criticism" which had "the attraction of a chapter of spiritual autobiography," said Robert Lynd
of it in *The New Statesman*.[61] The sober reviewer in *The Times*,[62]
however, while he recommended the book as very interesting, disagreed
with it on every important point. It was wrong to assume that Dostoevsky ascribed the terrible pain which was his experience, the
"personal accident" of his life, to a universal scheme of things. His
epilepsy "constantly affected his mind and made all experience to him
what music is to a man with a headache. But he was one of the greatest
of all artists because he knew all the time that the music was music
and the headache was in his head." It was wrong to speak of Dostoevsky's Christianity as if it had been uniquely his. What Murry said
about it was "true of every Christian, of every man who is possessed
by religion." It was erroneous to interpret Dostoevsky's view of man's
mortal relation to his world as offering two alternative solutions: to
act or to suffer. They were not "the same to Dostoevsky." To him,
man was "in his nature a being" that experienced; not one that acted;
"action was the result of the manner in which he experienced." And
the absence in his novels of a sense of time, was "due to his conception of reality as experience not as action." Still, Murry's book

was recommended, for the more one differed from it, the more was one "provoked to thought."

Robert Lynd's remarks in *The New Statesman* were not so much a review as an article for which Murry's book had supplied the occasion. George Moore's epigram about Dostoevsky, he said, had "a certain amount of truth in it." "In the last analysis" Dostoevsky might be a "great mystic" or a "great psychologist" but he "almost always" revealed his genius "on a stage crowded with people" who behaved like those "one reads about in the police news." His "visible world was a world of sensationalism." If he "had had less vision he would have been Strindberg. If his vision had been æsthetic and sensual, he might have been D'Annunzio"; he was, like them, "a novelist of torture." He invented "vicious grotesques" as Dickens had invented "comic grotesques." He never painted "Everyman" but always projected "Dostoevsky, or a nightmare of Dostoevsky"—which was the reason that *Crime and Punishment* belonged "to a lower range of fiction than *Anna Karenina* or *Fathers and Sons.*" Raskolnikov's crime interested us "like a story from Suetonius or like Bluebeard." But there was "no communicable passion in it such as we find in Agamemnon or Othello." Raskolnikov was "a grotesque made alive by sheer imaginative intensity and passion." And so, the reason for Dostoevsky's popularity was "easy to see": "no melodramatist ever poured out incident upon the stage from such a horn of plenty" nor presented people so "energetic and untamed, like cowboys or runaway horses. . . . Runaway human beings," one might describe them. There was certainly a measure of truth in Mr. Murry's contention that Dostoevsky's characters were "disembodied spirits." "Dostoevsky was no realist." But he "dramatized his spiritual experiences through the medium of human actions performed by human beings"; and, as for the "timelessness" of his world, that was "a novelist's device rather than the result of a spiritual escape." Had not the Greeks taken "the same license with events," "crowding an impossible rout of incidents into a single day"? This was "not to deny the spiritual content of Dostoevsky's work—the anguish of the imprisoned soul." There was "something" in him "of Caliban trying to discover some better God than Setebos"; and the novels were "the perfect image of the man" whose portrait as it had been given by Vogüé might "almost" have been "inferred" from them: "a figure that at once fascinates and repels," an author whose books would endure "as the confession of the most terrible spiritual and imaginative experiences that modern literature [had] given us."

Lynd's was measured praise in comparison with what was customary at this time. According to the editor of *Lippincott's Monthly Magazine*[63] Dostoevsky had felt in the Russian peasant "the pathos of those who suffer under burdens, the heartbreak of hopeless toil, the unexpected beauty gleaming in the midst of ugliness, honey hidden in the carcas of the lion"; "no finer tribute could be paid to a man" than that which he deserved, to be called "the apostle of humble folk." In *The New Witness*[64] Thomas Seccombe wrote that "the floodgates of the Russian temperament" were being opened and that "the remonstrances of a few intellectuals" were "less than futile. We welcome the on-coming flood." He recalled that when twenty years before, he had been "summarily called upon to write an article on Dostoevsky for an Encyclopedia," he had only *Poor Folk, Crime and Punishment, Buried Alive in Siberia,* and Vogüé's *Russian Novel* to turn to. But now Dostoevsky was "beatified, canonized, sainted. . . . It would hardly do now to describe him as 'Gaboriau with psychological sauce.' You must talk about him and Holy Russia and the religion of suffering very respectfully indeed." And showing himself among the worshipful, Seccombe said that there was "something of Michael Angelo about his work, something of the major Hebraic prophets." The author of an essay in *The North American Review*[65] declared that Dostoevsky had fallen into "the hands of the living God"; that his work was "so much reality spread out before one's gaze"; that it was imperative to consider his art "from an intensive standpoint as so much psychology, but a psychology which would strain one of our modern laboratories"; that his characters were divided into beasts and angels, which two states were sometimes seen to coexist in one man; that this "anthropology" made of Russia "a peculiar blending of Tartar and Buddhist"; that Dostoevsky made "Milton's Satan and Nietzsche's blond beast appear quite amateurish and unconvincing"; that according to his "amiable psychology of strength, everybody loves crime" and "as a matter of fact, . . . always wants to kill his father"; but that "side by side with such frank frightfulness, for which even the German U-boat fleet can hardly prepare us," Dostoevsky loved "tales of excessive want and extravagant self-abasement," passing "from tropic to poles . . . without literary inconsistency"; that, finally:

there must be some superior way of evincing the spiritual character of man's inner self, so that we will no longer need to follow Dostoevsky through all the perturbed ramifications of the stricken soul;

but that pending the elaboration of this desirable philosophy, one might "keep in mind Dostoevsky's idea that man, far from being a brick in the industrial wall or a cell in the social organism, is an inner world-order, fantastic, terrible yet beautiful." In *The Manchester Quarterly*[66] D. E. Oliver announced that before the "marvellous story," the "wonderful story," *Crime and Punishment,* he could do no more than admire speechlessly. He felt that the "various characters" in it transcended his "feeble powers of description." He could "ponder and read, dwell at inordinate length upon the sublimity of its theme; concentrate his thoughts with an ever-deepening intensity on the ethical aspects of human desire and aspirations, but in the end he would fain admit his incapacity to probe the mysterious depths of mind and soul to which the terrible genius of Dostoevsky directed him. A penny twine ball would not fathom the ocean of immensity nor a toy telescope pierce the heaven of infinite space. Therefore, content with the modest role of student fully conscious of his inability to express the depth and intensity of his feelings" he counseled his readers to judge for themselves. "The literary sandwichman," he consoled himself, had "his uses, be the calling ever so lowly." Fear was expressed in *The Academy*[67] that Dostoevsky was "in danger of being boomed after the manner of Strindberg," which was "a fate he [did] not deserve."

Frequently Dostoevsky was mentioned in passing in articles that did not primarily concern him. Thus, it was said of James Joyce's *A Portrait of the Artist as a Young Man* that had it been written by Dostoevsky, "it would have been a masterpiece";[68] and of Grigorovitch, whose novel *The Fisherman* had been translated, that he could "neither stage his incidents nor dramatize them subjectively" as Dostoevsky did.[69] Dostoevsky's opinion of *Anna Karenina* was cited in an article on the Russian Revolution;[70] and in another one, on "The Slav Ideal,"[71] he was mentioned as one of the exponents of "Slavism" in a "modified, broader, and more progressive form." Havelock Ellis, in an essay on Tolstoy,[72] commented on Dostoevsky's religious self-abnegation in contrast to Tolstoy's egotism. Such references are scattered but conclusive evidence of an ever growing interest and familiarity.

An article by Rebecca West in *The New Republic*[73] might be taken as further evidence of the same kind. Miss West had "spent Easter at a conference of Socialists" who "would not think of the war . . . would not open their hearts to one of the million sorrows of Europe," just because, it seems, they wanted to be different. "Nothing in them was real except the passion for contradicting the rest of humanity." In the train which took her from this conference she was confronted by a very drunken Jew who wept because he was drunk and because he must drink for the sake of conviviality essential to his business, and because he would die, he had been told, if he did not stop drinking. It suddenly flashed on Miss West that both the Jew and the Socialists were straight from Dostoevsky: the Jew from *The Brothers Karamazov*, wherein he would be a minor character:

Certainly it would be *The Brothers Karamazov*. For my despair over this body which had not been redeemed by all its achievement of love was my discovery of the realization which is the subject of that great book which is the allegory for the world's maturity, as *The Pilgrim's Progress* was an allegory for its childhood. [*sic*]

The Socialists, mistrusted by Dostoevsky as people who had taken utilitarianism for intelligence, would be from *The Possessed*. The essay was entitled "Redemption and Dostoevsky."

A Guide to Russian Literature by Moissaye Olgin was now published in New York "to answer the persistent question coming from many quarters. 'What shall I read to understand Russian character and Russian life?'" Dostoevsky was here listed as "a constructive genius" who had "the power to put all his visions, queries, doubts, anguish, rebellions, analyses, curses, blessings, into broad, gripping, scourging pictures saturated with elements of reality, of human life, human nature." An unusual feature of this guide was that it quoted Russian critics "as supplements, or as appreciations of individual books."[74] Concerning Dostoevsky, there were excerpts from Merezhkovsky, Vyetrinsky, Batyushkov, Volynsky, and Ovsyaniko-Kulikovsky.[75]

Randolph Bourne in an article entitled, "The Immanence of Dostoevsky,"[76] compared the interest taken in the gradual appearance of his work in English translation to that accorded Dickens' and Thackeray's novels in the previous generation:

It is impossible not to think of Dostoevsky as a living author when his books come regularly, as they are coming, to the American public every few months. Our grandfathers sixty years ago are said to have lived their imaginative lives in anticipation of the next instalment of Dickens or Thackeray. I can feel something of the same excitement in this Dostoevsky stream, though I cannot pretend that the great Russian will ever become a popular American classic.

The interest aroused by Dostoevsky was, of course, very different from that felt for the Victorians and the "belated Victorians like Mr. Chesterton." The difference lay in a changed psychology: the naïve duality, on the one hand, of "the sane and the insane, the virtuous and the villainous, the sober and the mischievous, the responsible and the irresponsible," which was characteristic of the Victorians; and, on the other, the modern attempt "to close up that dualism." What the modern reader had begun to discover was that Dostoevsky far from being morbid was actually the most healthy and understanding of novelists. For, although it was "still common to call his fiction unhealthy, morbid, unwholesome," all that was meant by this was "that the sudden shock of a democratic, unified, intensely feeling and living outlook" was "so severe to the mind that thinks in the old dual terms as to be almost revolting." What became "more and more apparent to the readers of Dostoevsky" was his "superb modern healthiness." He was healthy because he was "not afraid of life as it is actually lived, in its unsatisfactoriness and its aspiration and its queer blindnesses" and because he had "no sense of any dividing line between the normal and the abnormal, or even between the sane and the insane." "For all his subtlety" he was "the reverse of anything morbidly introspective." He was "introspection turned inside out." He was, said Randolph Bourne, "the decisive force" needed in the "American creative outlook"; and the only story in all English literature which had anything of his "fierce, absorbed intensity" was *Wuthering Heights*.

It was customary now, contrary to Galsworthy's minority opinion, to prefer Dostoevsky to Tolstoy. *The New Age*[77] printed a translation of an essay by the Russian critic A. Volynsky in which Dostoevsky was held to be superior to Tolstoy by virtue of his "fiery selfconsciousness and his extraordinary mental strength." He was "profound and more exalted than Tolstoy"; the "psychology of his heroes" was "essentially the psychology of every living man" and if it were not for such "great madmen" as Dostoevsky, "man would not know his real depth, nor, perhaps realize so clearly his relation to the inner, higher worlds." In America James Gibbons Huneker expressed his preference. "I am anxious to begin a comparative study of 'Dostoevsky and Tolstoy.'—Note the order," he wrote to E. C. March.[78] His "judgment of twenty-five years ago," he said, held good;[79] indeed, was "being verified critically, i.e. Dostoevsky [was] the *real thing;* Tolstoy was an amateur by comparison. But—the bigger artist, and Turgenev [topped] both as a writer." Once upon a time, he had made a scenario of *The Gambler;*[80] it was still in his desk. He thought this story "almost the best thing Dostoevsky ever wrote," that is, "for the public." *The Insulted and Injured* was not "the best of Dostoevsky," but *Poor Folk* was, though it had been in England "for twenty years or more" in one edition only "with a foolish preface by—George Moore, of all men."

His essay on the Russians, "Dostoevsky and Tolstoy, and the Younger Choir of Russian Writers," appeared first "very much curtailed," in *The Forum*[81] and then, in full, in *Ivory Apes and Peacocks.*[82]

If you think *Resurrection* strong [he wrote in it] then read Dostoevsky's *The House of the Dead.* If *Anna Karenina* has moved you—as it must, take up *The Idiot;* and if you are impressed by the special magnitude of *War and Peace,* study that other epic of souls, *The Brothers Karamazov,* which illuminates, as if with ghostly flashes of lightning, the stormy hearts of mankind. Tolstoy wrote of life; Dostoevsky lived it, drank its sour dregs, for he was a man accursed by luck and, like the apocalyptic dreamer of Patmos, a seer of visions denied to the robust, ever fleshly Tolstoy.

Dostoevsky, he said, was a realist of realists, "such as the world had never before seen, and yet at times as idealistic as Shelley." His "harrowing" recollections of Siberia made "the literature of prison life, whether written by Hugo, Zola, Tolstoy, or others like the literary exercise of an amateur." It was "this sense of reality, of life growing like grass over one's head" that rendered his novels " 'human documents' "; but the "fundamental theme of his work" was "an overwhelming love of mankind, a plea for solidarity." Nietzsche and he "were fellow spirits in suffering," and Huneker quoted Brandes' letter to Nietzsche about Dostoevsky and Nietzsche's own remark that one regretted Dostoevsky had not lived in the neighborhood of that "most interesting decadent," Christ, for he would have known "just how to perceive the thrilling charm of such a mixture of the sublime, the sickly, and the childish." Dostoevsky's "veritably tragic" books Huneker compared to Russian music. And his epilepsy he called a "fissure in the walls of his neurotic soul" through which "he peered and saw its strange perturbations, divined their origin in the very root of his being, and recorded as did Poe, Baudelaire, and Nietzsche—the fluctuations of his sick will." The "Hamlet-like introspection" of "this Russian" became "vertigo, and life itself [faded] into a dream compounded of febrile melancholy or blood lust." The "tragic side"[83] of Moussorgsky reminded him of Dostoevsky. "Who but Dostoevsky, if he had been a composer, could have written the malediction scene in *Boris?*" And there were also many other likenesses between them: intense Slavophilism, adoration of Russia; carelessness as to the externals of their art, "an obsession of the abnormal," similarities of temperament.

Maurice Baring and Edward Garnett must be accounted very influential in promoting Dostoevsky's fame. It was to Garnett, as has been seen, that Conrad, D. H. Lawrence, Galsworthy expressed their views on the Russian. "But aren't you writing a book about Dostoevsky?" Lawrence wrote him, and "how does your life of Dostoevsky go?"[84] Apparently, however, Lawrence was mistaken or Garnett abandoned the project, for there is no book on Dostoevsky by him.

Baring's most important work on Russian literature has been cited already.[85] Another one, *Mainsprings of Russia,* appeared in 1914, and in 1922, *The Puppet Show of Memory,* which related the history of his interest in Russian literature.[86] In *Mainsprings of Russia,* Baring was careful to emphasize that Dostoevsky's works must not be taken as literal pictures of Russia. "It stands to reason," he wrote, "that if all Russians were as melancholy as they are depicted as being in many Russian novels and plays written by men of genius, the great majority of the Russian nation would have cut their throats a long time ago." What the "creations of a Russian novelist such as Dostoevsky" afforded was "a synthesis of the Russian soul." They were "no more portraits of the average Russian than Lear" was that of "the average Englishman; and yet they [were] profoundly Russian, just as Lear [was] profoundly English, and Faust [was] profoundly German."[87]

The first biographical study of Dostoevsky in English appeared in 1912, J. A. T. Lloyd's *A Great Russian Realist.*[88] As was pointed out in *The Saturday Review,*[89] the book was neither "a purely literary study . . . nor precisely a biography." It might be termed, perhaps, an essay in "comparative thought," for it was an attempt to explain Dostoevsky's philosophy and method by comparing them with those of better known novelists of the realistic school: with Balzac's, Dickens', Flaubert's. "The nineteenth century," Lloyd wrote, "essentially devoted to the development of the bourgeoisie" was so mirrored in its novels, both English and French. In England "even the great novelists had to submit. . . . The very greatest of them [had] been perturbed by the pitfalls of English social life, rather than by the catastrophe of humanity. Thackeray himself [was] perpetually haunted by the lorgnette of the English county family in his telescopic sweep of the cosmos." In France, Balzac "accomplished with the French bourgeois almost what Aeschylus accomplished with Greek heroes." He "expressed the habit of thought of the West with all its pride in competition," "saluted success" in accordance with bourgeois morality; his heroes were "men of intense volition, each of whom with his 'à nous deux maintenant' [was] ready to shake his fists at Paris." Flaubert "inwardly remote and detached from those whom he observed and analyzed" was the psychologist of the bourgeoisie, as Balzac was its tragedian. But his pessimism which "lay at the very roots of his temperament" destroyed "the very objectivity for which, with his torment of style, he craved." Flaubert became "the castigator of humanity." Dostoevsky "on the other hand, represented the habit of thought of the East, with all its meditative yielding to necessity." He "knew nothing of our Anglo-Saxon religion of the front pews, of our policeman morality, of our insurance-policy piety"; he had nothing in common with "French logic and English devotion to muscular Christianity." Social issues had become for him national and universal. He "was not at all a being whose thoughts had soared wholly beyond this world"; he was not unaware of middle-class philosophy, but "the bourgeois, who in the hands of Balzac, had become a veritable Frankenstein's monster, and in the hands of Flaubert the dwarfed excrescence of M. Homais" was for Dostoevsky "the enemy of a national ideal." An epileptic, like Flaubert, and so of necessity, somewhat aloof from the world, he was, unlike the French author, "to lose his almost physical shrinking from the crowd, and was to become passionately anxious to be merged in it, forgotten in it. He was to become not the castigator of humanity but its suppliant."[90]

"Pity and intellectual curiosity" were his most characteristic traits, the latter leading him to what had been called "cruel" in his work; for pity and cruelty were extraordinarily blended in him. Pity "passed into scientific cruelty, the confessor passed into the vivisector of human souls"; "he had become confessor because of the sympathy of his heart, he had become inquisitor by reason of the terrible curiosity of his brain." He was, as Merezhkovsky had called him, " 'the great delineator' of the passions of the mind as distinct from those of the heart"; his observation, however, was not that of an onlooker but of "a suffering human being" whose pity for sufferers was that of a "fellow-sufferer." He never condemned according to rule, nor laid down programs of conduct. He was "not a protagonist of particular views" but a "creator of individual characters"; and in this he was comparable to Shakespeare and to the ancient Greeks—indeed Natasha of *Injury and Insult* was a Russian Phaedra.[91]

He combined an extraordinary gift of introspection with an understanding of others; and his realism was a synthesis of these two qualities. As a psychologist he went farther than any other novelist, went beyond "such artists as Turgenev, who [revealed] the emotional experiences of men and women in so far" as they were "fully conscious"; beyond "such moralists as Tolstoy who revealed the moral struggles of men and women, whom the need of confession had made minutely introspective." Dostoevsky's revelations were of the "subconscious, the hidden potentialities of human nature, which only rise to the surface under the most violent stimulus." The confession of Tolstoy himself was "a mere rough, first reading of truth to this curious inquisitor of the human soul." "To the very few," Lloyd concluded, Dostoevsky would "appeal as a novelist who seemed to have divined the most perplexing secrets of criminology." To a few he would "survive as the psychologist who realized, perhaps to the fullest extent, those two opposing truths—that of the God-man, and that other of the Man-god. But to the great mass, not only of Russians, but of all mankind, he would survive as the novelist of pity, of compassion, of inalienable tenderness towards all those from whom the world turns arrogantly away. Not Hugo, for all his splendid rhetoric, but Dostoevsky was the real interpreter of les misérables."[92]

The Times[93] critic thought that "Mr. Lloyd . . . might well have saved room for more about Dostoevsky himself"; it would be "a relief" if one could be "less certain" that whenever Dostoevsky was mentioned Tolstoy and Turgenev were "punctually at hand." His "characterizations" were "often useful and acute" but they were "too diffuse, too full of repetitions." It was "easy to distinguish between a crowded street, an illimitable plain and a shaven lawn of grass"; one "never thought of confusing them"; the differentiation was "otiose" and Mr. Lloyd gave "too much space to his variations on this simple theme." In *The Saturday Review*[94] also the study was described as tending "rather to prolixity"; it left one "aware of the grandeur" of the subject, which was "really nothing less than the psychology of the great Christian nation of Russia: but the epic of Dostoevsky had yet

to be written." The review in *The Nation*[95] summed up the state of
Dostoevsky's reputation in England at the time. That Lloyd's was the
first study of Dostoevsky to have appeared "curiously attested . . .
the blank indifference of the English-speaking world to Russian
thought." "One would have thought that Stevenson's ancient testimony to *Crime and Punishment* . . . might have stimulated public
curiosity in Dostoevsky to the extent of at least keeping in print the
imperfect translations of the 'eighties. But, no!" It was "only within a
year or so that two of these versions [had] been made accessible in
'Everyman's library,' perhaps helped a little by the publication of Mr.
Baring's essay in his 'Landmarks of Russian Literature.' Verily, the
gulf between English indifference and Slav genius was not to be
bridged even by the creation of Anglo-Russian banks and Anglo-
Russian syndicates." True it was that his "astounding skill in pathology" was obnoxious to the English. "The English mind" with its
"positive aversion from all ideas which it could not translate cautious-
ly and by degrees into action" would look upon Dostoevsky's "favorite characters, obsessed with tumultuous passions, morbid impulses,
mystical hallucinations, need of repentance and self-abasement, or
occupied with self-realization and spiritual regeneration" as "hopelessly unhealthy or positively alarming." But apart from pathology,
what Dostoevsky's works conveyed was an anti-materialistic philosophy, and what the English, if they read him, would find "chiefly
valuable" in his work, was "his enlargement of those straightened
valuations of good and evil which nineteenth century 'science' and
'common-sense' " had "too readily . . . taken for granted." *A Great
Russian Realist* was "valuable for the information it brought together,
not hitherto accessible to the English reader"; it "must be welcomed
for its sincere, if only partially successful, attempt to grapple with a
most difficult subject . . . in default of a really critical exposition of the
great novelist's work, based on the whole body of documents." In *The
Literary World*[96] Lloyd's book was considered to be a study that
would not "easily be superseded"; and a new, cheaper edition of it
was published the following year.

   In an article on the Russian novel, published a few years later,[97]
Lloyd characterized Dostoevsky as possessing "neither the grand indifference of Homer which had passed into Gogol's manner nor yet the
Sophoclean charm" of Turgenev. "He was essentially the psychologist
of pity in the sense of Euripides, whose pity was of the brain as well
as of the heart." All his books were "torn from life" but it was in *The*

Brothers Karamazov that one found "in all its fullness the long odyssey of Dostoevsky's suffering" as well as "the blind inchoate struggle upwards of the Russian people":

> It is Russia herself who is symbolized in this savage sunken family. It is Russia with all her swift blazes of revolt, all her black stagnation, her rage, and her grief, her barbarism, and her deep, uncalculated pity—it is Russia herself, and as the symbol of her future Dostoevsky has chosen, not Smerdyakov the parricide, but Alyosha, the follower of the Russian God, in whom, more than any other character in these stupendous works, there is foreshadowed the beginning at least, of a comprehension of that vast synthesis—the synthesis of the God-man with the Man-god. In no other book, not even in *The Idiot*, did the spiritual thirst of the Russians, that spiritual thirst which survives in the midst of sinfulness, find such clear expression.

Middleton Murry in the preface of his study had mentioned two other works on Dostoevsky, Merezhkovsky's, which he thought the only illuminating one in English and Eugenii Soloviev's which he called "spiteful, shallow, and misleading."[98] This work which had appeared in English six months before his own,[99] had been written in 1891 by the "earliest of the Marxist critics"[100] in Russia. It was a short biography which had come out originally "in a popular series entitled 'The Lives of Celebrated People,' sold at 25 copecks (6d) the volume,"[101] and made no pretense to thoroughness, as was indeed indicated by its subtitle, "a biographical sketch."

The subject, one feels, was certainly oversimplified. Dostoevsky, for example, was described as "a man of exceedingly sensitive nature" who "never tyrannized, for his character had in it not a shadow of cruelty";[102] his nationalist and mystic ideas were dismissed with the comment that they were "dull paradoxes" for which "his nervous, hysterical temperament" could be held responsible, but that "shorn of its mystical and chauvinistic angularities," his outlook "was so clear and simple as to be intelligible to every thinking person."[103] His mind was described as too complex for analysis. "To portray" it in its "entirety would be a vain and sysephean task."[104] And there were passages of statements so generalized as to say very little indeed.[105] Still, Soloviev's interpretation of Dostoevsky, as a hysterical, poor, psychopathic "intellectual proletarian" as he had called himself—a man, that is, formed by his temperament and his environment, had something in it which Murry's own study lacked. It must have been to it that Huneker referred in a letter to March: "thanks for the study of Dostoevsky— one of the best I've read."[106]

The first collection of Dostoevsky's letters to appear in English was translated from the German in 1914,[107] and in 1921 Aimée Dostoevsky's biography of her father was published. Concerning the letters opinion was divided. To *The Literary World*[108] they revealed their author's "very heart and soul" and gave us "the right point of view from which to understand and appreciate his work"; but to the reviewer in *The Nation*[109] they seemed to throw "scarcely a ray of light on the inner phantasmic world of Dostoevsky's imaginative conceptions": they left one "with the impression of a writer whose mental tenement was two-storied—viz., an upper one for healthy intercourse with his family and friends, for his natural absorption in his literary work and his patriotic intellectual interests, and the lower one, a subterranean chamber, where the author evoked and interrogated his figures." "Impossible not to feel moved" by their "intense sincerity"; and as for the beliefs which they revealed: his "mystical patriotism" and his " 'veneration and love for the Russian people,' " the one was "based on an aversion for all progress . . . not inspired by Christian ideals"; and the other contained "a great truth" which one wondered "whether educated Europe [had] ever really grasped," for even to-day "the ignorant peoples [felt] their brotherhood dumbly, while their rulers sent them against one another in war." In *The New Statesman*[110] a letter of Dostoevsky about Germans, was quoted:

'My God, how terrible are our prepossessions with regard to foreign countries! Are Russians simpletons, then, that they can believe it is through their schooling that the Prussians have come off conquerors? Such a view is positively sinful; it's a fine schooling whereby children are harassed and tormented, as it were, by Attila's horde, and even worse,'

with the comment: " 'So we go round the ruddy ring of roses' . . . It is all there—even down to Attila himself." In the American *Current Opinion* the review was entitled "Russian Hatred of Western Ideals."[111] To *The London Spectator*[112] the letters were a "disagreeable surprise." They revealed "not the vast, morbid, epileptic and mystic personality described in the novels, but a rather meanly egotistical nature, disagreeable, complaining, fault-finding—apparently without a trace of nobility." The book was of a sort "to make one pray that the correspondence of Shakespeare [was] not lurking in some Jacobean cupboard, ready to spring upon a dismayed and disillusioned world." In *The London Times*[113] also disappointment was expressed, with allowances made, however, for the inadequacy of the collection. Regarding Dostoevsky's unappreciative comments about

Italy, it was remarked that even though "the spirit whose response to such names" as Florence and Venice was "no livelier" than what financial considerations might prompt was "a spirit poverty-stricken in other ways than want of francs," to conclude "for an instant that the author of *The Idiot, Crime and Punishment, The Brothers Karamazov* was a man of imaginative poverty" was absurd. These few letters, only seventy-seven of them, all written at a time of Dostoevsky's exile from Russia, could not be the "whole account of the matter." It was a pity that the rest were withheld from publication.

Aimée Dostoevsky's biography was originally composed in German, and before its appearance in English[114] had already come out in three other separate editions: two in German and one in Dutch. A Czech version was "on its way" and arrangements had been made for French and Danish translations. The popularity of the book must be attributed in large part to its sensational nature. An intimate, highly emotional, and, on the whole, untrustworthy record, it gave information about Dostoevsky that had not been hitherto revealed: his affair with Apollinaria Souslova, for example, and the circumstances of his father's death. In this much it was valuable, but the picture which it drew was fantastic. Aimée Dostoevsky, wishing to consider herself of Lithuanian rather than of Russian origin—(she had read Gobineau, said *The Times*)—elaborated, on the scantiest evidence of truth, a mythical Lithuanian descent, made it the center of her study, and attempted constantly to prove its effect on her father's character and actions. With reference, for example, to Dostoevsky's part in the Petrashevsky affair, she wrote that it would be "indeed inexplicable" if one ignored her father's Lithuanian origin. "He plotted against the Tsar, because he did not yet understand the real meaning of the Russian monarchy." Yet his later patriotism could be accounted for on the same grounds, for patriotism was always deepest among "mature" nations such as the Lithuanian rather than among young nations like the Russian. Dostoevsky "having at last understood the Russian Idea, . . . eagerly followed the example of the illustrious Slavo-Normans whose literature he knew so well," and became an ardent Russian patriot.[115]

There was "no room in his daughter's head for the only Dostoevsky who matters" wrote Middleton Murry in *The Nation and Athenæum*,[116] "the Dostoevsky who wrote three of the greatest novels in the world." Maurice Hewlett[117] said that Mademoiselle Dostoevsky's book was "curiously naïve" and "argumentative"; one closed it "this much to the good, that Dostoevsky was a man of whom one must know more." To *The Spectator*,[118] the study "made strange reading"; the review in *The New Statesman*[119] concluded that "the standard biography of Dostoevsky" remained "unwritten"; and the comment in *The Times*[120] was that in reading the book one felt "as if one had been admitted to the kitchen where the cook was smashing china, or to the dining-room where the relations were gossiping in corners, while Dostoevsky sat upstairs alone in his study."

New developments in the realm of psychology, combined with interest in Dostoevsky's personality, encouraged psychoanalytic and "psychophilosophical" interpretations. Thus, for example, J. D. Beresford[121] writing on "Psychoanalysis and the Novel" attempted to explain Dostoevsky as the victim of an "inferiority complex." Although up to the age of seven, he said, information about Dostoevsky was insufficient, it was "fairly safe" to infer "from the later evidence that at some time in the course of those earlier years he suffered either some shock of terror or stress of misery that initiated the trauma which was later confirmed and emphasized by his experience on the scaffold. . . . For the remainder of his life" he suffered "beyond all shadow of doubt . . . from a neurosis that, even if it were not the cause, was the accompaniment and not the result of his epilepsy . . . an 'inferiority complex.' " He himself had "analysed the condition so perfectly" in his *Notes from Underground* that "this one story would be almost sufficient testimony" as to his own condition; but there was "further evidence" in "almost any" of his novels: in Smerdyakov in *The Brothers Karamazov,* in Prince Myshkin, in "more than one example" in *The Possessed.* It was a type that "dominated" both the "characterization and the atmosphere of all his works," and that was especially evident in his own letters. But it was not his own condition alone that Dostoevsky described; it was true of the whole of Russia:

Dostoevsky wrote of the Russian as he knew him; and has not Russia as a country exhibited precisely the symptoms of the neurosis we have been describing? Centuries of suppression and humiliation have been at work to foster and confirm the complex which we now see in its typical expression, although passing, as did that of the French in the last years of the eighteenth century towards its natural sublimation.

In *The New Age* during January, February, and March 1918 appeared ten articles on Dostoevsky by Janko Lavrin,[122] which attempted to get to the core of Dostoevsky's philosophic meaning and artistic significance. Of two possible kinds of art, said Lavrin, which might be designated *horizontal* and *vertical,* the one concerned with "the surface of reality," the other with " 'reality for reality's sake,' " Dostoevsky's was the latter. Always the "result of an inner spiritual necessity," his work was "seldom 'pleasant' " but it could be "majestic and elemental," the only truly tragic work in contemporary art.

The depth of Dostoevsky's perception was due to the degree to which his personal problems were identified with dilemmas confronting humanity, and the intensity with which he lived these problems. The central point of his struggle was the search for an absolute value, the formulation of which was based for him on a consciousness of psychological dualism, his special interest as a psychologist being with the split personality, of which he himself was an example. Philosophically, he carried this duality to the extreme limit expressed in the antithesis of God-Man and Man-God, a philosophical distinction which was but the expression of a psychological necessity, the reflection of personality's assertion in the face of the impersonal Universe, which might follow either the "mystical" path of consciousness, man recognizing himself as part of the cosmos, the God-Man, or the "magical" path, wherein the individual strove to become an absolutely autonomous and independent entity, the Man-God. Dostoevsky's characters typified this duality. They were either like Raskolnikov and Stavrogin "God-seekers," men who needed God but could not find him; or like Ivan Karamazov "God-strugglers," who believed in God but revolted against Him. In the harmonious intuitively religious characters, Myshkin, Alyosha, Zossima, Dostoevsky demonstrated what was to him the only possible solution, "a spiritual Imperative." His "will to value" had led him to the "will to belief." He never really solved the problem of Absolute Value. "Instead of certainty he was left with faith alone."

Dostoevsky was a "transcendental or symbolic realist." In his attempt to fathom the essence of the real, he strained the normal to the utmost limits: to the pathological, to the man at war with forces of his own consciousness, not with the environment or social conditions. He "made the boldest attempt to bridge the abyss between reason and Spirit, between rational and irrational," understanding "deeper than anybody" that the "truth of our rational reason and the truth of irrational consciousness may be different and quite opposed." It was this new insight that made him rather than Nietzsche the prophet of to-morrow. "Before Nietzsche and deeper than Nietzsche" he realized that " 'reason is reason, and no more.' " Nietzsche remained "a victim of the scientific view" in spite of his scorn of it. But Dostoevsky "undermined the scientific idea as such"; he "transvalued not only the value but also the transvaluer, i.e. Nietzsche himself" in his demonstration that " 'science and reason' cannot give a sufficient basis of life."

Lavrin's articles precipitated a month's discussion in the pages of *The New Age*. There was an answer by Ramiro de Maetzu[123] which pointed out that if Lavrin's explanation was correct, Dostoevsky was simply a characteristic Manichean, that he did not " 'belong to the future' " but was "a tomb," a "man of the past, a pertinacious past, a past that insists upon adopting the mask of the future." Another article, by Kenneth Richmond,[124] elaborated further certain of Lavrin's ideas and declared that the problem he had "set himself," "to trace the movements of the soul of Dostoevsky the artist" was "of infinitely wider significance" than would have been the other interesting problem, "to trace the causes that made him, personally, think and feel as he did." To the first article Lavrin replied,[125] correcting misinterpretations and explaining that Dostoevsky's theory of dualism was fundamentally psychological and not theological. He was answered again by Maetzu[126] who insisted on his argument, pointing out further that Dostoevsky's "damning error" had now tragically worked itself out in practice: "the West is bleeding on the Cross, but stands firm on its harmony of Matter and Spirit . . . while Russia has fallen—and let us say no more." Lavrin had the last word,[127] which was that the Russian Revolution illustrated "European values" and not Dostoevsky's, that there was "no trace whatever of Dostoevsky in it," Dostoevsky having "preached . . . a free universal brotherhood on a religious basis," not "a compulsory utilitarian union on the basis of 'economic interests.' "

In 1920 Lavrin's articles were published in book form, *Dostoevsky, and his Creation, a Psycho-critical Study*. The book was none too well received, even though it was noticed in *The Times*[128] as "an able piece of work" which had got "nearer to a clear picture of Dostoevsky's mental struggles" than that of any other writer the reviewer had "yet come across." In *The Athenæum*[129] Lavrin was accused of being "fond of pigeon-holing" and of neglecting "subtleties." "Lazy metaphors" such as his "horizontal" and "vertical" division of art had "no place in critical writing"; and even if there were "pure God-strugglers in the world, Dostoevsky explored their struggles only because they were pertinent to his own,"—which was a point not made in the book.

"Every study," however, "of so huge and strange a writer must be a partial study." The opinion expressed in *The English Review*[130] was that the reader must be "a psychoanalyst or humanist" to appreciate the "very limited appeal" in Mr. Lavrin's interpretation of Dostoevsky's central problem. On the other hand, Edwin Muir[131] praised the author for having attempted to pierce "to the heart of the mystery" of such a figure as Dostoevsky before whom the usual attitude was one of "guarded acceptance, followed by an indication of minor blemishes." It was a relief, "after the pæans of those who . . . canonize Dostoevsky as a pathological novelist" to read that his " 'pathology' " was not "the end but the means"; but Lavrin was wrong in saying of Dostoevsky that he " 'sought for the abnormal.' " Dostoevsky "found it infallibly, and he could have found nothing else." He "wrote of the unconscious as if it were conscious" which was the reason his characters seemed 'pathological,' while, in reality they were "only visualized more clearly than any other figures in imaginative literature." Every man "seen distinctly enough is abnormal, for the normal is only a name for the undifferentiated, for a failure to see the inescapable nuance."

The view that Dostoevsky's strange characters were fundamentally not strange at all was voiced also in an essay by Clutton-Brock, published originally in *The Literary Supplement* of *The Times* and then in a collection called *Essays on Books*.[132] Dostoevsky was read, said Clutton-Brock, not for the discovery of a strange world "in which people talked and acted like no one that we have ever met" but as a reminder "of what we had forgotten about ourselves." If Dostoevsky's novels were strange, they were strange because his interests were different from those of other novelists; for whereas the usual novel was centered about the success of the hero, his achieving happiness in one way or another, "in the greatest of Dostoevsky's books . . . the interest [was] not the happiness or unhappiness of the hero" at all, but the revelation of his soul; and this object made his "peculiar method." He was "well acquainted"—no modern novelist better—"with evil and misery," but whereas other novelists wrote "about them as moving exceptions in life; he wrote about them because, in his experience, they were the rule." One felt in reading him, "that a man [was] telling us about life who [had] ceased to fear it."

Dostoevsky's "realism," in other words, was more and more often explained as the expression of his own emotional and mental experience and not so much as the result of a policy of detached observation;

and this view made the "morbid" and painful elements of his work
appear more understandable. It was said that Dostoevsky had written
"not so much what he observed as what he felt,"[133] even in those
"parts of criminal psychology, those profound analyses of the state
of mind of scheming or conscience-smitten murderers" which one
found in his *Recollections of a Dead House*. That argued, of course,
"an abnormal state of mind," but "no normal brain" could have been
"in the head of so profound a psychologist," whose equal had not been
found among novelists, although psychology was "very much in vogue
now." In one respect Dostoevsky was superior even to Shakespeare,
for whereas Shakespeare's dialogue was "very often spoiled by the
necessity the dramatist [was] under to be witty and funny," Dostoevsky's "classics [had] nothing to do with humour"; they were the
"embodiment of a grim and determined earnestness." An article in
the American *Open Court*, "The Gloom and Glory of Russian Literature,"[134] was intended to show that suffering was "the foundation of
Russian literature" as it was also "the essence of Russian life." Sixty-
eight Russian authors were listed in it, from Ivan Pososhkov (1670-
1726) to Artzibashev, whose lives were, all of them, tragic. Dostoevsky
was presented as the best example of Russian pity for suffering, and
Signora Pardo Bazán, Vogüé, and Brückner were quoted in support of
this view. To Dostoevsky, it was said, Christianity was "reduced to
the three parables of the repentant thief, the prodigal son, and the
woman taken in adultery." Nevill Forbes, who in an article in *The
Russian Review*[135] gave a brief account of Dostoevsky's life and
sketched his principal novels, noted "his two chief characteristics" as
"morbid curiosity and overwhelming pity," and concluded that "there
may have been greater artists" but never, although it was "impossible
not to perceive his delight in torturing his own nerves, and those of his
public," any "with a greater heart." So also Professor Otto Heller, of
the Washington University of St. Louis,[136] who considered that
Dostoevsky's

greatest proficiency lay, as [was] apt to be the case with writers of a
realistic bent, in dealing with the darkest side of life. The wretched and
outcast portion of humanity yielded to his skill its most congenial material.
His novels . . . [took] the reader into company such as had heretofore
not gained open entrance to polite literature: criminals, defectives, paupers,
and prostitutes. Yet he did not dwell upon the wretchedness of that submerged section of humanity from any perverse delight in what is hideous or
for the satisfaction of readers afflicted with morbid curiosity, but from a
compelling sense of pity and brotherly love. His works [were] an appeal

to charity. In them, the imperdible grace of the soul [shone] through the ugliest out-ward disguise to win a glance from the habitual indifference of fortune's *enfants gâtés*. Dostoevsky preceded Tolstoy in frankly enlisting his talents in the service of his outcast brethren.

Much was said of Dostoevsky's relations to Western writers. *Current Opinion*[137] quoted the view of "the erudite" James Huneker that the influence of Dostoevsky, "the greatest explorer of the psychic underworld," had been "enormous," as was most lately evidenced by *The Inferno* of Barbusse, which developed the notion, found also in *The Brothers Karamazov* and *The Possessed*, "that Infinity is contained within us," that "Eternity is Now." Professor Ashley H. Thorndike of Columbia University[138] thought that Dostoevsky's interest in poverty made him similar to many an English novelist, notably to Dickens by whom he "surely must have been influenced." In *Modern Philology*,[139] Edgar C. Knowlton expressed the opinion that Stevenson's *Markheim* was "a Dostoevsky's *Crime and Punishment* on a greatly reduced scale, a cameo version of a colossal frieze," that although Stevenson had "altered with great skill the method of expressing the mental emotions of the murderer, the fundamental developments" of the two stories "were similar." He pointed out that at the time he composed *Markheim*, in 1884, according to Balfour's account, Stevenson had been much concerned with "the duality of man's nature and the alternation of good and evil," that *Markheim* was meant to express this duality and that *Dr. Jekyll and Mr. Hyde*, published two years later, dealt with the same problem more forcibly. It was "perhaps in the same letter" which criticized the conclusion of *Dr. Jekyll and Mr. Hyde* that J. A. Symonds "referred to his own enjoyment of *Crime and Punishment*" which called forth the letter from Stevenson, already cited.[140] Mr. Knowlton then adduced a series of parallels to show "how vividly the mechanical details of *Crime and Punishment* impressed themselves" upon Stevenson, and concluded that

in view of Stevenson's acquaintance with *Crime and Punishment*, the likeness of *Markheim* to the Russian novel [was] so great as to make it clear that the titanic Dostoevsky should be added to the list of the literary forbears of the 'little romanticist.'[141]

The novelist W. L. George[142] stressed Dostoevsky's importance for modern fiction. "The time had gone," he wrote, "when novels were written for young ladies, and told the placid love of Edwin and Angeline." Now, the novel, grown "ambitious," laid hands "upon science, commerce, philosophy." The Press was teaching "the people to look to the novel for a cosmic picture of the day, for a cosmic commentary." The "old narrative form" was broken up, thanks largely to Dostoevsky and Romain Rolland; and if the coming novelists of England, J. D. Beresford, Gilbert Cannan, E. M. Forster, D. H. Lawrence, Compton Mackenzie, Oliver Onions, Frank Swinnerton, were to "become the men of to-morrow" it would be because they broke "away from the old traditions, the tradition of aloofness and the tradition of comment." They did not "rigidly stand outside the canvas, as did Flaubert and de Maupassant," nor did they "obviously intervene as did Thackeray." Their models were Dostoevsky and Stendhal; that was to say, they stood "midway the expression of life and the expression of themselves"; they tried indeed "to express both, to achieve art by 'criticising Life' "; they attempted "to take nature into partnership." In the American *Current Opinion*[143] it was declared that "whether or no" one appreciated Dostoevsky, his influence was "profound on contemporary fiction." Arnold Bennett, it was said, did "not hesitate to apply the adjectives 'unapproachable' and 'sublime' to his work" and the "most distinguished group of French realistic writers, including Marguerite Audoux and the incomparable Charles-Louis Philippe"— who was quoted in support of the statement—acknowledged Dostoevsky "as their master." Simeon Strunsky was also cited to the effect that both Dostoevsky and Tolstoy "towered above the younger generation of novelists" because, although they were " 'remorseless realists' " they had " 'escaped pessimism.' " Professor Otto Heller thought Dostoevsky "was one of the earliest writers of romance to show the younger generation how to found fiction upon a deeper psychological knowledge," and considered that he had "probably an even stronger influence upon modern letters than Tolstoy himself."[144] George Bernard Donlin[145] wondered at the strange history of Dostoevsky's reputation. Turgenev and Tolstoy had been "accepted at once," he wrote,

but with Dostoevsky the case [had] been different. The interval between those who praise and those who depreciate is greater than with other writers; nor is this the most puzzling aspect of the affair. We cannot foresee the reaction of a given temperament. Thus we hear Nietzsche . . . confessing that the chief exemplar, in our time, of his 'slave morality' is the only man who can teach him psychology. Yet Mr. Henry James, who is a psychologist or nothing finds *Crime and Punishment* so little to his mind that he cannot finish it. If we turn to America, we hear Professor Phelps asserting that 'of all masters of fiction, both in Russia and elsewhere, he is the most spiritual.' On the other hand Mr. Paul Elmer More plunges us at once into the abyss by simply recording the impressions he carried away from *Crime and Punishment*.

And he quoted Paul Elmer More:

'Filth, disease, morbid dreams, bestiality, insanity, sodden crime, these are the natural pathway to the emancipation of the spirit; these in some mysterious way are spirituality. And the same lesson runs through Tolstoy and Strindberg and a dozen other moralists who are, as it were, the Prophets of our young.'

But Paul Elmer More notwithstanding, Donlin concluded that one came from Dostoevsky "with an uneasy realization of the superficiality of our average judgments, the thinness of our spiritual experiences." He increased our "sense of wonder and our capacity for awe," and added "immeasurably to our understanding of the pathetic dignity of the downtrodden and oppressed."

Nationalist animosity, wrought to highest pitch during the World War, was naturally reflected in criticism of the time. Dostoevsky was now more often contrasted with German than with English writers. Thus, in a review of *Crime and Punishment*, in *The Athenæum*[146] it was noted that despite similarities, "the conclusions at which Nietzsche and Dostoevsky arrived were . . . diametrically opposite": the latter was a Christian, the former was not. They represented two antagonistic cultures, of which Dostoevsky's was the superior. "During the last three-quarters of a century," Russia's "culture, as manifested in the sphere of novels and short stories, [had] far surpassed that of Germany, and had not been outdone—if, indeed, it had been equalled—by that of any other country." But when the complete edition of Dostoevsky was first planned, "the publisher could hardly have foreseen the importance, political as well as literary, that now attached to all books" which promoted appreciation of "our Allies."[147] In *The Saturday Review*[148] also Dostoevsky's message was declared to be "a corrective to the preaching of Nietzsche and many of the modern German prophets"; and Dostoevsky was said to be "almost the only writer of the last century whom sane critics could mention in the same breath with Shakespeare." In an essay in the *McGill University Magazine*,[149] Ralph Flenley presented Dostoevsky as the embodiment of Russian ideals, which he said were "more in consonance with English civilization than those of a German philosopher such as Nietzsche." And such might be England's reply to "the German taunt" that "she had allied with a reactionary, a semi-barbarous nation." Interest in Russia had begun before the war, but it was "safe to say" that among "many as yet problematical results of the war" would be the "growth of a more intimate knowledge of Russian life and ideals." It was time "that writings of one who to Nietzsche was representative of the Russian spirit—as of the Gospel teaching—became more than a mere name to us." The article sketched Dostoevsky's life, discussed his "realism," the limitations of his form, the religious element in his work. It compared him to Charlotte Brontë in the degree to which they were both "incarnated in their work":

The depth of inspiration which raises the work alike of Dostoevsky and of Charlotte Brontë above nine-tenths of the novels of their age is primarily due to their having lived so much of their writing.

Dostoevsky, as soon as he became better known, would, without doubt, take a permanent place in England, although he would never be "a popular novelist in English-speaking countries," his works being "too far removed, both in structure and character, from those which flood and largely overflow the English-reading market."

But the most profound explanation of Dostoevsky as an embodiment of Russian ideals was written before the War, although it did not appear in English until 1919. This was President Masaryk's *The Spirit of Russia*, originally written in German in 1913.[150] The work was an account of the main progress of Russian thought, a philosophic interpretation of history, which took into consideration literature and philosophy as much as political events. "What I wrote about Dostoevsky," said Masaryk in a foreword which explained how he had come to write the book, "is the core of the undertaking. Properly speaking the entire study is devoted to Dostoevsky, but I lacked the literary skill requisite for the interweaving of all I wanted to say into an account of that author." It would be impossible, Masaryk realized once he had begun a work on Dostoevsky, to do him justice "without discussing his predecessors and successors"; and so the present work was evolved. He hoped that it would show that he had been "right in choosing" Dostoevsky as his "main text"—and this, "although or for the very reason," that he differed "profoundly from Dostoevsky's outlook."[151] In the course of his long study he referred several times to the work which he would next undertake, ending with an appeal "to the reader's interest in behalf" of this sequel, which would deal with Dostoevsky, "the greatest analyst of the Russian revolution."[152]

Dostoevsky had been, he showed, the most influential spokesman of the main philosophies that agitated Russia in the nineteenth century. His "philosophical significance" was "to be found in his contest with Nihilism." He was "the first to force upon Nihilism reflection upon its own relationships in the field of metaphysics and in that of the philosophy of religion; he was the first to make a serious attempt to grasp its general significance." "All the great writers of that epoch" dealt with the problem, but Dostoevsky "above all." He was, in a certain measure, a Slavophile; had "imbibed the ideas of Kireevski," but "developed his views towards religion and the church independently," so that he became, "to put the matter paradoxically . . . too slavophil to be reckoned among the slavophils." He was the "greatest prophet" of the "great mystical movement which affected so large a part of the Russian intelligentsia in the closing decades of the nineteenth century." He was opposed to "individualistic anarchism" the main conceptions of which were incorporated "in the figure of Ivan Karamazov"; and he was an anti-liberal, representing "the devil as a liberal bourgeois." He "devoted much attention" to the philosophic problem raised by German Idealism and Marxism which occupied the Russian thinkers of his day; and "devoted his life to the exhaustive consideration" of the theological problem which these philosophies raised, that of "revelation and tradition versus experience and science."[153] Reviewers of the book noted, of course, the place in Russian thought which it assigned to Dostoevsky.[154]

Before 1921 enthusiasm for Dostoevsky had been considerably reduced. One wonders, naturally, how much the Russian Revolution had to do with this change. Several articles written by the Reverend George W. Thorn, although far from being absolute proof, might be taken as indicative of the trend of public opinion. In 1915 he published an article on "Dostoevsky as a Religious Teacher,"[155] in which he sought to show that Dostoevsky was wrongly reproached for dealing "only with the darker and more terrible experiences of life." He was a master of tragedy, who "recognized . . . as unmistakeably as Aeschylus or Sophocles" that "the utmost possibilities of our nature can be tested" only in tragic circumstances, in "the terrifying adventures of the human soul as it fathoms the depths of suffering and sin," at which time only "all spiritual resources of faith or hope the soul possesses stand revealed." This even the "most enthusiastic admirer" of Dostoevsky's work "failed to perceive." Dostoevsky's own experience, his familiarity with the New Testament, and his theory of the Russian Christ, had much to do with his view of tragedy and religion.

Dostoevsky "was always on his knees before the suffering of humanity. And he discovered that through the experience of compassionate
love to mankind he became more sure of the reality of God." Two
years later in another essay, entitled "Dostoevsky as a Psychologist,"[156] Thorne praised Mrs. Garnett's translation; held the war
responsible for having "greatly stimulated . . . the already deep and
growing interest in Russian literature"; quoted Stevenson's letter to
J. A. Symonds about Dostoevsky; referred to Merezhkovsky; and explained Dostoevsky's psychology as a study of "inward duality" with
a religious answer to the problem of the "divided self." His psychology
was "the method by which he [revealed] to men the real malady of
their souls." His religion was "the remedy he offered and that religion
[was]—Christ." But the following year, under stress of events occur-
ring in Russia, Thorn presented Dostoevsky in a somewhat different
light.[157] "Dostoevsky's portrayal of the Russian soul," he said, was
"more helpful to an understanding of existing conditions than many of
the explanations of them offered us." What Dostoevsky had understood
about the Russian temperament was its "overplus of impulse . . . which,
once overpowering the forces which restrain it, may result in hideous
crime." The murder in *Crime and Punishment,* the suicide in *The
Possessed* and in *The Brothers Karamazov,* Smerdyakov's justification
of robbery and murder on the basis of Ivan's teaching, all illustrated
the Russian tendency to carry out theories "to their extreme logical
conclusion." What these tendencies became in a revolutionary epoch
had been shown in *The Possessed* which "in 1871, seemed to be a gross
caricature . . . but which in the light of later history and of recent
events, [had] been more than justified."

On the other hand, in defense of Russia C. Hagberg Wright under-
took in *The Contemporary Review,* April 1918,[158] to answer all those
people who were "talking about Russia" and for the most part "abus-
ing her." He was "not surprised" that Gorky and Dostoevsky should
seem "repulsive" to men and women who had "always breathed our
wholesome English air," nor that the question "which Byelinsky
heard in his day" should now be heard again "from English lips:
'What can one learn from a book in which some miserable wretch
who has drunk himself to perdition is described?' " Yet Dostoevsky
and Gorky were "no fabulists"; they wrote of what they had personally experienced, and if Russia was to become, as seemed "probable," the "voice of the world's commonweal," the "Dostoevskys and

Gorkys of the future" would have "material better than the secrets of the prison-house and the lazar-house."

Among Dostoevsky's greatest admirers was Katherine Mansfield. She read him with such devotion that ordinary experiences of her life called up images from his work. "There's such a sad widower here," she would write Middleton Murry from Bandol, "with four little boys all in black. . . . They are *silly,* so *stupid:* that's what makes one sad to see them. Like a Dostoevsky sixth floor family."[159] Or again:

I had been awake nearly all night, too. It was all so noisy and at two o'clock my French windows burst open—out popped the candle, the blinds flapped like sails. As I rushed to the rescue I thought of that Appalling Moment when Kirillov rushed at Pyotor Stepanovich.[160]

At another time:

Why believe liars? Everybody lies. I don't know; but there you are. Dostoevsky at least understood through and through. . . . Why do I feel like this about Dostoevsky—my Dostoevsky—no one else's—a being who loved, in spite of everything adored Life even while he knew the dark, dark places?[161]

In 1919, when *An Honest Thief* was published, she wrote an essay on Dostoevsky for *The Athenaeum.*[162] "Will you please say if my Dosty is all right?" she asked Murry, "I sent it rather in fear and trembling, but I meant it."[163] She feared and trembled perhaps because its tone was facetious. She sketched amusingly, but not unkindly, the atmosphere of adulation which now surrounded Dostoevsky's name, but intimated that this admiration was on the wane. She imagined it "not at all impossible to see in Dostoevsky's influence upon the English intellectuals" of the day "the bones of a marvellously typical Dostoevsky novel." She pictured his arrival in the "small provincial town" of, let us say, London:

Could he himself exaggerate the discussions he has provoked, the expenditure of enthusiasm and vituperation, the mental running to and fro, the parties that have been given in his honour, the added confusion of several young gentlemen-writers declaring (in strict confidence) that they were the real Dostoevsky; the fascinating arguments as to whether or no he is greater than Jane Austen (what would Jane Austen have said to the bugs and the onions and the living in corners!), the sight of our young egoists puffing up like undismayed frogs, and of our superior inner circle who are not unwilling to admit that he has a considerable amount of crude strength before returning to their eighteenth century muttons?

Ohé Dostoevsky! Où est Dostoevsky? As-tu vu Dostoevsky?
Few indeed have so much as caught a glimpse of him. What would be the
end of such a novel? His disappearance without doubt, leaving no trace
but a feeling of, on the whole, very lively relief. For if we do not take
him superficially, there is nothing for us to do but to take him terribly
seriously, but to consider whether it is possible for us to go on writing
our novels as if he never had been.

This, she said, was "not only a bitterly uncomfortable prospect"; it
was "positively dangerous; it might very well end in the majority of
our young writers finding themselves naked and shivering, without
a book to clothe themselves in." But, she continued,

the danger is not a real one. There are signs that the fashion for him is
on the wane. How otherwise can we interpret the avidity with which opinion
seizes upon the less important, extravagant side of Dostoevsky, making
much of it, making much of that and ignoring all else, than that it has had
its fright as it were, but now has been assured that the monster at the fair
will not remain.

Dostoevsky's virtue was, she said, that "more than any other writer"
he created the "mysterious relationship with the reader," the "sense
of sharing." With him, "we are never conscious that he is writing at
us or for us. While we read, we are like children to whom one tells a
tale."

And a month later, to Middleton Murry: "How long was Dostoev
sky in prison? Four years, wasn't he? And he came out and did his
finest work after."[164] Then passing to other matters, and now dealing
with G. B. Shaw:

There's no getting over it: he's a kind of *concièrge* in the house of literature
—sits in a glass case, sees everything, knows everything, examines the letters, *cleans the stairs,* but has no part, no part in the life that is going on.
But as I wrote that, I thought: Yes, but who is living there, living as we
mean life? Dostoevsky, Chekhov and Tolstoy and Hardy. I can't think of
anybody else.

1921, the centenary of Dostoevsky's birth, was marked by the
publication of his daughter Aimée's biography and by an essay in *The
Fortnightly Review*[165] in which J. A. T. Lloyd elaborated the comparison he had previously drawn between Dostoevsky and Flaubert.[166] "They live," he wrote of them, "each after his fashion . . .
in this year—1921, and it is not dangerous to predict that, a hundred
years from now, not only in Russia and France, but throughout
Europe and the world, the birthdays of Feodor Dostoevsky and Gustave Flaubert will be remembered." But, on the whole, apart from

Lloyd's essay and a special article in *The Times*,[167] Dostoevsky's first
centenary passed unnoticed. In America it was belatedly recalled
the following year in a garrulous article in *The Methodist Review*;[168]
and there were also a few sketchy pages about him in a negligible little
history of Russian literature,[169] and mention of him by C. Hagberg
Wright in an article on Russian literature,[170] but only as an author
who was not fairly representative of Russians and so not appropriate
to his study. In America a Doctor's thesis on his ideology was presented to Columbia University by Avrahm Yarmolinsky;[171] and in a
volume on the modern English novel by Abel Chevalley,[172] the following statement was made about his influence:

Il est visible qu'après l'influence de Flaubert et de Maupassant qui s'exerça
pendant toute la fin du xix⁰ et le commencement du xx⁰ siècle, celle des
écrivains russes et notamment de Dostoïevski s'est fait sentir fortement
sur eux avant, pendant, et depuis la guerre. La Russie fut alors l'objet
d'une véritable mode littéraire. Nul ne pouvait aspirer au rang d'intellectuel et à l'épithète d'avancé sans être verni de slavisme révolutionnaire.
Il est peu de romans littéraires qui n'aient, entre 1912 et 1918, été fortement marqués de cette influence russe. Aucun livre n'a été plus lu en
Angleterre durant cette période que les *Frères Karamazoff*. Un mélange
de mysticisme et de sensualité, de violence et d'amour, une sorte de sadisme
intellectuel, pénétrait alors la mince portion du public anglais qui se pique
de littérature.

There were also several allusions to Dostoevsky in Percy Lubbock's *Craft of Fiction*,[173] which came out this year. Dostoevsky's
tense and close atmosphere was there contrasted to the broadness
and lucidity of Tolstoy. In the "ominous circle" of the *Brothers Karamazov* was not to be found "the serene and impartial day that arches
from verge to verge in *War and Peace*." With Tolstoy "nobody doubts
that an ample vision opens in every direction. It may be left untold,
but his men and women have only to lift their eyes to see it." But
with Dostoevsky "night stops the view—or rather no ordinary,
earthly night but a sudden opacity, a fog that cannot be pierced or
breathed." Dostoevsky "intensified," by "shutting off the least glimmer of natural day," the "blaze of light" which illuminated "his
strange crew." The illumination was "like the glare of a furnace-
mouth; it searched the depths of the inner struggles and turmoils in
which his drama was enacted." For Dostoevsky's method was essentially dramatic. On it depended the strength of *Crime and Punishment* where drama was "pushed into the theatre of a mind," where a
man's mind was "uncovered" and the reader forced to look into it.

But, of course, Dostoevsky's subject had made this method appropriate. There would have been "no reason," for example, for Dickens to adopt it in *David Copperfield,* "since the subject was not essentially in David at all, but in the linked fortunes of a number of people grouped around him. David's consciousness, if we watched it instead of listening to the story, would be unsubstantial indeed."

But these references were hardly called forth by the occasion of Dostoevsky's centenary. It may have been with the centenary in mind, however, that Constance Garnett's translation of Dostoevsky was brought to a conclusion[174] with the publication of *The Friend of the Family,* at the close of the preceding year.

V. THE LATEST PHASE—1922-1936

BY 1922, then, Dostoevsky was well known in English literary circles. His novels had been ably translated and some biographical material had appeared. His influence on the western novel was said to be extensive and profound, and several popular authors had declared their enthusiasm for him. His fame indeed had reached its zenith and had already begun to decline. In the following years much of his work appeared in new editions, and some of it was translated for the first time.

Of new translations the most important were *The Plan for the Life of a Great Sinner* and *Stavrogin's Confession,* rendered into English by S. S. Koteliansky and Virginia Woolf, and published in one volume in 1922.[1] In 1923, 1929, and 1930 various of Dostoevsky's letters appeared,[2] and in 1926, a portion of his wife's diary, which in 1928 was published in full but from a German translation.[3] All this material that revealed Dostoevsky the man tended to qualify admiration of Dostoevsky the author; when the one was shown all too human, it was difficult to continue thinking the other divine.

Through all the new records Dostoevsky appeared for the most part ununderstandable—"no more clarified and settled for our minds . . . than Shakespeare the Man by his two signatures"[4]—and when understandable, a far from admirable figure, "a worried, uneasy, tortured, sensitive, expostulating, explaining shadow."[5] When we looked "in a spirit of worship and horror, from the work to the man, trying to discover the matrix in which his sublime serenity was molded" we found a "pitiable epileptic, a disease-exasperated being, driven like a tormented demon from one to another of the gambling hells of the Continent."[6] He was obviously, as Tolstoy had described him, "a man with a kink." His works "in some curious way" left one "in the air," and the "troubled condition" which he aroused in readers came from "the feeling that this man was open to anything." He was "without the inhibitions that kept us safe." To him "not only were all things theoretically lawful, but emotionally possible." Such a man was "beyond or beneath good and evil"; it was hoped, a little doubtfully, that "such an explorer of human possibilities" had existed "for the good of mankind."[7] Mme. Dostoevsky's diary "should serve to correct to some extent the 'heroic' or 'demoniac' views" of her husband. The quality that made "the novels the great things" they were, was "to be found only in the novels; it was not in the man himself."[8]

Indeed, "the most remarkable thing" about the diary was its revelation that the wife had apparently "remained immune" from all her husband's "spiritual poisons and preserved her simplicity and serenity of soul in such dangerous proximity."[9] In short, however justifiable might be "idolatry of Dostoevsky as a novelist, or as a poet," Dostoevsky the man, it was "difficult to respect."[10]

As for *The Plan for the Life of a Great Sinner* and *Stavrogin's Confession,* revealing a crime which, according to *The Saturday Review,*[11] it was "difficult in decent language to hint at," Dr. Freud and his disciples might be interested in it, but "no one else would be the better for it." In *The New Statesman,*[12] Hugh Owen Meredith declared himself "too much of a philistine . . . to appreciate Dostoevsky." He wondered "at his incomparable power of presenting the stream of consciousness"; no one he thought got "nearer to an articulate expression of life," but "his characters and situations . . . mudsplashes from the chariot wheels of life" were not "important"; they had not "as one might say, 'a stake in the country.' " *Stavrogin's Confession* left him "yet colder" than the Grand Guignol. "Between tragedy and Dostoevsky," he wrote, "there is a considerable gulf. . . . For the tragedians have concentrated on the breaking of men who are within an ace of being unbreakable. . . . To call Dostoevsky a tragedian is as though one should match the frustration of lions with the sad history of lice."

On the other hand, for those whose interest in Dostoevsky could withstand these revelations, the new material had the fascination of an important discovery. His letters revealed "a very impressive sincerity."[13] And although they were uniformly "nightmarish" in atmosphere, and dull, they were "of high psychological interest . . . as monotonous and interesting as life itself,"[14] of the "greatest value" to students of Dostoevsky's character, "indispensable" indeed "for the study of his life."[15] There was "something morbid" in Dostoevsky's "obsession of detail" which they revealed, but "something on the other hand" that struck one "as the biographical material out of which much of his artistic methods grew up . . . an exaggerated importance attached to the infinitesimals and details of life" being "one of the essential features" of his style.[16] The diary of his wife also showed how his "novels developed from his life, and why he forestalled all modern schools of psychology of the 'unconscious' and also (what was more important) transcended them."[17] The diary was "entrancing," said Leonard Woolf. There was "a type of greatness

about the great Russians" which for his part he could not think
"spurious or imaginary." He got it "even in books about them; even
occasionally in the dreariest of Dostoevsky's letters."[18] According to
the *Times Literary Supplement*,[19] Dostoevsky's art contained what
his life had lacked; nor did one "need elaborate study to account"
for this. What Dostoevsky lacked was will; what his novels contained was the "heroic idea of the will." His "profession of mystical
humility [was] only an after-thought; it [was] Ivan not his brother
Alyosha . . . whose spiritual drama [was] significant." Dostoevsky's
"abnormal power of analysis went with abject weakness of character." *Stavrogin's Confession* was "a precious survival," which had
"value in itself, by reason of the beauty and the terror" in it, value
also for what it showed "of Dostoevsky's most secret and intimate
thoughts," but value mostly as "a monument of his spiritual integrity." Its "least importance" was the sensational revelation imputed
to it by rumor. The "significance of the act confessed" was "small
beside the significance of the act of confession" and was a "symbolic
significance." It was "a symbolic representation, which would sadly
disappoint the amateur of pornography."[20] *The Plan for the Life of a
Great Sinner* was "proof" that Dostoevsky's novels were "a kind of
battle-ground in which he fought for a belief";[21] it showed that this
"irregular genius of chaotic energies and fervent incoherencies
planned, meditated and slowly evolved his plots and his ideas."[22]

Following the publication of these biographical records, studies
appeared which dealt with isolated episodes in Dostoevsky's life.
Several of them had to do with Apollinaria Souslova, whose diary
had come to light in 1928. There was a short article about her by the
Russian scholar Leonid Grossman, translated for the *Calendar of
Modern Letters*, March 1925;[23] a long but undistinguished essay
in the *Cornhill Magazine* by W. L. Blennerhasset;[24] and, in the *Fortnightly Review*,[25] a more sound and interesting one by E. H. Carr,
who published excerpts from her diary, and unlike Blennerhasset,
thought her not at all a "passionate, emotional, direct, imperious, and
resolute" woman, but, most unsentimentally, a "minx," a rather
ordinary, unprincipled flirt. Elsewhere,[26] Carr discussed the Turgenev-
Dostoevsky quarrel. Through the complete correspondence between
the two authors which had been collected and published in Leningrad
in 1928, he traced their relationship from the literary friendship at
the time *Poor Folk* was published, through the stages of mutual
jealousy, hurt feelings and insults, to the "serio-comic" episode at the

Pushkin celebration when Dostoevsky referred to Turgenev's Liza, Turgenev rose and blew him a kiss, and at the end of the performance, the two solemnly embraced. "Were they sincere?" Carr asked. "Yes. Would the reconciliation have been lasting? No. . . . Turgenev lived to pen, in a letter to Saltykov, one of the bitterest epitaphs ever written by one author on another." In another article, in 1931,[27] Carr reviewed the memoirs of Dostoevsky's brother, which had just been published in Russia. They contained material for "a curious study of heredity," and the "first detailed account of the murder of Dostoevsky's father," as well as the father's letters to his wife, "printed here for the first time," which gave "a remarkable foretaste of the passionate but suspicious devotion of Feodor Dostoevsky's letters to Anna Grigorievna." But the "greatest 'find' " in the collection was a series of "more than twenty hitherto unpublished letters" of Dostoevsky himself, "the first dating from childhood, the last written just two months before his death." The letters were none of them of "first-rate importance," but would probably become available in no other form since "literary jealousies" had prevented "their inclusion in the standard edition of Dostoevsky's letters now in course of publication in Moscow."

Other essays on special phases of Dostoevsky's life and thought dealt with his Slavophilism,[28] with his relation to the Russian Revolution,[29] with his influence on modern Russian Literature,[30] with his attitude to Judaism.[31]

Of particular interest have been the psychoanalytic studies of Dostoevsky published in the last ten or twelve years. In 1926, Dr. Alfred Adler, in the course of a series of lectures delivered in England, discussed Dostoevsky as a perfect example of a frustrated will-to-power.[32] Dostoevsky was a second son, he said, and, as such, in his childhood, subjected to the twofold dominance of father and elder brother. As in the case "of a great many young criminals" he had failed to achieve his "personal liberation by conscious readjustment to environment"; and, as a matter of fact, "before he was thirty . . . was actually sentenced to death." "The shadow of the scaffold hung over Dostoevsky in his own mind." And his own conflict was expressed in Raskolnikov's crime, committed "half out of vanity and half from conviction of the worthlessness of life." That Raskolnikov's confession was made to a prostitute was another typical and revealing circumstance. He went to her just as Dostoevsky, as a child, had run to a peasant in his terror of a wolf. For it was true, not only of Dostoevsky but of "others in like situation," that they were magnetically attracted "towards the company of lower-class and intellectually feeble people . . . as though only in such company [was] the superiority so unutterably longed for established beyond question." It was "once more significant" in Raskolnikov's case that the "anti-social deed" was "revealed to the social outcast, the uniqueness of the murderer and his humiliation being linked again"—another resolution of that doubt which tormented Dostoevsky as well as Raskolnikov: "am I a Napoleon or a louse?" Epilepsy, furthermore, very much resembled "the realization of a power fantasy, since all the world runs to serve one in that condition." Finally, Dostoevsky, consciously or not, "took the most diabolical revenge possible on authority in his society." Tottering authority may withstand criticism, but not fulsomeness; and Dostoevsky's worship of the Church and the Czar was "the too servile praise of a hanger-on" which "destroys the prestige of the adored object." Dostoevsky may have been "genuinely reactionary, but the manner of his later years was certainly that of the criminal, entirely overpowered by his environment, who waxes in cunning to make up for his deficiency in courage." In his "thwarted effort towards liberation" he "has received the lion's share of responsibility for the destruction of society as it was in his time."

Sigmund Freud in 1929, in a study contributed to *The Realist*,[33] explained Dostoevsky's epilepsy as the manifestation of an Oedipus complex. Although there existed insufficient data, he supposed the cause of Dostoevsky's epilepsy to have been functional rather than organic. The trances of Dostoevsky's boyhood and his fear of death were to be seen in relation to his feeling of guilt for some unknown crime. All were symptoms of well known cases of neuroses. He deduced that Dostoevsky's first epileptic fit occurred upon the news of his father's murder. He saw special significance in the parricide of *The Brothers Karamazov*, and in Dostoevsky's feeling of reverence for criminals, shown in the famous scene between Dmitri and Zossima—the criminal, according to this interpretation, being in a way a Saviour, preserving others from the necessity of crime—and he pointed out the fundamental similarities which, on this basis, existed between *The Brothers Karamazov, Hamlet,* and *Oedipus Rex*. Richard Montgomery, in *The New Age*,[34] discussed Freud's and Adler's analyses of Dostoevsky. He thought Adler's views the more plausible; but his essay was a comparison of psychoanalytic methods rather than a study of Dostoevsky.

The following year in *The Psychoanalytic Review*,[35] S. C. Burchell supported the Freudian hypothesis that Dostoevsky's sense of guilt was related to his feeling toward his father and to his epilepsy.

The Karamazov 4 in 1, [he wrote] is a sort of morality play in which levels of the psyche are substituted for the conventional Mr. Goodman and Mr. Badman. It is in a way a psychological *Gulliver's Travels* which may be read either as a story or as an allegory. The characters represent progressive stages in the psyche from the criminal *id* of Smerdyakov to the ideal super ego phantasy of Aliosha. That the situation was autobiographic is obvious from the internal evidence alone.

Crime and Punishment, which "tapped a universal stream of guilt," was the "most enlightening novel on the power of his guilt sense" and "a profound contribution to criminology."

But E. H. Carr, referring to Freud and other analysts,[36] declared it "natural, though unfortunate, that these scientific investigators" should be imperfectly "familiar with the literary evidence on which our knowledge of Dostoevsky's epilepsy" depended. On the basis of this literary evidence, which could be classified in three groups: I. Statements of Dostoevsky, both those recorded by himself and those recorded by others; II. Statements by others; III. Evidence to be derived from his literary work, Carr came to the conclusion that there was no reason to suppose Dostoevsky's epilepsy to have existed before his exile to Siberia, nor any reason to connect it with his father.

But interest in Dostoevsky was evidenced also in more imaginative form than that of scientific analyses. For example, a poem about him by Louis Grudin appeared in 1922 in the magazine, *Broom:*[37]

A man with a face like a thin green wave
that rose in a drawn treble against the darkness,
stood in a small bare room;
it fled in four directions
from the frantic gas light.

Faces vaguely resembling his own
ranged about him and hung in straight lines,
like an abandoned quest.

Hungers with tired hands
and hatreds breast to breast
groped toward him, crying
that their struggles were unavailing,
and in their midst a ceaseless wailing
suddenly choked itself, explaining
that it did not know how to die

a man and woman relinquished each other
and pointed to their futile bruises;
a violent ghost leaped before him
and fluttered with a pain without words;
among them hovered
a woman with an invisible face
and shoulders like a heavy scent
which she had wearied of pursuing;
a giant stared at his own phosphorescence
and begged with a guiltless candor,
from a heap of implements and rags,
to be told what he wanted.

The young man stumbled among them and they
    clung to his clothes,
their voices struck him like hail,
and he cried that he was only a child.

He fled till he knew they would not vanish,
then he lay, whispering their questions,
tasting them warily, as though
he had learnt how to sip poison;
it flamed gently in his veins,
and he knew the gaiety of those
that need no sunlight and can no longer die.

There was a parody by Duncan Marks, in the *New Statesman*,[38] entitled "The Aunt, the Dog, and the Nose," supposedly translated "from the Russian of Dostchekovski." It was the tale of a Prince Stepan Yaroslav Baryoulska who, one day, could not control his impulse to pull the nose of a perfect stranger. The stranger thereupon introduced himself, "Vaselin Gramateich Zebroski," and took the offender with him to visit his aunt. At the aunt's the prince was so irritated by her pet pug that he threw an old Sèvres vase at him, and was arrested for murder. First found guilty, he was then declared insane, and released with apologies.

Among the most sensitive appreciations of Dostoevsky in English is that in Edmund Wilson's novel *"I Thought of Daisy,"*[39] where, in a long monologue, of central philosophic importance for the book, the hero meditating the problem of the relation between literature and life, starts with the consideration that the perversity of Dostoevsky was not repaid by the "flights of his Christian idealism." "The Svidrigailovs and the Stavrogins," he thinks, "those malignant growths which seemed to sprout and, almost without the author's intention, to swell to such monstrous proportions . . . were they not the price which one had to pay for the Myshkins and the Alyoshas?" It was, to his mind, too great a price. But, he reflects, the people whom he himself admires, were they not, all of them, precisely as regards their most admirable qualities, "the victims of deficiencies and derangements?" And then, remembering Dostoevsky's "miseries," where, he asks, in the presence of such a life as his, "where was there place for ironic patronage?" Dostoevsky "had been forced to live at close quarters with the basic contentions and discords, the basic horrifying anomalies of our common life"; he had "attempted to explain them, to resolve them." And were not these contentions and discords, after all, "the prime provokers of literature," the basis of the greatest poetry? "Was there, indeed . . . from the point of view of barbarous behavior, very much to choose between Sophocles and Dostoevsky himself. . . . Myshkin's epilepsy, Zossima's putrefaction and Stavrogin's rape" were they not "quite matched by Philoctetes' ulcer, by the unburied corpse of Polyneices and by the incest of Oedipus?" Realization of Dostoevsky's meaning, that is, shows the hero the springs of artistic creation and both the aesthetic and moral significance of evil.

Most important for English-speaking students of Dostoevsky were two full length biographies which now appeared: one in England, by E. H. Carr, 1931; the other in America, by Avrahm Yarmolinsky, 1934.

To Carr's biography, Mirsky contributed a preface in which he described it as "an eminently sensible book." He said there was "no nonsense" in it and that it was "probably the first book on the subject (published outside Russia) of which so much could be asserted." It was, furthermore, "the first life of Dostoevsky in any language to be based on adequate material." Altogether, it was "something to be thankful for" after "the sensational gossip of the novelist's daughter, after the Pecksniffian sob-stuff of Mr. Middleton Murry, after the perverse and arbitrary sophistications of André Gide and the unutterable rot of a legion of pseudo-profound Germans."[40]

Thoroughness, scholarship, common sense and imaginative sympathy are indeed the distinguishing characteristics of this biography. Mr. Carr having no axe to grind and interested in nothing so much as a scientific exposition of his subject, presents his material chronologically, discussing each work from the centre of the immediate circumstances which shaped it. And the serious carefulness of his approach is evidenced in his use of sources whose validity he always weighs with all that is possible in an investigation of this kind of scientific detachment. He discounts, for example, the picturesque but untruthful comments of Dostoevsky's daughter, of the unfriendly Strakhov, Dostoevsky's "official" biographer; he is suspicious—perhaps too suspicious—of Freud; he examines all available evidence regarding Dostoevsky's quarrels with Belinsky and Turgenev, and the various sentimental relationships in which Dostoevsky was involved; he points out repeatedly the danger of reading Dostoevsky's productions as autobiographical documents;[41] and he distinguishes always between ascertained fact and plausible conjecture. One might cite as typical, the opening of Chapter V, "The House of the Dead":

The account given by Dostoevsky of the four years spent by him in the prison fall into three categories—the letters which he wrote from Siberia during the two or three years after his release; *Memoirs from the House of the Dead* published, under the transparent guise of a novel, after his return to Petersburg at the beginning of the following decade; and numerous references, direct and indirect, in his subsequent writings. Each of these three categories reveals markedly different characteristics. In the first, memories of suffering and insult are still green and bitter; the letters, sent for the most part by private messengers and not exposed to the risks of censorship, provide a healthy corrective to the rosier hues of the later accounts. In *Memoirs from the House of the Dead*, though they conceal nothing of the horror and hardships of a convict's life, the mellowing influence of time has combined with fear of the censor to reproduce an attitude of unresentful detachment. In later references, beginning with the epilogue to *Crime and Punishment* and ending with *The Journal of an Author* and *The Brothers Karamazov*, Dostoevsky carries to its conclusion the moralising process of which faint traces may be found here and there in *The Memoirs*, and treats his prison years, not without an occasional hint of smugness, as a vital and salutary stage in the salvation of his soul. These later writings are, from the strictly biographic point of view, valueless.[42]

Carr shows the psychological and social basis in the development of Dostoevsky's philosophy; never loses sight of the milieu, with all its determining intellectual forces—but neither does he overlook the entirely individual physical and nervous factors which would have predisposed him to certain ways of thought. We see, for example, Dostoevsky spurred to writing as a career at a moment when for the first time in Russia authorship had become possible as a profession; we see him, in like manner, led to journalism by the social ferment of the sixties; we see him influenced by the most powerful literary current of his day, French and German Romanticism, combined with the Realism of Gogol. And, at the same time, we are made aware of the concentrated, enclosed tenseness of his work as peculiarly his, the result, in part, of his social isolation. We see the psychological insight which he gained from his close relationship with several women; but, above all, we see how all these influences combined logically in the formation of his philosophy.[43]

The people whom Dostoevsky met are vividly characterized: Baron Wrangel, for example, Anna Korvin-Krukovskaya, Martha Brown, the hosts of the artistic salons which Dostoevsky frequented.[44] There is a full account of the genesis and growth of *Crime and Punishment* and of *The Idiot,* and the religious and philosophic background of the great novels is given in detail.[45] Carr points out that Dostoevsky's psychology derived directly from the French romantics but indicates also wherein it transcended its origins. The all important concepts of sin and suffering and of dualism receive his special attention. He demonstrates how elements of Christian apologetics combined with romantic enthusiasms to form the background of Dostoevsky's philosophy; and how the philosophy of Hegel, French romanticism, and Dostoevsky's personal urge to explain himself worked together to form his all important concept of the Double. His references to the differences between the ideals of Russia and the West are occasionally mystifying—"as if he actually believed," says Mirsky, "in the existence of such a thing as an abstract Russian divorced from circumstances of time and class"; but, on the whole, they are grounded in historic fact and are illuminating.

Reviewers, in *The London Mercury,*[46] *The Spectator,*[47] and *The New Statesman and Nation,*[48] agreed for the most part with Mirsky in his estimate of the book. "We sigh with relief," said Richard Church, in *The Spectator,* "to find Dostoevsky treated as a man and not as a latter-day Messiah." "For the first time Dostoevsky is shown life-size, and in such a sane light that the man, his work, and his complicated career fit together into a unity as understandable as it can possibly be to an onlooker." And this is done "with such fairness, tender intuition, and subtlety of understanding" that he "stands up as a man so distinct and humanly recognizable that all the former emanations as prophet, magician, saint or devil, conjured up by other zealots, vanish from our minds." Another critic thought the work not only fair and valuable, but "exciting" reading.[49] Alone the reviewer in *The Times Literary Supplement,*[50] although complimentary on the whole, had much in the book to criticize. He found that the author's matter of fact, scientific approach was insufficiently appreciative of Dostoevsky's Christian doctrine. "A true life of Dostoevsky," he thought, could hardly be written "save from a point of view which admits at least the symbolic truth of Christianity." The approach of the present biography was that of historical materialism which was "an inadequate basis for the appreciation of spiritual genius," for there was "such a thing as spiritual reality, even though historical materialism" had "no room for it." The "curiously unsympathetic introduction" [unsympathetic, of course, to Dostoevsky, not to Carr] seemed "singular" until one remembered that Prince Mirsky had "lately proclaimed his complete conversion to the doctrine of historical materialism."

Avrahm Yarmolinsky's biography of Dostoevsky is the fullest to have appeared so far in English. Like E. H. Carr's it is based on all available material, but it is more circumstantial than Carr's in its narrative, less compact, more "popular" in tone, more journalistic. Whereas the English biographer had been interested in explaining Dostoevsky as a writer, Yarmolinsky was interested in him as a man. He attempted to identify himself with his subject and thus to recreate the story of his life sympathetically, from the inside, as it were. He reproduced scenes of Dostoevsky's life in vivid detail: the cold weather and the prisoner's clothing, for example, were not forgotten in the narrative of the execution scene, nor the detail that it was Christmas eve and that Dostoevsky on his way back to the fortress must have passed his brother Michael's house; so also, with equal vividness, the evening in which Dostoevsky proposed marriage to Anna Korvin-Krukovskaya, and was rejected; an incident of a journey taken by him in his boyhood, and many others.[51] Apparently insignificant episodes were dramatically presented and given their due in the development of Dostoevsky's character. Much attention was devoted to the emotional side of his nature, the stage for the neurotic author being carefully set in the picture of the nervous child: his fear of his father, and his devotion to his mother and to his older brother, his ardent schoolboy attachments, the terrifying tales told him at night by his nurse, his early religious training, the rigor of his military school and his hatred of it and unhappiness there.[52] One is made to feel how exaggeratedly the sensitive and nervous boy suffered a series of humiliations, and how exaggeratedly also, his early triumph. The work reads like fiction. There is even, in spite of the sober detachment of its analytic portions, an air sometimes of almost condescending familiarity; "Dostoevsky was scribbling away at a great rate,"[53] for example,—which may be explained, perhaps, as the assumption of thorough understanding. For this assumption there is indeed ample reason. Although the work reads like fiction, no detail of it—one may be certain—was invented or inserted without careful weighing of evidence.

Nowhere is this care better shown than in the review of the scandalous legend surrounding the long suppressed *Stavrogin's Confession*,[54] or in the estimate of psychoanalytic explanations of Dostoevsky's epilepsy.[55] Whereas other critics had contented themselves with hasty allusions to and hastily impatient dismissals of these problems, Yarmolinsky considered them with patience and came to measured conclusions, accepting the credible, dismissing the fantastic.

His primary interest in Dostoevsky the man shows itself in his analyses of his works. Carr had pointed out the danger of reading them as autobiographic revelations. But Yarmolinsky, considered that literature was for Dostoevsky a means of expressing the events of his psyche, though not the factual occurrences of his life, "not escape from himself, but rather a form of confession." He thought it "conceivable" therefore that in "identifying himself" with the "dwarfed thwarted souls" of the early stories Dostoevsky "was gratifying his secret sense of his own insufficiency." *Notes from the Underground* had "plainly . . . much in common" with its author, and *Crime and Punishment* was "in a deeper sense than his earlier works, a confession." For this reason the least interesting of his novels was *The House of the Dead* which, unlike the others, "obviously autobiographical," left his "inner life . . . out of the picture." From *The Idiot* one carried away the "impression that it was the work of a man who smothers a curse in a shout of hallelujah"; and in the characters of *The Brothers Karamazov* he "embodied his own mental conflict, his emotional disorder, his carnality." Through Smerdyakov "he could give his own dark impulses their freedom" and in Alyosha, could present "the man he would so gladly have been."[56]

The difference between Yarmolinsky's approach to his subject and Carr's can be best seen, perhaps, in a comparison of their versions of one instance in Dostoevsky's experience, of for example, his behavior after the first enthusiasm about *Poor Folk* had died down. Carr had written:

A naïvely optimistic temperament, combined with complete ignorance of social usage, led him to mistake encouragement for adulation, and friendly gestures for passionate devotion. The literary world had come to gaze with interest on a young writer of promise; and he fondly imagined it prostrate at his feet. . . . In short, Dostoevsky made a fool of himself.[57]

Yarmolinsky gave the following account:

Turgenev described him as a mole who had crawled out into the light of day.
He had moments of abysmal shyness. His eyes would hide behind their lids;
his head would seem to withdraw like a turtle's; his words came out in gasps.
But as his visits became more frequent, his bashful manner gave place to
a tactlessly forward one, which these clever literary people failed to interpret as another sign of shyness. They saw merely that he was obstinate
and cocky. . . . They behaved like a crowd of schoolboys baiting an inoffen-
sive newcomer.[58]

In short, this biography sees the man first and the author second.
A final chapter gives a succinct summary and interpretation of his
work and of the fortunes of his after fame in Russia and abroad.[59] He
is interpreted as a Realist, but a Realist of a special kind whose novels,
however accurate and well-documented they may have been, were
"veiled, distorted, and transfigured" projections of the "forces and
potentialities within himself," his greatness residing in the light which,
through this inwardness, he has thrown on all men.

These two biographies, which sought to render Dostoevsky com-
prehensible, were welcome in an age which had grown dissatisfied
with the criticism of mystification. Some years earlier already, in
1925, Dorothy Brewster and Angus Burrell had classified, with some
impatience, the existing schools of Dostoevsky critics.[60] According to
them, they were three in number; the "sweetly solemn . . . Christian
interpreters" such as William Lyon Phelps; the "symbolic and metaphysical" ones like Middleton Murry and Janko Lavrin; and those
who saw his work as a lunatic asylum: Percy Lubbock, Kropotkin,
Merezhkovsky. In reply to all of them Brewster and Burrell had maintained that the characters of *The Brothers Karamazov* were much
more understandable as men than as symbols and that with the help
of new psychological theories they appeared neither abnormal nor
strangely foreign. There were American families, living in New England, they said, who offered perfect analogies to the Karamazovs.
One needed only to imagine the events of ten years in their lives
compressed and speeded up to quicker tempo and the novel would
be recreated on American soil. What seemed abnormal in the Russian
characters was really the effect, as Merezhkovsky had pointed out,
of the "laboratory experiment" to which Dostoevsky subjected them,
raising the "pressure of life . . . to the nth power, instead of leaving
us at the comfortable 2nd or 3d at which we usually function!" These
" 'abnormal people' in Dostoevsky's world" were "they not potentially ourselves?"

The "symbolic" school of interpreters, however, still had its representatives. There was the German poet Herman Hesse, for example,
whose essay on Dostoevsky was published in translation in 1922 in
The English Review[61] and in *The Dial.*[62] In it Dostoevsky appeared
as a "prophet," and a prophet, said Hesse, was "something like this.
. . . A sick man, like Dostoevsky . . . the sort of sick man who has lost
the sound sense of taking care of himself," and who, therefore, "has
that strange, occult, godlike faculty" of vision into the future, "which
the Asiatic venerates in every maniac." One looked, therefore, at the
characters of Dostoevsky's books, "these criminals, hystericals, and
idiots" in a way quite different from that in which one saw "the
criminals or fools in other novels," for they revealed Dostoevsky's
prophetic vision of the Downfall of Europe, "foretold and explained
with extreme clearness" in his works and stated "in the most concentrated form" in *The Brothers Karamazov*. The Downfall of Europe
was indeed the overwhelming of the "European soul" by the "ideal of
the Karamazov, primeval, Asiatic, and occult." It was "a return
home to the mother, a turning back to Asia, to the source, to the
'Faustischen Müttern.' " The "rejection of every strongly held Ethic
and Moral in favour of a comprehensive laissez-faire," the "new and
dangerous faith that Elder Zossima announced, the faith lived by
Alyosha and Dmitri, a faith which was brought into clearer expression by Ivan Karamazov." It was a "faculty to feel the Godlike, the
significant, the fatalistic, in the wickedest and in the ugliest, and even
to accord them veneration and worship." By this new Ideal, embodied
in the Karamazovs, "the roots of the European Spirit" were being
"sapped." The " 'Russian man'," who had "long existed," who existed
"far outside Russia" was "on the road to become the European man";
and "part of the dreaded explosion" had indeed "in these last years
been audibly evident." It showed itself in that Europe was "tired . . .
in that Europe [wanted] to turn homewards, in that Europe [wanted]
to rest, in that Europe [wanted] to be recreated, reborn." The " 'Russian man' " was "dangerous, emotional, irresponsible, yet conscience-
haunted; soft, dreamy, cruel, yet fundamentally childish." He was
"far older than Dostoevsky" but Dostoevsky had "finally shown him
to the world in all his fearful significance." He was "assassin and
judge, ruffian and tenderest soul, the complete egotist and the most
self-sacrificing hero"; he feared "nothing and everything, [did] nothing and everything." He was "primeval matter," he was "monstrous
and soul-stuff." In him the "outward and inward, Good and Evil,

God and Satan" were united. And his dominance was evidenced in the Downfall of Europe, for Europe, "at all events half Eastern Europe" was "on the road to chaos. In a state of drunken illusion" she was "reeling into the abyss, and, as she [reeled] she [sang] a drunken hymn such as Dmitri Karamazov sang. The insulted citizen [laughed] that song to scorn, the saint and seer [heard] it with tears." To be sure, one could regard *The Brothers Karamazov,* if one were so minded, from a purely literary standpoint.

When the unconscious of a whole continent and age has made of itself poetry in the nightmare of a single, prophetic dreamer, when it has issued in his awful, blood-curdling scream one can of course consider this scream from the standpoint of a singing-teacher.

But our age, said Hesse, was not an age for singing teachers. The time for artists had "bloomed itself away." That was why Flaubert's work by comparison to Dostoevsky's became "quite a small artistic affair," why in Dostoevsky "European and especially German youth were destined to find their greatest writer . . . not in Goethe, not even in Nietzsche" and why "in the most modern poetry" however "callow and imitative," there was "everywhere an approach to Dostoevsky." Hesse admitted that every symbol had "a hundred interpretations, of which every one may be right," that the Karamazovs, too, therefore, might have a hundred interpretations, of which his was but one. But that they were a symbol, of that there could be no doubt. "This book of Dostoevsky's" had "hung a symbol round the neck of mankind," and "erected a monument for it just as an individual might in a dream create for himself an image of his warring instincts and forces."

In the same ecstatic tradition was an essay on Dostoevsky by Stephan Zweig, published in English in 1930,[63] meant to be, according to its author, not "an introduction but . . . a sublimation." What was most remarkable in Dostoevsky, he wrote, was his *"amor fati"* which permitted him "to see in every hostility, fulfilment, and in every trial, salvation. . . . While the foam still flecked his lips he rallied his energies to sing a hymn of praise to the deity who sent such trials." His genius, which owed "as Merezhkovsky [had] brilliantly pointed out . . . as deep a debt to [his] illness, as Tolstoy's to his radiant health" was shaped by this ability to suffer gladly. No one before him "had been able with such skill to lay bare the polarity of the emotions, the perpetual swing from ecstasy to annihilation, the extremes of joy and pain." He was "the most perfect example of antinomy, the greatest dualist, that art, and maybe humanity" had ever known. His "inherent contradictions" touched "both God and the Devil" and had "the universe between their extremes." It would be "foolish to try to excuse his moral lapses; unpardonable to force into the petty leading strings of bourgeois harmony, that which had the elemental beauty of the unmeasurable."

Because life was lavished so abundantly upon him and opened up such vistas of emotional suffering, he was able to love all that was terrible and good, divine and incomprehensible and everlastingly mysterious, in life.

In sum,

he was the archetypal man, subject to the everlasting powers; in him was resurrected . . . the bard of a mystic age, the sorcerer and seer, the frenzied prophet, the man of destiny.

Zola and Flaubert were "savants"; Dostoevsky was a "magician." His novels were "mighty epics of the heart" wherein the tragedy transcending its Russian origin broadened to "include all mankind." The "symbolic destiny" of his figures was "explicit and staggering":

Again and again, we live through the mystery of self-birth, of the myth created by Dostoevsky himself; the birth of the new man from the universal humanity which resides in every pilgrim here below. Self-birth; that is the word I have chosen wherewith to describe the advent of the new man in Dostoevsky's cosmogony.

As for the form of his novels, it must not be decried. Dostoevsky needed "massive dimensions," "just as the pyramids required gigantic foundations." His novels were like the great rivers of Russia: they "rolled on their way like the Volga or the Dnieper." It was Dostoevsky who made his nation known to the world: "during the Great War we could not but feel that we owed all our knowledge of Russia to Dostoevsky."

O Life, how wonderful you are, [the essay concluded] that you create martyrs for yourself, martyrs who, knowing what is before them, yet go to their martyrdom singing a hymn of praise as they go: O Life, wise and awful one, who through suffering innumerable makes thralls out of the greatest among men so that in the end they may proclaim your triumph.

In this category of personal appreciations should be listed Nicholas Berdyaev's book on Dostoevsky,[64] the purpose of which was avowedly to exemplify the author's own religious philosophy as much as to analyse his subject's. It was possible to do this Berdyaev explained, because the core of his own thought was also Dostoe..ky's,[65] which through the implications of the essay appeared to be a vision of human progress on an entirely abstract level, with all that is of value in human experience taken as having least to do with man's realization of himself as a material being. "Culture," for example, is something "spiritual" having nothing in common with the masses of people; and social and economic necessities have relatively little significance in the life of man. What is important is "man's original relationship with God and with the world," which is a "spiritual" relationship, opposed to Humanism. "Humanism," according to Berdyaev, "destroys man, but he is born again if he believes in God." Historically, the "Humanistic conception" had reached its fullest expression during the Renaissance, a "conception of the world . . . directed towards its psychic and not its spiritual aspect." But Humanism ran its course: "the time came when . . . man began to feel that the earth was not solid under his feet as he had thought. . . . Human freedom . . . plunged into the depths of the spiritual world"—a plunge that was "like a descent into Hell," but holding promise of salvation. In time, man would find there "not only Satan and his kingdom, but also God and Heaven"; and this descent and this discovery was the spiritual experience that Dostoevsky had predicted.[66] Dostoevsky's special value, then, was that he possessed foreknowledge and spiritual vision. His eyes were "turned towards the unknown future, the Becoming." His "art [was] prophetic: it [unveiled] the secret of man." And as a prophet of social change, he had predicted the Russian revolution which "took place in the way he said it would." He was "an apocalyptic being who [took] the side of Christ in his supreme struggle against Anti-Christ." The essence of the moral problem which he presented was the problem of "freedom," of the degree, that is, to which man is capable of acting of his own free will. "All his novels—his tragedies" were "concerned with the experiment of human liberty." Dostoevsky was not a "psychologist but a 'pneumatologist'; a symbolistic metaphysician" who could be understood only by a chosen few: "really to 'get inside' " him it was necessary "to have a certain sort of soul," a "Russian soul," for the "far-reaching spiritual experiences" which Dostoevsky narrated were "possible only to the Russian soul." Men of the West, therefore, might as well realize that to them the door was shut, for "it must be understood that the structure of the Russian soul is all its own and completely different from that of Westerners."[67]

Different in approach but not less subjective than Berdyaev's study was Spengler's *Der untergang des abendlandes* which was translated into English in 1928.[68] Here Dostoevsky and Tolstoy were once more confronted, Tolstoy being taken as representing the West in its decline, Dostoevsky, the ,emergent unwesternized civilization. Tolstoy belonged to the "pseudomorphosis of Petrinism." He was "tied to the West." He "could never shake it off. Hating it, he [hated] himself and so became the father of Bolshevism." This hatred was unknown to Dostoevsky whose "passionate power of living" was "comprehensive enough to embrace all things Western" as well as all things Russian. " 'I have two fatherlands,' " he had said, " 'Russia and Europe.' He [had] passed.. beyond both Petrinism and revolution, and from *his* future he [looked] back over them as from afar. His soul was apocalyptic, yearning, desperate, but of this future *certain.*" Everything that Tolstoy saw about him took "the hate-period, megalopolitan, and Western form of a *problem,*" whereas Dostoevsky did not "even know what a problem" was.

The reality in which Dostoevsky [lived], even during his life [was] a religious creation directly present to him. His Alyosha has defied all literary criticism, even Russian. His life of Christ, had he written it . . . would have been a genuine gospel like the Gospels of primitive Christianity . . . Tolstoy, on the other hand, [was] a master of the Western novel.

In these two authors "we have beginning and end clashing together." Dostoevsky was "a saint," Tolstoy "only a revolutionary." Bolshevism proceeded only from Tolstoy, "the true successor of Peter, and from him only." The "real Russian" was "a disciple of Dostoevsky." Although he had not read him "or any one else, nay, perhaps because he [could not] read, he [was] himself Dostoevsky in substance. . . . Tolstoy's Christianity was a misunderstanding. He spoke of Christ and he meant Marx. But to Dostoevsky's Christianity the next thousand years belong":[69]

Tolstoy, the townsman and Westerner, saw Jesus only as a social reformer, and in his metaphysical impotence—like the whole civilized West, which can only think about *distributing,* never *renouncing*—elevated primitive Christianity to the rank of a social revolution. Dostoevsky, who was poor, but in certain hours almost a saint, never thought about social ameliorations —of what profit would it have been to a man's *soul* to abolish *property?*

Again, Dostoevsky demonstrated "the immeasurable difference between the Faustian and the Russian souls." It was a difference that was "disclosed" even in "certain word-sounds." Compare, for example, the Russian and the German words for *sky* and *fate: nyebo* and *Himmel, sudba* and *Shicksal. Nyebo* contains in its *n*

a negative element. . . . Western man looks up, the Russian looks horizontally into the broad plain. . . . *Shicksal* rings like a trumpet call, *sudba* is a genuflection. There is no room for the upstanding 'I' beneath this almost flat-roofed heaven. That 'All are responsible for all'—the 'it' for the 'it' in this boundlessly extended plain—[was] the metaphysical fundament of all Dostoevsky's creation. That [was] why Ivan Karamazov must name himself murderer although another had done the murder.[70]

Not less exalted in tone was Julius Meier-Graefe's study of Dostoevsky, translated from the German in 1928.[71] It differed from the others, however, in its emphasis on artistic considerations. "What we are mainly concerned with," wrote Meier-Graefe, "is the æstheticism of the work freed, as far as possible, from extraneous matter."[72] Granted that the events of Dostoevsky's life had the closest relation to his writing, still it was dangerous to infer "a closer connexion between the man and his creation than actually [existed]"; and so Meier-Graefe spent little time in biographical detail but much in descriptions of Dostoevsky's works, giving enormous space to paraphrases of the principal novels—no less than fifty pages to *The Idiot*[73] and almost ninety to *The Brothers Karamazov*.[74] He saw in these novels, a certain progression of thought: *Crime and Punishment* developed further the idea introduced by *The Letters from the Underworld; The Idiot* began where *Crime and Punishment* had left off; and *The Brothers Karamazov* was the "unambiguous" proof of the Christianity that had led to "the legend in *The Idiot*." But the development was not only of thought but also of form. "Already in *Poor Folk*" one detected a "purely poetic" impulse, and this "lyric note" was extended and modified into the "novel-drama" of his principal creations. Dostoevsky's style Meier-Graefe analyzed into

three consecutive effects: first the crude tension of a detective story . . . secondly, the enigmatic and intimate relationship of the stories to latent parts of our own existence . . . thirdly, the gladdening relaxation bringing spiritual harmony.[75]

And he saw merit in the lengthiness of his novels. "However much his lengthiness may irritate us," he wrote,

it was never the outcome of loquacity; on second reading his long-drawn passages . . . long as Jupiter's nose and El Greco's saints . . . shrink, and we scarcely notice their length. The more often we take up *The Brothers Karamazov* the more compact it appears.[76]

As for the nature itself of Dostoevsky's creation, he considered that, in spite of its "tendentiousness," his ideas ascended "from moral motives into the realm of art, and not, it would seem, from art into the realm of morals." Dostoevsky wanted "to teach reform. But to him doctrine was not an immutable law" but a "living organism in perpetual motion"; it avoided "a rigid formula because that would weaken its effect."

A distinctive characteristic of Meier-Graefe's study was the frequency of its allusions to the realm of painting. Dostoevsky was, in one way or another, like Rembrandt, like Vermeer, like Fra Angelico, like Cézanne, like Van Gogh, like Leonardo—the most extensive comparison being with Rembrandt.[77] There were "pictures by Rembrandt whose relationship to Dostoevsky shoots like a flame out of darkness." There were "phrases of the Russian, occasional, arbitrary, contorted, acute-angled phrases, like drawings by Rembrandt." And the similarity was not alone of motifs, but of "the stage on which the play [was] set; this thoroughly theatrical drama carried right into the midst of life with the unmistakable central illuminations all that we, with our satellite understanding, call form and technique."

It should be noticed about these subjective studies that they were all translations, and that two of them, at least, Berdyaev's and Spengler's, belonged to an earlier period. But even more revealing of a change in the temper of criticism is the comment with which these works were greeted. For example, Meier-Graefe's book, thought Edwin Muir,[78] was "interesting but very unsatisfactory," lyrical, rhapsodic, not at all illuminating, and full of inaccuracies and falsifications. Meier-Graefe had fallen into the erroneous ways of many of the commentators on Dostoevsky, "nearly all" of whom indulged in a kind of "special pleading" which found Dostoevsky's "greatness as a writer" to be "something more than greatness." He was "either condemned by rote in the fashionable French style, or praised at the expense of literature" in a manner that was "not peculiar" to Herr Meier-Graefe. Of course, it was "better that he should be praised in any way at all than condemned by rote, but one would like to see him praised," Mr. Muir complained, "in a different way for a change." In *The New Statesman*[79] one who signed himself "Affable Hawk" said there was "a too-muchness" about Herr Meier-Graefe's *Dostoevsky*. His style conveyed "his excitement and his own intense interest more clearly than his thought. He [burrowed] into his subject, which [was] to the good, but he often [remained] buried in it, which [was] not." Such "pot-shot phrases as 'painting which frees itself from the burden of events' and literature which 'overcomes the sequence of words and becomes an undulating surface' " were "contemptible." It was "a writer's business, above all a critic's to get nearer than that to what he means." There was certainly "considerably less cry and more wool" in Gide, Lavrin, and Merezhkovsky. John Freeman in *The London Mercury*[80] described the book as "large and comprehensive, eager, bold, provocative, voluble." Herr Meier-Graefe "exalted, adored, and seldom questioned," and Dostoevsky's ghost perhaps "smiling horribly from purgatory" felt "uncomfortable at this new tribute." The volume "could have been halved in size, and doubled in value." This also was the opinion of *The Times*[81] reviewer who held that even "the commonly accepted" view of Dostoevsky's "contribution to the scheme and intention of the contemporary novel" did not justify Herr Meier-Graefe's extravagances. After all, "however searching Dostoevsky's ideas," the "discomfort" he produced was "not altogether the discomfort of learning something new" but "rather the sensation of contact with a rash, undisciplined, diseased imagination." Dostoevsky was "unquestionably . . . very great literature," but "in his astonishing way" he was "too indiscreet, too far-fetched, too given to pretense to sustain the burden of a 'spiritual prophet.' " About Zweig's essay the reviewer of *The Times*[82] remarked that there was "no need to say much." "Herr Zweig [prostrated] himself with the utmost humility and [passed] from one solemn and enraptured extravagance to another." One wondered why the work had been translated. Concerning Berdyaev's study E. H. Carr reminded the readers of *The Spectator*[83] that it had been written fifteen years earlier when "it would not have sounded absurd, or even original, to write in an English journal that Dostoevsky had been one of the great turning-points in the history of human thought." Since then, the "cult of Dostoevsky" had "gone the way of all fashions"; and the publishers of Berdyaev's study were to be "congratulated on their courage." But certainly "the history of the past ten years" had not made the problem of Dostoevsky "less actual"; he was "too important to be disposed of by the whims of highbrow critics" and Berdyaev was undoubtedly right in explaining Dostoevsky "as the first forerunner of the anti-rationalist and anti-democratic reaction" which had "swept over Europe since the War," although the importance which he set on Dostoevsky's political views and his interpretation of Dostoevsky's political prophesies were open to question. On the other hand, in *The Times Literary Supplement*,[84] whose reviewer, it will be remembered, had been irritated by Carr's "historical materialism," Berdyaev was upheld in his method and purpose. Dostoevsky needed "to be interpreted by minds which [had] felt the full force of his impact. Merely 'literary' criticism of Dostoevsky [was] irrelevant and wearisome."

Carr's position, however, was more in keeping than that of *The Times* reviewer with the critical spirit of the age, which favored analysis rather than unexamined praise. As regards Russian literature D. S. Mirsky's influence in this direction is especially noteworthy. His introduction to Carr's biography and to Dostoevsky's *Letters to His Wife,* and his review of Mme. Dostoevsky's Diary have already been noticed.[85] In 1925 his *Modern Russian Literature* was published and in 1927 his *History of Russian Literature,* the best surveys of the field that have appeared so far in English. In the former, concerned exclusively with Russian literature since 1880, Dostoevsky was mentioned only in passing, with reference to his critics and to those whom he had influenced; in the latter, a chapter was devoted to him. There, considering Dostoevsky's work in the light of the development of Russian literature, Mirsky pointed out its affiliation with Gogol; its change of tone after 1849—(the chapter on Dostoevsky indeed was divided into two parts,[86] "the great series beginning with *Memoirs from Underground* and ending with the Karamazovs" being "so closely connected with later developments" that such a division in a history of literature was only logical). Dostoevsky was seen as a complex, unique, extremely significant figure, "prophetic" in that his mentality belonged to a period later than his own, but by no means an unapproachable, inexplicable, godlike phenomenon. It was "necessary to distinguish not only between the various periods of his life, and the various currents of his mind, but between the different *levels* of his personality. The higher or rather deeper, level [was] present only in the imaginative work of his last seventeen years, beginning with *Memoirs from Underground.* The lower, or rather, more superficial, level [was] apparent in all his work, but more particularly in his journalistic writings and in the imaginative work of before 1864." He was to be explained partly by the circumstances of his life, partly by his peculiar experience of thought: his "faculty of 'feeling ideas' . . . as others feel cold and pain," the "white-hot temperature" of his "intellectual passion" which made him comparable to "certain great religious thinkers . . . St. Paul, St. Augustine, Pascal, and Nietzsche."

The deeper, the essential Dostoevsky [was] one of the most significant and ominous figures in the whole history of the human mind, one of its boldest and most disastrous adventures in the sphere of ultimate spiritual quest. The superficial Dostoevsky [was] a man of his time, comparable, and not always favourably comparable, to many other Russian novelists and publicists of the age of Alexander II.

Artistically, his method, though allied to the realistic school, was perhaps even closer to the symbolist. His absorption in the intellectual experience of life, the "ideological character" of his novels, the fundamentally symbolic function of the "realistic" elements in his work, of setting and characterization,—actually only embodiments of his own "infinitely fertile spiritual experience,"—marked him off from the one and linked him with the other. That was why he had been justly appreciated only since the symbolist movement and why novels of his kind had been "written only . . . by novelists of the symbolist school." In a later work,[87] Mirsky declared that what had "come to be regarded as the fullest expression of the " 'Russian soul,' " the work of Turgenev, Dostoevsky, and Tolstoy, was "in reality . . . only the expression of a single phase in the development of the intellectual élite of the Russian educated classes"; that "its specific qualities and its philosophy were conditioned by the nature of social groups that produced it—the middle gentry faced with the disintegration of all the social system to which it belonged, and the mixed intelligentsia that had no satisfactory place in existing society and was by definition maladjusted and 'rootless.' " That explained the "comprehensive humanity of the world of 'the Russians' " which was "natural in an élite essentially unattached to any definite forms." On the other hand, "many of its masterpieces, including all Turgenev's novels and Dostoevsky's *The Possessed*" were "immediate echoes of transitory phases of social life." In that, their realism had its source; and one of its "greatest lessons" was that "no amount of 'actuality' [detracted] from the 'permanent' value of a literary work."

Mirsky's studies and those of Carr are historical in approach and thus, naturally tend to be "objective." But even less scholarly criticism has been since the 1920's impatient of rhetoric and subjectivity, for it has proceeded more from a wish to understand and to explain than to impose opinions. This is true of the "appreciative" essays of E. M. Forster and of Virginia Woolf, of the "psychological" studies of André Gide, of Thomas Mann's remarks, which can be called "appreciative" only in the Latin meaning of the word, and even of the more dogmatic pronouncements of D. H. Lawrence.

In his *Aspects of the Novel*,[88] E. M. Forster asserted the "unpleasant and unpatriotic truth" that "no English novelist" was "as great as Tolstoy," that none had "explored man's soul as deeply as Dostoevsky." In comparison with these, English novels could be seen for what they were, charming "little mansions" but "not mighty edifices" when one "stood them for an instant in the colonnades of *War and Peace* or the vaults of *The Brothers Karamazov*." Of Dostoevsky he had most to say in the chapter which he called "Prophecy," a term that meant to him not at all its "narrow sense of foretelling the future," but a quality which he described as "an accent in the novelist's voice." It was something more and other than "fantasy," that element which strains credulity, more even than the author's fundamental attitude or predisposition towards his subject, for a distinction could be made between "the prophet and the non-prophet." The difference might be best pointed in an illustrative comparison, for which Forster chose passages from two novelists who had much in common, George Eliot and Dostoevsky, and having quoted that in *Adam Bede* where Dinah visits Hetty in prison, and that other in *The Brothers Karamazov* where Mitya, first accused of his father's murder, has a moment's sleep and wakes up saying "I've had a good dream, gentlemen," he asked:

Now what is the difference in these passages—a difference that throbs in every phrase? It is that the first writer is a preacher and the second a prophet. George Eliot talks about God, but never alters her focus; God and the tables and chairs are all in the same plane, and in consequence we have not for a moment the feeling that the whole universe needs pity and love— they are only needed in Hetty's cell. In Dostoevsky the characters and situations always stand for more than themselves; infinity attends them. . . .

It was not that Dostoevsky's characters were mystical or symbolic.

Mitya does not conceal anything (mysticism), he does not mean anything (symbolism), he is merely Dmitri Karamazov, but to be merely a person in Dostoevsky is to join up with all the other people far back. . . . Dostoevsky's characters [asked] us to share something deeper than their experiences. [They conveyed to us] a sensation that [was] partly physical, the sensation of sinking into a translucent globe and seeing our experience floating far above us on its surface, tiny, remote, yet ours.

There were only four writers who illustrated the quality of prophecy as Forster meant it: Dostoevsky, Melville, D. H. Lawrence, and Emily Brontë. Hardy, who as a "philosopher and a great poet, might seem to have claims," did not qualify. His novels were "surveys"; they did not "give out sounds." The writer "sat back, it [was] true, but the characters did not reach back." Never "could Jude step forward like Mitya and release floods of our emotion by saying 'Gentlemen, I've had a bad dream!' " Conrad, too, must be excluded and also Joyce. Unlike Dostoevsky's, the work of Hardy, Conrad, Joyce, was "talk" but "never song."

The essay called "The Russian Point of View," in Virginia Woolf's *The Common Reader*[89] is, I believe, well known. In it Mrs. Woolf dealt with Chekhov, Dostoevsky, and Tolstoy, of whom Tolstoy she considered to be the greatest—indeed, "the greatest of all novelists,"—but all of whom exemplified a common view of life which could be recognized as peculiarly and unmistakably Russian. When, for example, one read:

Learn to make yourselves akin to people. I would even like to add: make yourself indispensable to them. But let this sympathy be not with the mind—for it is easy with the mind—but with the heart!

one had no hesitation in knowing the passage to be "from the Russian," although one could not, perhaps, ascribe it to any one author. This passage, in fact, was the quintessence of "the Russian point of view." Its call for sympathy of heart and not of mind was "the cloud which [brooded] over the whole of Russian literature; which [lured] us from our own parched brilliancy and scorched thoroughfares to expand in its shade." The lure, of course, was disastrous, for the English temper was not suited to this peculiarly Russian demand. The English could not say " 'Brother' with simple conviction. . . . The English equivalent for 'Brother' " was " 'Mate'—a very different word, with something sardonic in it." But with the Russians at any rate with the Russian writers of fiction, so far as an Englishman could judge, the "soul" seemed to be the chief consideration. It was this that created the colossal emotional tension of Dostoevsky's books, and made for their new vision of men as, at one and the same time, both good and evil:

If our voices suddenly rise into shrieks of laughter, or if we are shaken by the most violent sobbing, what more natural?—it hardly calls for remark. The pace at which we are living is so tremendous that sparks must rush off our wheels as we fly. Moreover, when the speed is thus increased and the elements of the soul are seen, not separately in scenes of humour or scenes of passion as our slow English minds conceive them, but streaked, involved, inextricably confused, a new panorama of the human mind is revealed. The old divisions melt into each other. Men are at the same time villains and saints; their acts are at once beautiful and despicable. We love and we hate at the same time. There is none of that precise division between good and bad to which we are used.

No restraints of class-consciousness, of those social differences which inclined the English novelist "to satire rather than compassion, to scrutiny of society rather than understanding of individuals themselves"—none of these restraints concerned the soul:

The soul is not restrained by barriers. It overflows, it floods, it mingles with the souls of others. The simple story of a bank clerk who could not pay for a bottle of wine spreads, before we know what is happening, into the lives of his father-in-law and the five mistresses whom his father-in-law treated abominably, and the postman's life, and the charwoman's, and the Princesses' who lodged in the same block of flats; for nothing is outside Dostoevsky's province; and when he is tired, he does not stop, he goes on. He cannot restrain himself. Out of it tumbles upon us, hot, scalding, mixed, marvellous, oppressive—the human soul.

That, then, was the essential difference between the English novel and the Russian. And that was why, perhaps, it needed "so great an effort on the part of an English reader to read *The Brothers Karamazov* or *The Possessed* a second time. The 'soul' was alien to him."

André Gide's book on Dostoevsky appeared in English translation in 1925.[90] It was composed, for the most part, of a series of six lectures which had been delivered in Paris in 1922, although it contained also some essays that dated as far back as 1908 and 1911. The war had prevented Gide from completing a study of Dostoevsky which he had undertaken; instead of resuming it, he had contented himself with gathering up his notes in several lectures and publishing them without revision.[91] The English version was somewhat altered; the first two sections were much abridged, with their substance given in a new Author's Preface; and there was added a short introduction by Arnold Bennett.[92] "Those who read Gide's *Dostoevsky*," Bennett wrote, "will receive light, some of it dazzling on both Dostoevsky and Gide." He could not recall another "critical work which more cogently [justified] and more securely [established] its subject." It enlarged "one's idea of Dostoevsky and of the function of the novel" and destroyed "all conventional charges against the greatest of the Russians—morbidity, etc., etc." Indeed the "progress made by Western Europe in the appreciation of Russian psychology" might be measured in a comparison of "the late Count Melchior de Vogüé's *Le roman russe* with the present work."

"I have but gathered from his works," said Gide in one of his lectures, "what I needed to make my own honey."[93] What he gathered was Dostoevsky's extreme individualism, the tortuousness of his psychology, his understanding of the New Testament, his complete devotion of himself to his art. The reason, said Gide, that, in spite of his increasing reputation, "certain minds" remained "obdurately prejudiced against" the work of Dostoevsky was that in the first place it dealt with a theme foreign to Western fiction, the "relation between the individual and his self or his God"; and that, in the second place, what he wrote was not easy to analyse and classify. The public could not say of Dostoevsky as it could of Pasteur "Yes, hydrophobia," or of Nietzsche, "the superman." There was no word or phrase in which he could be comprised, not even Vogüé's "bright idea," the "religion of suffering." Conservative, but not hidebound by tradition; monarchist, but of democratic opinions; Christian, but not a Roman Catholic; liberal, but not a progressive, Dostoevsky remained "ever the man of whom there was no way to make use!" He was "of the stuff which displeases every party." His novels "though pregnant with thought" were never "abstract." His characters, "representative" as they were, never forsook "their humanity to become mere symbols." That indeed was his "miracle."[94] The dominant feature of Dostoevsky's psychology was his understanding of duality, but in his view, the different realms of the human personality existed within each man and manifested themselves simultaneously, not alternately as in Stevenson's *Dr. Jekyll and Mr. Hyde,*—which, together with "the fact that each character never [relinquished] consciousness of his dual personality with its inconsistencies" was the "most disconcerting feature" in Dostoevsky's work.[95] Feelings with him, were rapidly supplanted one by the other; they seemed to be incompatible, but were only the converse of each other, related by their very oppositeness, and having indeed a common root: the experience of humiliation. Dostoevsky was "obsessed without ceasing by the idea that humiliation damns, whereas humility sanctifies."[96] All of his characters despite their "extraordinarily rich diversity . . . [grouped] and [arranged] themselves" in this "one plane only," of humbleness which is self-denial, and of humiliation, which is hurt pride. It was self-denial that triumphed with Dostoevsky; "the will to power led inevitably to ruin"; and in this respect his heroes, surrendering will and intellect and personality, differed from those of Balzac who were creatures of intellect and will. It was indeed to Blake that Dostoevsky was comparable in his "mysterious inversion of values," according to which the "realm of mind" became "the first region" of Hell, the "antithesis of love, . . . less hate than the steady activity of mind." In other respects, there was similarity between Dostoevsky and Browning, not only in narrative form and use of monologue, but also in the special character of their optimism, which had "no affinity with Goethe's" but brought "them both very close to Nietzsche and to William Blake." Indeed, Nietzsche, Dostoevsky, Browning, and Blake were "four stars of one single constellation."[97]

Gide presented Dostoevsky the man as one driven by æsthetic passion, tormented more by the effort of creation than by any of his other ills, devoting himself to his work, taking enormous joy in it—a fact which Vogüé had "missed entirely." He was complex, self-abnegating, "steeped in the teaching of the Gospel," which formed the essential difference between him and Nietzsche, who was "jealous of Jesus Christ, jealous to the point of madness."[98]

In one lecture Gide considered "whether several of Dostoevsky's characteristics" which seemed "perchance more than strange" to Westerners were "not common to all Russians," and concluded that they were.

Gide's book, said H. P. Marshall in *The London Mercury*[99] demanded and deserved "serious attention," for "whatever pose the intelligentsia" might be adopting "at the moment," Dostoevsky was "a great writer." One could not approach him with "an academic phrase": dignity might be "all very well in its place" but it was "a poor thing beside reality." And Dostoevsky was "real" because he was concerned with "man's conscience," the "desire for absolute truth." For those who believe that the "hope of mankind" lay "only in an increase of spiritual endeavour" he "must always be supremely important." *The Edinburgh Review*[100] could assure success for Mr. Gide's "extremely interesting" and "provocative" study, for the "vogue of Dostoevsky [appeared] to be growing." *The Brothers Karamazov* had always seemed to the reviewer "merely a confused nightmare" but M. Gide had "at least shown him some of its author's intention," which he acknowledged, even if he could not "agree as to its effect." Edmund Gosse, curiously reversing his former judgment, wrote to Gide:[101]

May I venture to wish, however, that you would try to release yourself from your bondage to the Russians, and particularly to Dostoevsky? We have all in turn been subjected to the magic of this epileptic monster. But his genius has only led us astray, and I should say to any young writer of merit who appealed to me, Read what you like, only don't waste your time reading Dostoevsky. He is the cocaine and morfia of modern literature.

Thomas Mann mentioned Dostoevsky in his essay on *Goethe and Tolstoy*.[102] He there divided all artists into two fundamental categories: those who, like Goethe, "wary of the fantastic, avoid speculative natural philosophy, guard [themselves] against losing touch with the earth"—artists of "intuitive" imagination,—"the inborn sympathy of the child of nature with the organic," whose "creative art . . . is . . . precise and based on the sense-perceptions,"—whose characters "evince their actuality by action"; and those others, artists of "thought, of the idea, of spirit," whose figures "possess the realism of sheer being," and not of actuality in action. The distinction had been made by Schiller himself who spoke of the " 'etwas Schattenhaftes' " in the work of the latter kind of artist—which, translated "from the sphere of German idealism into the Russian and revelational" became "a sort of national pendant to Schiller's world of idea, rhetoric, and drama, the shadow-world of Dostoevsky, over-life-size and exaggeratedly true." Dostoevsky's was a world in conflict "with the epic attitude toward art," a conflict that was "neither new nor old" but "eternal," "between contemplation and ecstatic vision." It found "complete expression in on the one side Goethe and Tolstoy, on the other Schiller and Dostoevsky":

Very much, yes, precisely as Goethe's 'profound and tranquil contemplation,' his precise and sensuous fancy, the life-likeness of his characters, stand in relation to the ideal visions of Schiller and the activism of his creations, so the mighty sense-appeal of Tolstoy's art stands to Dostoevsky's sickly, distorted dream-and-soul world.

Mann spoke of the "fleshliness of Tolstoy's art as contrasted with the holy soulfulness of Dostoevsky's" and quoted Merezhkovsky's distinction between Tolstoy "the great seer of the body" and Dostoevsky "the visionary of the soul," though unlike Merezhkovsky it was Tolstoy whom he admired and not Dostoevsky, Tolstoy who represented "the truth, power, calm and humility of nature" as against Dostoevsky's "disproportionate, fevered, and dogmatic presumption of spirit."

D. H. Lawrence declared in his introduction to *The Grand Inquisitor*,[103] that Dostoevsky was false to the truth he had found, the Inquisitor's truth that the cruellest gift of God to man is the gift of freedom, for man cannot live freely but requires for life three things: mystery, miracle, and authority, because for the most part he cannot see the "distinction between bread, or property, money, and vivid life" and must therefore be governed by the few elect who do see the distinction and must bow down to them; that Jesus, therefore wronged man by demanding of him the impossible. Dostoevsky understood all this. His "diagnosis of human nature" was "simple and unanswerable," but, "as always" his "amazing perspicacity" was "mixed with perverse and poisonous hate of Jesus; his moral hostility to the devil [was] mixed with secret worship of the devil." Dostoevsky was "always perverse, always impure, always an evil thinker and a marvelous seer." The authority which he saw as necessary to men he represented in the "diabolic" figure of the Grand Inquisitor. Why, if the Inquisitor represented truth, and Jesus illusion? "Why should Dostoevsky drag in Inquisition and *autos-da-fé,* and Ivan wind up so morbidly suicidal?" They, Dostoevsky and Ivan, should have been "glad" they had "found the truth again."

Among the most important works on Dostoevsky in any language is that by the Russian philosopher and critic Leo Shestov, who is little known in England.[104] His *Dostoevsky and Nietzsche, the Philosophy of Tragedy,*[105] never translated into English, belongs to an earlier age. It was written in 1903, but an epitome of it, "The Conquest of the Self-Evident" appeared in English in 1929, the first essay in a volume entitled *In Job's Balances.*[106] *Dostoevsky and Nietzsche,* is an original and remarkable piece of criticism, and since it gives more fully the substance of the extremely condensed shorter essay, I hope a discussion of it here may not be thought inappropriate.

Dostoevsky's central problem Shestov saw as the struggle of the "free" individual against the bondage of general commonplace, the bondage of the "self-evident," "the omnitude" of commonly accepted ideas. His solution was a personal one, if indeed an answer put in the form of a question might be called a solution at all. Like Nietzsche Dostoevsky also spoke "not for the sake of spreading [his] beliefs and enlightening [his] neighbors" but because he himself was "in search of light." His works were "not an answer, but a question, the question: is there hope for those people who have been repulsed by science and morality?" Like Baudelaire and like Nietzsche he loved the damned, those who had been so repulsed, knew and accepted evil, loved it indeed as desirable. But this acceptance proceeded, as was true also of Nietzsche, from a painful disillusionment. They had both broken away from their early ideals. Dostoevsky spoke of the "rebirth of his beliefs, Nietzsche of the revaluation of all values. In reality both expressions" were "but different words to indicate one and the same process."

Memoirs from Underground was the central point of Dostoevsky's work. Before that, in *Poor Folk, The Double, The Insulted and Injured,* Dostoevsky's ideal had been the humanitarian pity of Gogol and the social humanitarianism of Belinsky. "No one had felt at that time, that together with the declaration of man's rights before society (humanitarianism), we were given also the declaration of his lack of *rights*—before nature." *The Dead House* also was humanitarian in its inclinations—but it stood on the threshold of the spiritual crisis marked by the *Memoirs,* which were "a heart-rending cry of terror, torn from a man who [had] been suddenly convinced that his whole life he had *lied,* had pretended, when he assured himself and others, that the highest aim of being, was—service to the least of men." With this work began "the underground epoch." Already in *The Insulted and Injured,* the prince had laughed at "ideals" and "Schiller,"—an indication of what was to come in the *Memoirs from Underground:* "a public declaration of the denial of one's past." The conclusion to which Dostoevsky now arrived was not that the ideal of human happiness was unattainable but that its very possibility was damnable. He cursed it in advance. He had learned that all moral teaching benefited the teacher and not the pupil, that "humanitarianism" was a lie. With this discovery "reason and conscience" were ended for him and a new era, of "psychology," began. It was a decision built on despair, the philosophy of the "underground" man.

The "underground" man had been known also to Tolstoy but was not accepted by him. The "underground" philosophy was that of helpless indifference. Everything was "just the same," one would not escape one's fate of sin and loneliness. "Tolstoy still had hope, and to the end of his days struggled with the terrible phantom of hopelessness, which never left him alone"; he clung to the ideal of the commonplace: " 'I bow before Rostov, and not before Pushkin or Shakespeare, and I openly announce this to every one,' "—that was the meaning of his epilogue to *War and Peace.* When Rostov passed abruptly from Princess Maria's theoretic discussion about one's duty to humanity, to the immediate and practical affairs of their household, and Princess Maria, unable to tell her husband as she would have liked to do, that man lives not by bread alone, simply took his hand and kissed him, "What wonderful audacity" was there! "What other writer," cried Shestov, "would have dared play so openly such a dangerous game. The Princess Maria 'always striving toward the infinite, the eternal, and the perfect,' consents as if nothing had happened, to the greatest hypocrisy. . . . But what is most interesting is that Count Tolstoy gives no hint that he is aware of the chasm he has just bridged. He is as usual clear, lucid, transparent. What 'psychology' Dostoevsky would have made of this!" Tolstoy's, that is, was a "diplomatic art." In the face of antinomies he knew that one must look "saintly, innocent, childishly-simple . . . otherwise farewell forever to all *a priori*, generalities, necessity, solidity." Dostoevsky was incapable of such diplomacy. "*A priori*, generalities, necessity, solidity" were not to be acquired at the price of honesty. He was an enemy of Idealism, and as was true of most such enemies, as had been true of Nietzsche, for example, he had once been an extreme Idealist. Disillusionment came when, face to face with actual life, he suddenly discovered to his horror that all "the beautiful *a priori* were lies." Then, "Socrates, Plato, humanitarianism, ideas" all vanished into space; and he experienced "that terrible isolation" which was the beginning of "the philosophy of tragedy." The "underground" man was the one who had had this experience. For him it was impossible to conquer pessimism and skepticism by means of Idealism. There was only one way left: to follow pessimism and skepticism to their logical conclusions. "Eternal truths," he saw, had been invented by the wise not for those who were in need of comfort but for the comforters themselves, for their own sakes. And so Dostoevsky like the "underground" man "ran away from reality; but, having met Idealism—went back," like King Lear between the bear and the sea.

The humanitarian ideal ultimately meant nothing to Dostoevsky. Supposing universal happiness were attainable, would the suffering of the past be thereby expiated? "The fact [was] Dostoevsky [did] not *want* universal happiness in the future, [did] not *want* the future to acquit the present." And so after *Memoirs from Underground*, one finds little in his work about the insulted and injured but much about crime and criminals. "Good" and "evil" were replaced by "the ordinary" and "the extraordinary." Raskolnikov, for example, passed "beyond good and evil" at a time when Nietzsche "was still a student dreaming of lofty ideals." "Beyond good and evil" was Dostoevsky's discovery, evolved in his struggle "against himself and only against himself. He alone, in the whole world, *envied* the moral greatness of the criminal." Raskolnikov's tragedy was not that he had overstepped the law, but that he had recognized himself as incapable of so doing. Dostoevsky's attempt was to "rehabilitate the rights of the underground man" but he could not show convincingly the man who had found himself. Myshkin, Zossima, Alyosha were poor creatures compared to Raskolnikov and Rogozhin, for his own "thought wandered through the deserts of his soul." Convinced of the ultimate *egoism* of man, he concluded that the happiness of the majority, progress, etc., could not solve the most important problem of life, the individual's assertion of himself in the face of all that destroyed individuality. Man's struggle was all the more bitter in that there was nothing tangible for him to turn against. He fought in a terrible loneliness; he had not the good fortune of the ancients' Prometheus who was never alone but was always heard by Zeus "whom he could anger and irritate with his unbending speeches. . . . The man of to-day, Raskolnikov or Dostoevsky" did not "believe in Zeus." Such then was the nature of tragedy on which Dostoevsky's philosophy was built; the tragedy of man turned upon himself in a void. His feeling was Baudelaire's who loved the damned because they alone had the courage of intellectual honesty. "Aimes-tu les damnés? Dis-moi, connais-tu l'irrémissible?" was the motto Shestov chose for his essay.

Dostoevsky's literary style and technique have occupied the attention of several critics. Boris Brasol[107] attempted, not too successfully, to show Dostoevsky's indebtedness to Pushkin, a task which has been more ably accomplished in a recent Russian study by A. L. Bem. In an article in the *Psychoanalytic Review*[108] Dostoevsky's knowledge of psychology was traced to a treatise published in 1846, Carus' *Psyche,* and the opinion was advanced that however accurate scientifically might be the cases of mental and nervous disease in the novels of Dostoevsky, they could not be considered anticipations of modern psychoanalysis. Edwin Muir examined *The Idiot*[109] at length and discovered that its tone depended largely on a special treatment of the element of time. All through the novel by constant hints, one was prepared for the outcome of Nastasia's murder by Rogozhin; the characters moved through the story "driven helplessly towards a fate they [foresaw] and could not escape." Their sense of time was like that of the man about to be executed, described by Prince Myshkin; and in the whole novel, as in the episode related by Prince Myshkin, Dostoevsky showed how "the knowledge of something to come [could] change, and at the same time bring out the values of time"; "almost from beginning to end Myshkin, Rogozhin and Nastasia [were] fighting against time and it [was] this that [gave] the book its hurried and urgent movement." It was comparable to and yet different from *Wuthering Heights*. In both novels "time passes . . . swiftly, but in the one with a rush of freedom, in the other with unwilling haste."

Professor Joseph Warren Beach,[110] in a study of the literary methods of various twentieth century novelists, discussed Dostoevsky's way of "dramatizing in the novel a systematized moral philosophy." The philosophy itself was "at root religious." The "important thing" to notice about it was that Dostoevsky had "at any rate, a philosophical system which he held in all sincerity in common with a good many people" and "that he [had] succeeded in bodying it forth magnificently in terms of individual character, speech, and action." He had done this more successfully than Tolstoy, Turgenev or Gorky. He was a "much more dramatic" writer than they. He was the "great builder of plots . . . the most remarkable of Russian storytellers." He was the best example of "how philosophy and story go hand in hand." He achieved his effects in the first place, by eliminating the imaginary narrator as much as possible; and when this could not be done, by making him a "dramatic creation on his own account"; secondly, he made use of themes "single, clear-cut, and calling for closer continuous treatment" which was "another element predisposing to drama"; finally, one found in him five "specific mechanical features of the dramatic method." They were: a consistent centre of interest—"it would be hard to find novels of the nineteenth century that keep single individuals on the stage so continuously as Dostoevsky's"; a limited point of view; limitations of place; limitations of time; and lengthy development of the events of a single day or suites of days following one another.

In certain ways Dostoevsky was comparable to other novelists. Henry James was like him in his use of a consistent centre of interest; Aldous Huxley, in *Point Counter Point*, Virginia Woolf, in *Mrs. Dalloway*, James Joyce in *Ulysses*, resembled him in their treatment of "continuous action"; and both Gide and Wasserman reminded one of Dostoevsky in their "craving to get away from too strict a logic in the motivation of character." With reference to Waldo Frank's *Rahab*, Beach exclaimed: "Oh, Sonia, Sonia! woman of Samaria! how large a progeny you have among the mystics of our day!" And he pointed out that Conrad, despite his frequently expressed dislike of Dostoevsky, was greatly influenced by him: "where do we come so near as in Dostoevsky and the Russians to the psychology of a

Lord Jim, a Baron Heyst? And where but in Dostoevsky did Conrad get the plot, the psychology, the very technique of 'Under Western Eyes?' " Like Dostoevsky, Conrad had "a profound feeling of the mysteriousness, the almost transcendental character of human motives."

More elaborate comparisons between Dostoevsky and other novelists were made by Janko Lavrin in the *Slavonic Review*[111] in 1927, and by Tatiana Vacquier in the *Sewanee Review*[112] in 1929. The one compared the Russian novelist with Marcel Proust, the other with André Gide. Lavrin explained that "his only excuse for confronting" Dostoevsky and Proust was "that of contrast." They were "poles apart," he said: "in the psychological novel, in temperament, in mentality, in artistic methods, in Weltanschauung, in everything." Dostoevsky was "dynamic," Proust, "static," Dostoevsky treated life "as an apocalyptic struggle between good and evil," Proust, "as an 'involuntary' day-dream"; Dostoevsky's "creation" showed a "frenzied impulse of self-divided consciousness towards a final unity and wholeness of man"; Proust's reflected a "dispassionate and subtle display of its final inner 'atomization' "; if Dostoevsky's "work symbolized in a new way the author's own fight for a new man and a new life, Proust's big novel was an ingenious substitute for life, on the part of a refined but imprisoned Epicurean." Dostoevsky gave the "impression of being more clairvoyant than observant," while Proust seemed "above all . . . an observant and inquisitive connoisseur." Dostoevsky, "a born sensualist . . . did his best to spiritualize his own chaotic sensuality. Proust on the other hand only intellectualized it." Dostoevsky's heroes, therefore, presented "a real spiritual tragedy," but Proust's provided a "fine sporting ground for the most observant psychological gourmand of recent times," a ground which was "more confused than tragic." Of Dostoevsky's "realism," Lavrin wrote that it was "entirely subjective." It was his method of relieving "his spiritual chaos," which "he could relieve . . . only by projecting it outside himself, by symbolizing it in living plots and characters."

Tatiana Vacquier demonstrated that Dostoevsky and Gide had much in common and that the French author was influenced by the Russian. Both of them possessed "dual personalities" and it was this "contradiction of opposed elements" that had "helped André Gide to sense the enigmatic soul of the Russian novelist"; both were "absorbed with the problem of man and his place in creation" and longed to "exhaust all the possibilities" of life; both were interested in the subconscious, not in what man could "accomplish" but in what he could *"know* about himself," in the opposition of introspection to action, in showing "that something monstrous, wholly unreasonable, invariably upsets the most elaborate and convincing principles"; both were fascinated by the problem of moral ambivalence, of the Madonna known only to the Sodomite; both experimented with the "superman" and the problem of self-affirmation; both excluded social views in their consideration of man's relationship to God; both attempted to solve the question of free-will; both were interested in crime and the abnormal, in the "motif of love-hatred," and in the psychology of young people; and many analogies could be drawn as regards their techniques. The "inner" similarities were of greater value than the "formal" ones, although these too had their significance; an examination of them gave, at any rate, "a better understanding" of Gide's "very interesting and important literary creations."

In spite of the difficulty of the enterprise, attempts are perennially made to dramatize Dostoevsky. In 1927 a dramatic version of *The Brothers Karamazov* was presented in New York, translated from the French of Jacques Copeau and Jean Croué and published "for the Theatre Guild";[113] and in 1928 the same novel was used as the basis for a play called *The Brass Paper Weight*, produced by Komisarjevsky in London. This was a violent, melodramatic play, very different from the original story; but the producer himself explained that he had not intended to represent the novel. "Go to see 'The Brass Paperweight' at the Apollo," wrote the reviewer in *The Nation and Athenæum*,[114] "it is an exciting entertainment." Despite numerous changes the characters remained "the complicated creatures of Dostoevsky's imagination" whose behaviour would be doubtless "very difficult to understand" for any one who had not read the novel. "But what a series of effective situations the play contained." "Perhaps meritably," according to *The Times*[115] report, those who knew the original were bound to find the play "slightly irritating," but it was not intended to reproduce the original, and "if it were possible to avoid memories, or—as many among the audience must have been— to be innocent of them" it "would probably seem an ingenious and an unusually intelligent variant of the theme of murder."

The Idiot was adapted and acted in 1926 by Michael Hogan who took the part of Rogozhin. The performance was widely but unfavorably reviewed. Michael Hogan had made Rogozhin commit suicide and had invented a concluding "idiot's monologue for Myshkin"; and in his acting, moreover, had had recourse to "physical contortions and grimaces" to "reinforce the interest of the part."[116] All in all, critics were inclined to think Dostoevsky did not lend himself to dramatization, the comment in *The Spectator*[117] that the adaptor had done "much better" than could have been expected, being the highest praise the play received. "The impression of the novel," according to *The Times*,[118] was of "a formlessness that [was] the formlessness of humanity; the impression that the conditions of the theatre [made] inevitable [was] of a vain struggle for an alien form." In *The Outlook*[119] Michael Hogan was commended for "courage and enthusiasm. . . . He had taken one of the greatest, and longest novels of modern times" and had tried to "cram it into three not very long acts and make it a stage play"; the result, "even for those . . . who knew the novel well" was "violent and exciting, but not very intelligible"; what it must have been for those who had not read the book, the reviewer could not imagine. In the opinion of *The London Mercury*,[120] "the mystic Russian hero" was "as difficult to conceive dramatically as . . . Don Quixote"; and in that of *The English Review*,[121] the play was not so much "in itself a failure" but "it was overshadowed by its original." Desmond McCarthy, in *The New Statesman*,[122] thought it "far more disappointing than all but the poorest" plays running at that moment. It was bound to be disappointing because Dostoevsky, although he was the "most dramatic of all novelists" could not be dramatized. His characterization depended on dialogue; yet it was impossible to string together various parts of his dialogue and make a play of them. Dostoevsky required "as many pages to describe the events of hours as Tolstoy . . . the events of years," and without this expansiveness, his "climaxes" appeared "hysterical or merely lurid."

In August 1934 took place in Moscow the first "All-Union Congress of Soviet Writers." It was addressed by leading Russian authors and publicists; and the principal speeches, translated and published in America,[123] should serve to dispel the criticism that has been often leveled against Soviet Russia, that she has tried to destroy and forget her artistic heritage.[124] Among the speakers was Gorky who, dealing with the differences between Soviet literature and the literature of the bourgeoisie, had much to say concerning Dostoevsky.[125]

To Dostoesvky [he said] belongs the credit of having painted with the most vivid perfection of word portraiture a type of egocentrist, a type of social degenerate in the person of the hero of his *Memoirs from Underground*.

With the grim triumph of one who is insatiably taking vengeance for his personal misfortunes and sufferings, for his youthful enthusiasms, Dostoevsky in the figure of his hero has shown the depths of whining despair that are reached by the individualist from among the young men of the nineteenth and twentieth centuries who are cut off from real life. This type of his combines within himself the most characteristic traits of Friedrich Nietzsche and of the Marquis Des Esseintes, the hero of Huysmans' *Against the Grain, Le Disciple* of Paul Bourget, and Boris Savinkov, who made himself the hero of his own composition, Oscar Wilde and Artsybashev's "Sanine" and many another social degenerate created by the anarchic influence of inhuman conditions in the capitalist state.[126]

[Dostoevsky, that is, had admirably shown] with what rottenness the soul of bourgeois personality is burdened.

In a state founded on the senseless and humiliating sufferings of the vast majority of the people, it is fitting that the creed of irresponsible self-will in word and action should be the guiding and vindicating principle. Such ideas as "man is a despot by nature," that he "likes to be a tormentor," that he is "passionately fond of suffering" and that he envisages the meaning of life and his happiness precisely in self-will, in unrestricted freedom of action, that only this self-will will bring him his "greatest advantage," and "let the whole world perish so long as I can drink my tea"—such are the ideas capitalism has inculcated and upheld through thick and thin.[127]

Not only in his writings, however, but also in himself, in his repudiation of liberal ideas at the end of his life, Dostoevsky had demonstrated this "rottenness" of the bourgeois soul. And so, said Gorky, it was necessary to devote so much space to Dostoevsky,

because without the influence of his ideas it would be almost impossible to understand the *volte face* which Russian literature and the greater part of the intelligentsia made after 1905-06 from radicalism and democracy towards safeguarding and defending bourgeois "law and order."

What one finds, then, on the basis of this historical criticism, is recognition of Dostoevsky's importance coupled with condemnation of what he stood for and expressed. His "genius" was "indisputable." In "force of portrayal" his talent was "equal perhaps only to Shakespeare." But as "a personality," as a "judge of men and the world," he is "easy to conceive in the role of a mediæval inquisitor."[128] And a mediæval inquisitor, Gorky implied, is a logical product of the capitalist system. It stands to reason that those whose dissatisfaction with the old regime is greatest should be most appreciative of an author who had best expressed its corruption.

Similarly, Karl Radek declared that Dostoevsky had "reached the summits of art" through his awareness of the society about him, "by analysing some of the types who inhabited suppurating semi-feudal

Russian cities—people stifling in the tiny garrets where the lower middle classes of the Russian cities were cooped up—oblivious of any way of escape from their situation." Not only that, however. The "vilest types, when revealed by the scalpel of Dostoevsky, became titans of suffering." The "drawing-room heroes of Proust," on the other hand, seemed to "cry aloud that they [were] not worth analysing, that no analysis of them [would] produce any results."[129] In other words, it is the implicit grandeur of the individual that the socialist critic, as much as any bourgeois writer, admires primarily in Dostoevsky.

That Dostoevsky's method should be unlike that of the ideal Socialist writer was to be expected. In historical perspective, it could be appreciated without being held up as a model. An article on Soviet literature in *The Nineteenth Century*,[130] by Gleb Struve, cited a Soviet critic, Nasimov, who in a discussion of "the relationship between Socialist Realism, as a method of psychological presentation, and the psychological methods of Dostoevsky and Tolstoy" had presented Dostoevsky as "the complete antipode of Socialist Realism." This view, however, does not necessarily imply condemnation. The Russian Ambassador to England, J. M. Maisky, was at pains to point out in *The Contemporary Review*[131] that although the new Russian writers represented a different stratum of society from the old, and were optimistic, whereas the others had been pessimistic, the "old classics" were still "very greatly appreciated" in Russia. "We are very proud of them," he wrote, "and we never had, nor have we now, any desire or intention of renouncing those great geniuses who produced masterpieces that will never die, as for instance, Leo Tolstoy's *War and Peace*, Dostoevsky's *Crime and Punishment*."

One final point. The nature of Dostoevsky's influence on the literature of the West has not been, to my mind, as yet satisfactorily determined. But, as I have already pointed out, the importance of this influence has been alleged over and over again. In the following chapter the subject will be discussed somewhat more fully, but here I should like to list a few characteristic statements relating to it, which have not been already quoted in the foregoing pages.

Janko Lavrin, in a brief history of Russian Literature,[132] published in 1927 in "Benn's Sixpenny Library" declared Dostoevsky to be "more important" even than Tolstoy from the "standpoint of European Literature," for "the whole of recent psychological fiction had been affected—in some way or other—by his work." Similarly, John

Carruthers[133] wrote that Dostoevsky as well as Tolstoy had influenced English fiction "rather overwhelmingly." He outlined as follows the English reputation of these two "indisputably . . . greatest psychological novelists in European literature":

Tolstoy was the earlier known in England, and will be found ultimately to have had the more powerful and lasting effect; but immediately, that is, for the period 1900-1920, Dostoevsky was the more important. Though *Crime and Punishment* had been translated into English as far back as 1885, and Dostoevsky's other novels were known to some readers through translations into French, it was not until Mrs. Garnett's masterly translations began to appear in 1912 that English writers in general woke to the significance of the author of *The Idiot* and *The Brothers Karamazov.* The first result of this awakening was oddly perverse. The greatness of Dostoevsky as a novelist—his astounding insight into human motive, his strong sense of drama, his mastery in dialogue, his power of integrating diverse and often contradictory revelations of character into concrete figures as real and unique in their own peculiar world as Tolstoy's in the actual world we live in—was for the most part overlooked. He was taken as first and foremost a great thinker. His ideas were discussed, wrangled over, and fervently preached by disciples. And in so far as his practice in the craft of fiction was considered at all, it was hastily assumed that he had dealt yet another blow, and possibly the final one, at form, or plot; whereas in fact he had a much stronger sense of plot than Tolstoy. Of the two writers, Tolstoy was the more analytical and formless, Dostoevsky the more intensely dramatic. But the formless 'slices of life' became fashionable, and at the same time fostered a new interest, due also in large measure to Dostoevsky, in morbid, abnormal, or actually pathological states of mind.

British enthusiasm for Dostoevsky was less amiably characterized in a volume on *Contemporary Movements in European Literature*[134] by William Rose and Jacob Isaacs. They considered that among the "waves of fashion" by which in the Twentieth Century England had been swept was

the Russian fever that, from about 1912, with Mrs. Garnett's new translation of Dostoevsky (who was, of course, known and translated in the unready eighties), increased in fury until about 1918 it became the predominant factor in the hectic evolution of young intellect. Its hectic quality is shown clearest in Middleton Murry's biography of Dostoevsky and in parts of his *Evolution of an Intellectual.*

Even more scornful is Mirsky's comment in the brilliant, bitter, essay, *The Intelligentsia of Great Britain*,[135] written by him in Russian soon after he became a Communist, and translated into English in 1935:

The cult of Dostoevsky began in Great Britain among the intelligentsia during the war. It was a cult which corresponded to the poems of Wilfrid Owen. But it was more than the worship of suffering that attracted in Dostoevsky. Now that the hopes of the nineteen-hundreds had come down to the catastrophe of the war, the incomparably mystical, exaggeratedly irrational cult of faith in Dostoevsky was just what was needed to replace the rarified naturalistically rationalistic faith of Shaw. Faith in vital forces disappeared, and a faith in the miraculous appeared. This kind of faith provided a foundation for a new manner of viewing life which was put forward in 1916 by a book on Dostoevsky by Middleton Murry. . . . But at last, not through any miraculous invention, but simply thanks to the natural grace of big battalions and big banks, British capitalism, though a little battered, came out of the war victorious and began a rather left handed sort of stabilisation. The intellectuals then became a little forgetful of Dostoevsky as prophet of a new heaven and new earth. Yet the less they believed in him as prophet, the bigger he became as a supreme embodiment of introspection and a great authority on agonised human hearts. The drawn-out war, being not merely the war of the trench hell, but also the beginning of the world crisis and of a decisive intensification of the crisis of British capitalism, now showed in a full flowering of all those decadent individualistic and introspective currents of thought which had appeared first in the 'eighties, had developed insidiously through the pre-war years, and at last became the governing mood of very large sections of the intelligentsia.

John Galsworthy's final estimate of Dostoevsky was no longer what it had been, but he was certain that his work would endure. He wrote as follows on August 26, 1932 to Mr. W. Kozlenko of New York:[136]

Dear Sir,—
    I will answer your questions in order and as best I may:
1. If I were still reading Dostoevsky I have no doubt that I should find him an interesting (and in some sort irritating) writer.
2. I doubt whether he is still a universal influence for the novelist. In morals and philosophy he was a dissolvent. Against dissolution there is always reaction.
3. On the whole he is not as great a man as Tolstoy, either as an artist or as a thinker.
4. He was very unbalanced, but his insight was deep and his fecundity remarkable. I think he will live.
                    Very truly yours,
                            John Galsworthy.

Dostoevsky's effect on French literature was mentioned in Mario Praz' study of the Decadence, *The Romantic Agony*,[137] which appeared in English in 1933. Dostoevsky had been, according to Praz, an important influence in the development of the Decadent movement in France. He had given "a more profound treatment to certain of Poe's themes." The " 'imp of the perverse,' " for example, was prominent in his characters. The French "found, or thought they found" in his novels

a sadism which had become mystical and more subtle; no longer limited to the grossness of physical torture, but penetrating like a worm-hole into all moral phenomena; they found also a thirst for the impossible, and impotence elevated to the height of mystical ecstasy. . . . Dostoevsky seemed to speak the very language of Baudelaire, not in aphorisms, but with a profusion of introspective eloquence.

He had gone a step farther than the Marquis de Sade.

In Sade and in the sadists of the "frénétique" type of Romanticism it [was] the integrity of the body which [was] assailed and destroyed, whereas in Dostoevsky one had the feeling—to use a phrase from *Letters from the Underworld*—of the "intimacy of the soul brutally violated."

As a matter of fact, however, Dostoevsky had introduced nothing new but had only cleverly used the old. He was a "belated manifestation of the Romanticism of 1830." He did "nothing more than make use, but with profounder understanding, certain themes used by the 'frénétique' French romantics" and because the taste for the "frénétique" had been revived by the Decadents, he became influential in the new movement.

What Dostoevsky had meant to the younger American writers of the post-war period was discussed by Malcolm Cowley in his "narrative of ideas," *Exile's Return*.[138] His generation, he said, "passed through a whole series of enthusiasms—Mencken, Huneker, Somerset Maugham, Laforgue," and then "encountered Dostoevsky who didn't fit into their scheme." The reason he did not fit was that he was too close to their own experience. Dostoevsky on his trip abroad with Anna Grigorievna was like the American expatriate of the 1920's; Dostoevsky meeting Turgenev in Baden-Baden was as if Ernest Hemingway or John Dos Passos had talked with Henry James: they were "symbolic" of the "younger generation of expatriates confronting the elder." Dostoevsky writing *The Possessed* was like Sinclair Lewis writing *Main Street:*

Change the names . . . change the style to something more colloquial, objective, and it [*The Possessed*] might almost have been written by a young American in Montparnasse as he leaned his elbows on a café table of imitation marble ringed with coffee stains.

There was, however, this difference, Mr. Cowley went on to say, that "instead of ridiculing a Russian Gopher Prairie" Dostoevsky ridiculed the "Russian Carol Kennicotts, the denationalized intellectuals who dreamed of escaping to Europe." And there was also "another difference" which was "enormous"; that, whereas Lewis, planning to write a "good satirical novel" had kept a "firm grip on plot and character," Dostoevsky "after the first few chapters, let his characters take hold of the story." Then Mr. Cowley pointed out what, by so doing, Dostoevsky had accomplished for Russian fiction. In Stravrogin, he said, Dostoevsky had "invented what used to be known as the Russian soul," which he himself called the "Russian god." Of course, we now knew that this god "was not the god of the Russian people" but only "the myth of the old intelligentsia." Yet, this myth had lifted a burden "from the shoulders of Russian literature," had liberated it from "backwardness and provincialism." From now on the Russian writer "could create his own fashions, could write for the world."

Concerning Dostoevsky's influence on English literature, the most searching study I have been able to discover is the leading article which appeared June 5, 1930 in *The Times Literary Supplement*.[139] Dostoevsky had left a "deep mark on the novel throughout the whole of Western Europe," was the opinion of its anonymous author, on the English novel as well as on that of other countries, although in England his influence was not "so perceptible on the surface" as in Germany, for instance, where Werfel, Herman Hesse, and Wasserman were under his spell, or in Russia with Pilniak and Leonov, or in that "literary annexe of old Imperial Russia," Paris, with Remizov and "the symbolist writers headed by Merezhkovsky," or in France proper with André Gide. In England Dostoevsky had caused greater "consternation" than elsewhere. "Still, without translations of Dostoevsky and Tolstoy, even without translations of Turgenev or Chekhov" it was "difficult to believe that the contemporary English novel could have become the thing it is"; and in this transformation which had been of "a startling abruptness," the role of Dostoevsky was "incalculably large." Dostoevsky's importance was not so much that he "*felt* ideas" as that he "spiritualized them," presented "souls" rather than people, and for this reason, because the soul, as Mrs. Woolf had pointed out, was formless, wrote formless novels.

More than any other novelist of the last century Dostoevsky helped to weaken the formal restraints of imaginative literature and to break down the conventional discipline of fiction. . . . What happened in effect, as the result of [his] researches into the soul, was that artistic reality for the novelist tended to approximate more and more closely spiritual reality— or to ideas of spiritual reality.

In consequence, then, the novel, "became at once increasingly one-sided and amorphous." There were, of course, other influences at work, nor was the effect of Dostoevsky perhaps "strictly definable"; it was "something in the air, a layer of the atmosphere in which the novelist breathed." But his "preoccupation with the soul" had become a "definite starting-point" for many of the novelists, for D. H. Lawrence, for example, who although he borrowed nothing "directly" from Dostoevsky and wrote of " 'a lot of little Stavrogins biting one another's ears' " and "rejected everything in Dostoevsky that seemed spurious to him," wrote *Aaron's Rod* at a time when the "transformation which had made the novel had already been accomplished," when the novel had become "freer, looser, less restricted, altogether more confidential," cultivating "a sort of intimacy . . . with real life" so that one thought it "more like life" as it was known. It "no longer set out to create a logical and self-contained little world," nor assumed "that human affairs [were] invariably tidied up in a final chapter." The novel had changed "in the last half century in response to the stimulus of *War and Peace* and *The Brothers Karamazov*."

Of course, no influence was lasting, and fiction itself continued to change. The Russian novelists seemed now "a decaying influence," there was "even a noticeable onrush of hostility" against them, and those like Mrs. Woolf or Mr. David Garnett who had "most readily assimilated the Dostoevskian tradition" now appeared "most anxious to restore the balance." "Newer trends" were being "woven into the fabric" of the novel; and "Dostoevsky's influence, germinating in an atmosphere of nervous intellectual excitation" seemed "to have exhausted itself." Today one realized that Dostoevsky's "profundities" were "shallower than we had thought," that his "spiritual excesses" however illuminating, were nevertheless "excesses," that his "welter of indefinable agitation, even regarded as a comprehensive symbol of the unseen world of the spirit," was "strangely like mere fantasy and make-believe . . . the realm of the purely irrational, of the miraculous." His "influence on the novel [presented] a strange paradox," and could be summarized as follows:

It is what Dostoevsky tried but failed to do, not what he genuinely accomplished, that has proved so powerful an inspiration. His desire to map out the whole uncharted territory of the human spirit erred on the side of rashness and pretentiousness, but it served as an example for writers of a less fevered turn of mind. Dostoevsky discovered no new ultimate values; he only affirmed the existence of the ultimate. Nor did he bring the soul into fiction; he merely sought to exclude everything else from it. It is in the looseness and formlessness of the contemporary novel that we can find the clearest evidence of the effect he has had; it is in the growing emphasis on artistic form that we can detect the failure of his type of symbolism. It was, that is to say, his technical method as a novelist, the sort of spiritual reality he postulated, which gave the novel new boundaries and a new vitality. He has bequeathed to later novelists the ambition to discover less questionable reality in the region of experience he so ingeniously explored.[140]

VI. SUMMARY AND DISCUSSION

DOSTOEVSKY, in sum, has been rewritten and multiplied by his critics; and, on the whole, it is on their minds rather than on his that the story of his fame throws light. Now, he has appeared a master of accurate documentation, his work described as "faultless photography," now, the most lyrical of authors who wrote only about himself, "projecting" his own emotions. It may be true, perhaps, that critics, in general, have nothing "in common with the ideas of those they criticize,"[1] and that of Dostoevsky they have built up a legendary figure only. Which indeed, of all those drawn in the preceding pages, is the real Dostoevsky? The present essay does not attempt an answer. Of what these pictures indicate concerning the thought of the time, however, there can be little doubt.

To understand Dostoevsky's earliest English critics, one must glance however cursorily, at the background of ideas which formed their opinions. The intellectual legacy of which the 1880's found themselves in possession was that of scientific Realism, grounded in Empiricism and predisposed to Naturalism. Nature—had been the assumption in the 1850's—lay open to the investigation of human intelligence, and human intelligence was adequate to cope with nature. All that was supernatural had been excluded from the philosophies of Darwin, Spencer, Mill, and Auguste Comte. The reality of the physical world had been postulated by them as ultimate and indubitable, and personal opinion or consciousness of self had been discounted as irrelevant in matters of serious intellectual investigation. Certitude rested on "proof" and proof was a matter of logical deduction from an accumulation of the empirical facts. The part of wisdom was to recognize that mind could not reach beyond the experience of sense, and this limitation could be all the more cheerfully accepted on the assumption that beyond experience of sense there was nothing worth knowing. "Insight" and "intuition" had no place in the philosophies of Positivism, Agnosticism, and Utilitarianism; they were objective in approach and analytic in method.

Their artistic counterpart was Realism which is, fundamentally, Empiricism translated into terms of art. For Empiricism, all knowledge, including knowledge of one's self, is derived from experience and predominantly from sensation. Knowing is largely a passive reception of given reality; and all reality, as given and as real, is equally valuable. Man's idiosyncracies of taste, therefore, are completely irrelevant for knowledge. In philosophic as in scientific investigation they must be eliminated. So also in art. The goal of art must be a truthful record of reality. The artist must strip himself of ideals and desires in his observation of the existing fact. He must be selfless in his interest and exact in his account. All self-assertion is an impediment to understanding. To see the world through the prism of one's emotions is to distort it; to record one's personal experiences is to be uselessly self-indulgent. The artist must make himself a sensitive instrument of receptivity and transmission; his mind must be a clear window through which he can look at life and see all of it. Realism, that is, demands of the artist a definite separation between his private concerns and the objective facts. The limitations it imposes on him proceed from a fear of illusion which is based on deep regard for the intrinsic value of objective reality, coupled with distrust of individual emotion.

Presently Zola gave a new turn to the doctrine of Realism.[2] Convinced that science represents the highest reaches of intelligence, Zola sought to raise art to the status of science. He started specifically from a work on medicine, Claude Bernard's *Introduction to Experimental Medicine*, and seized upon the distinction made there between the sciences of observation and those of experiment. Fiction he then classed in the second category, and called the new literary method which he advocated "Naturalism." The novelist's purpose, he held, must be that of all scientific investigators: to find the relationship between a given phenomenon and its immediate cause. In his own province, that of the passions and of the intellect, the novelist must be concerned not with the *why* but only with the *how* of things. His problem must be to discover what a given passion, acting in a given milieu and under given circumstances, will produce with reference to the individual and to society. His method is to take facts as he observes them in nature and then to study their mechanism through carefully instituted modifications of circumstance and environment. These modifications must never depart from the laws of nature; the novelist must operate on characters, on passions, on human and social facts, as the chemist and the physicist operate on inorganic matter, as the physiologist operates on living organisms. The naturalistic novel is a real experiment on man. Its method is not merely photographic, nor is Fatalism its philosophy. Experiment involves more than simple observation; and scientific Determinism, for which causality is held to be within the series of events, differs from Fatalism which rests on belief in externally operating causes. The ultimate purpose of the novelist should be the attainment of socially useful knowledge; for once the ways of individuals and of society have been determined, it becomes possible to dominate and direct the lives of men.

Naturalism, then, differs in one important way from Realism. For although both theories rest on a profound respect for scientific method and have faith in the æsthetic sufficiency of the empirically existing fact, Naturalism, with its emphasis on experiment and *usefulness*, implies a degree of manipulation and thence of "subjectivity" which Realism does not admit. Zola's naturalistic novelist, to be sure, is permitted no more concern with his own emotions than the Realist, but he is obliged to be "in" his work in the role of experimentor, as the Realist may not be. No longer does he merely look at life as through a clear window; he re-arranges the life before him and then records what happened. Thus, although he is still "scientific," he is not completely "detached." Naturalism, therefore, although historically further removed than Realism from Romanticism, stands closer to it in one important respect.

Be that as it may, Zola was doubtless right in claiming that his doctrine was timely and consistent with the temper of his age. The enormous vogue which his novels achieved, however, depended only in part on their advocacy of a popular doctrine. The interest with which they were received was due much more to their novelty, and mostly to their flagrantly scandalous nature. Their success in England as in France was a success of scandal as much as of esteem. They raised a storm of protest. Vizetelly was tried and imprisoned for publishing them. Zola was spoken of in the journals as "sickening," "revolting," "coarse beyond expression,"[3] "a bourgeois Juvenal" whose "influence for evil" it was "difficult to overestimate," a writer who "prostituted talent approaching to genius to the artistic execution of the most repulsive photography."[4] Tennyson wrote of "maiden fancies wallowing in the troughs of Zolaism."[5] In the unpleasantness of his effects, his seriousness of purpose was overlooked or mistrusted. The Victorian reader believed in Realism but would not grant that an honest devotion to it might lead to repulsiveness. He asked for Truth but predetermined its limits, hedged it into the moral boundaries of his optimistic belief in human dignity and the fundamental goodness of life; any exhibition to the contrary was for him necessarily false and immoral. In brief, the unexamined prejudices on which popular criticism of the 80's operated were that art must be pleasing, virtuous, beautiful, and truthful; by which was meant that it must

present a view of life in accordance with current, conventional understanding of right and wrong; that it must give evidence of crafts-
manship in effects of harmonious order; and that it must represent
"life as it is." In the presence of a work of art the critic asked, what
is its message? Is its message good, that is, socially desirable? Is its
statement true? And is it useful and hopeful? It is an attitude which
assumes that the method of art is reproduction, and its function,
moral teaching. Failure to recognize the obvious possibility that moral
fervor may come in conflict with respect for truth is often the root of
what usually appears to us now as prudish or sentimental rationaliza-
tion. George Eliot, for example, who was a general favorite, was
praised for having both painted reality and "ennobled" life,[6] without
awareness of the contradiction, that to ennoble implies an initial lack
of nobility, and that therefore if George Eliot ennobles life, her work
must be not a copy of reality but invention.

This equivocal position, so clearly the result of wounded moral
sensibilities, which obscured logic and dulled æsthetic judgment, was
opposed by certain critics of cosmopolitan interests and open minds.
Henry James, for example, wrote an essay in praise of Zola;[7] Edmund Gosse declared himself "tired to death of the criticism on both
sides of the Atlantic" which refused to see what Realists were. He was
not, he said, a "great lover of what they produced" but when they
were "advised to give up their studies and paint pretty girls on
bridges" he was "almost stung into partisanship."[8] W. L. Courtney
lamented that the world "shut its eyes to the deeper aspects of existence" because it resented all "unpleasantness";[9] and in America, Professor Boyesen declared that fiction would not improve so long as
it was expected to be "a weak lemonade mixture, harmless and mild-
ly exhilarating, adapted for the palate of ingénues."[10]

It was at this time, when the assumptions of an æsthetic utilitarianism were being brought in question, that Dostoevsky was introduced
to England. Reviewers praised or blamed his novels on the basis of
their usefulness. They asked the familiar questions: did his work or
did it not give a good and honest picture of Russian people, Russian
customs, Russian institutions? Was it or was it not ethically desirable?
Was one "the better" for having read him or not? They stressed
Dostoevsky's humanitarianism, but also seemed to grope for less
tangible qualities in him, which could be felt but for which terms of
description were lacking. They said that his was Realism, but with a
difference. It is not hard to see why Vogüé's "Introduction" to his

Russian Novel, the most influential example of this "realistic-humani-
tarian" school, had had, as Edmund Gosse said of it later,[11] the force
of a "manifesto . . . at the precise moment when the reading public was
ready to accept it."

Vogüé's "Introduction" was an essay which, in revulsion from
Naturalism, and yet, fundamentally, not breaking with it, was oriented
toward Idealism. It praised Realism in literature as the natural expression of an age of science and democracy just as Classicism had
been that of absolutism and monarchy, as an "art of observation
rather than of imagination" which, like science, concerned with the
evolution of microscopic and obscure objects, gave its attention to
minute, ordinary events rather than to the sudden and the catas-
trophic. Vogüé praised in Realism its effect of simplicity and naïveté,
its imitation of Nature's "unconsciousness" in its avoidance of rhetoric. The aim of Realism was to represent man as he was observed to
be, not as on the basis of an absolutist conception of the heroic, he
should ideally be. No French "Realist," said Vogüé, had achieved
that aim, for nothing was less simple and naïve, nothing less impatient nor more rhetorical, than the genius of the French. Stendhal
had attained no more than an "abominable dryness," Balzac had described not life but his dream, "dreamt with such precision of detail"
that it had been taken for real. Zola himself was not a Realist. His
most forceful effects, creations of a "synthetic monster," were distinctly romantic. Flaubert alone might lay claim to the title, but even
with him, Realism was vitiated by a strong element of subjectivity, a
bitterness without charity, which led to that "grotesque Iliad of
nihilism, *Bouvard et Pécuchet.*" French "Realism" was either not
Realism at all or it had failed, having arrived at nothing but pessimism through its narrow exclusion of the "human" and the divine.
It was to the North that one must look for Realism, to those Slav or
Anglo-German races whose genius was not the "genius of the absolute," who were not constrained by traditions of precision and clarity,
whose soul was "large and turbid" because it saw "many things at the
same time" and neither easily nor willingly restricted its observations
for the sake of simple lucidity, because it judged that "representations
of the world must be as complex and contradictory as the world itself."
These Northern races gave the most exact attention to the study of the
actual but also "lent an ear to the murmur of abstract ideas." They
were "scientific" but their science led them to see goodness in man
and nobleness in nature; and this was the right view. They did not

forget, as the French had forgotten, that man was more than dust, that the breath of God was in him, and it was their appreciation of the divine in man that gave greatness to their work. Posterity would hesitate in its choice among the novelists of Russia and England: Tolstoy, Turgenev, and George Eliot.

Thus Vogüé stood philosophically midway between Realism and Idealism. He respected science but loved divinity and objected to idealization because nobility seemed to him inherent in the scheme of things. He thought man good but Nature great; and asked of art that it be objective, sensitive, and honest. Æsthetically, although he valued emotional above rational perception, he rejected Romanticism because its subjectivity falsified, "Art for Art" because its motives were trivial, Naturalism because it was too rational and too limited. He stood for Realism, because unlike Art for Art, it gave a moral purpose to æsthetic expression, unlike Naturalism did not exclude the "divine" in its conception of the human, unlike Romanticism preferred objective to subjective evaluations.

The enormous success of *The Russian Novel*, then, was due largely to the exactness with which it echoed unformulated artistic inclinations of its day. When it appeared, theories of "Realism" were thirty years old.[12] The term was used principally to describe the method of accurately reproducing facts and the choice for artistic treatment of objects commonly known as against those poetically imagined, and more particularly was applied to the deliberate choice for art of the ugly or the salacious. The chief exponents of Realism in France had never attained more than a scandalous popularity; they were associated with a squalid and ostentatious bohemianism and a taste for the gutter, "la nostalgie de la boue." Their efforts had culminated in the shocking and "soul-less" brutality of *Germinie Lacerteux* and *Nana*. The reading public, scandalized, wanted reassurance of human dignity, without relinquishing belief in a scientifically discoverable, objective reality; and, weary of admiring art only for its informative value, were glad to extend the province of the real from the merely observed to the emotionally experienced. They were glad to turn to the "kinder" Realism of Dickens and George Eliot, and they welcomed Vogüé.

Vogüé, then, with his argument for feeling as an inherent part of an objective reality, straddled the eras of Positivism and of Idealism. Shortly after his book, it will be remembered, came a long period (roughly from 1890 to 1912) when interest in Dostoevsky had de-

clined noticeably. And this was the time when in the dominant trend
of thought, Idealism and Mysticism came into their own, when the
realm of perception lost its certainty as it widened its horizon,
knowledge of the Beyond gained ascendency over cognizance of the
Here and Now, and evidence of "spirit" and of insight outweighed
that of the senses. This was the time of the idealistic reaction in
philosophy, when scientific Realism was re-examined and found wanting. Utilitarianism with its arithmetical morality, Agnosticism with its
cheerfully accepted limitations, the simple dogma of Positivism were
found to rely for certitude upon important exclusions: the assumption that similarities are more accurately descriptive of truth than
individual differences; that the discovery of laws of nature and of
behavior, of historical tendencies, is more vital than the consideration
of separate unduplicated events; and that documentary "proof" is an
adequate equivalent for faith. In short, it was seen that these doctrines took too little account of individual differences, of hardly classifiable variations, and left no room for the non-logical certitudes of
emotional understanding. And in the reaction against them, Helm-
holtz, Wundt, and Von Hartmann reasserted the philosophical importance of the self-conscious ego; Bradley, of the idea as well as of
the fact. Those ways of thought were now favored which tended to
ascribe ontological value to modes of perception that had been neglected in the procedure of "scientific" philosophies. This was the time
also when the school of Art for Art's sake lived and died,[13] when the
Society for Psychic Research was established, when spiritual séances
were held, and when Nietzsche became popular.

Art for Art was a transitional step between an outworn Realism and
a new Romanticism. (Just as in the corresponding metaphysical development, Neo-Hegelianism was a transitional step between Positivism and Intuitionalism.) It had, indeed, something in common
with Naturalism, in spite of differences which placed them at the opposite extremes of the literary gamut. Naturalism had rebelled against
the confusion of ethics and æsthetics, against the assumption that the
value of art lay in its ethical guidance. Art for Art was an extension of
this view, including in its condemnation not only ethical but also
metaphysical and scientific considerations. But whereas Naturalism,
half-consciously or unconsciously, took art to be the handmaid of a
certain philosophic attitude, Art for Art declared itself independent
of all philosophy, other than its own æstheticism. Both schools
achieved a certain dispassionateness which distinguished them from

the Romantics. They differed in their view of the artist's relation to his work: Naturalism would exclude his avowed interpretation of the material with which he dealt; Art for Art, his interest in any implications of his material beyond its suitability to a pleasing effect— "pleasing," of course, being broadly interpreted to admit the possibility of even the ugly and the painful. The Naturalist's frame of reference, that is, was scientific; the other's, æsthetic. With the Naturalist it was the concrete fact which took the place of individual emotion and judgment; with the Æsthete, the pattern into which emotion, judgment, observation had been arranged. The first was concerned exclusively with sensuously perceptible objects, the other might deal with observations given only to introspective insight. The danger of the first was platitude, of the second unintelligibility; the former stressed the generally understandable and was fundamentally social, the latter, loved the esoteric and was definitely anti-social. As indicative of the progress of thought this is the most important difference between them. Art for Art was objective only in so far as attention to form implies emotional detachment; it gave a new importance to subjective evaluations.

When Nietzsche died, in 1900, Georg Brandes expressed amazement at the rapid ascendancy of his philosophy, at the way in which "in the course of five or six years" his "intellectual tendency" had become "the ruling tendency of a great part of the literature of France, Germany, England, Italy, Norway, Sweden, and Russia."[14] It had been Georg Brandes himself who twelve years earlier, having become interested in Nietzsche and got acquainted with him through a lively correspondence, delivered a course of lectures on him at the University of Copenhagen, at the conclusion of which, he wrote, the applause "took the form of an ovation," for which he himself claimed no credit. He had only reproduced, he said, "clearly and connectedly, and intelligibly to a Northern audience" what Nietzsche had "originated." But now Nietzsche's name was "very popular in all intelligent circles in Copenhagen and all over Scandinavia it [was] at least *known*."[15] These lectures were followed the next year by a study entitled "An Essay on Aristocratic Radicalism," the phrase having been used by Brandes in one of his early letters to Nietzsche and enthusiastically approved: "the cleverest thing I have yet read about myself."[16] From this time on, translations and articles poured forth and Nietzsche's philosophy became known outside of Scandinavia. The authorized English translation of his works, in eighteen volumes, ap-

peared between 1909 and 1913, a translation of Elizabeth Förster-
Nietzsche's biography in 1912, and approximately a score of other
studies from 1911 to 1930. *The International Index* for 1907 to 1915
lists thirty-one articles about him, the *Reader's Guide,* thirty-seven
from 1910 to 1914.

Nor need Brandes have been surprised by the sudden popularity of
this aristocrat in an age of democracy, of this iconoclast at a time of
religious reaction, of this anti-humanitarian and immoralist at a
time of social and ethical preoccupation, whom the "voltairians of the
age could not claim . . . since he was a mystic; and contemporary
anarchists had to reject . . . as an enthusiast for rulers and castes."
For in "some hidden way" he was indeed "in accord with much" that
was "fermenting" at the time. His "indomitable energy" and "self-
reliance," his gift as a lyricist, his "psychological profundity and ab-
struseness," the "fascinating combination" of "his lyrical and critical
qualities"[17] were precisely those factors of emotionalism and strenuous
individualism which could have won an age of reaction from rationalist
and utilitarian philosophies. Idealism emphasized subjective judgments; Mysticism, intensely personal religious experience; Art for
Art tended toward the esoteric in æsthetic appreciation; and the culmination of Individualism was certainly attained in the doctrine
of the Superman. Nietzsche's work was the eloquent statement of the
ruling predispositions of the age.

And so when Dostoevsky was re-introduced to England, in 1912,
truth other than that of accurate observation was being asked of
art, something more than the useful morality of kindness, and also
something other than a simple "wholesomeness" of outlook. Personal
judgments and individual emotional perceptions, rather than the
methods of a depersonalized rationalism, had come to be valued as
modes of critical appraisal and philosophic discourse. A new psychology, furthermore, was showing the individual psyche to be a more
complex system of impressions, response, and adjustments than had
been hitherto suspected, and a new art had demonstrated what differences existed between æsthetic and ethical criteria. The age offered
no surer solution than that of "tentativeness from day to day"[18]
and no greater satisfaction than the highly personal one of mystic
certitude. It leaned to primitivism and emotionalism, sanctioned
for art the record of impressions, and for ethics, codes of behaviour
that centered about the individual rather than the group. Neither life
nor art, it began to assert, reached, amidst the "pleasant clatter of tea

things" on "vicarage lawns,"[19] the depths of experience and of truth which lay open to them. And so Dostoevsky was now praised not for his accuracy but for his "sincerity," his "depth" and "intensity," his "insight," for the "soul," the "volcanic" power of his creations. He was a "poetic" or "transcendental" Realist, his Realism was mingled with romance. His understanding of Russia was not that of an observer but of a being who was somehow mystically united with it. His books were more than thoughtful fictions; they were national symbols, prophetic allegories of the fates of nations. His "humanitarianism" was not that of the socially directed consciousness of the West. It was a quality of compassion that had no primary purpose of social utility, but stemmed from a personal emotion so intense that it cut through barriers of class to an imaginative identification of man with man, "the pity . . . of a suffering human being for a fellow-sufferer." The example set by him, very different from the inculcated Christianity of dutiful kindness, was that of unpremeditated tolerance without other conviction than the heart's immediate response. What mattered was the spontaneous impulse to compassion and not a self-willed striving for it. The criminal had become "our brother" not as a member of a group to which sympathy was due but as an individual human being. What was now admired in Dostoevsky was his ideal of extreme individualism which made heroes of such unconventional and anti-social beings as Myshkin and Raskolnikov. Idealism weighed the balance of ethical judgment on the side of personal codes of behaviour independent of society's demands. No longer were Dostoevsky's people queer Russians. They were everybody, seen by a genius. Nor was the "unpleasantness" of his novels to be excused as an evil redeemed by good intentions; it itself constituted the value of his work. Vogüé's simile of the surgeon's knife had lost its meaning. It was the "soul," man's residuum in social isolation, that was Dostoevsky's concern, a kind of quintessence of humanity to which the Englishman's practical interest in life's material demands made him a stranger.

Shestov, Merezhkovsky, Middleton Murry, Janko Lavrin, Spengler, are the chief exponents of this anti-rationalist, anti-social school. For the first three of these, one feels, Dostoevsky stood as an expressed statement of their own spiritual experience. He was to them a kind of mirror into which they looked, with torment like Shestov, or ecstasy like Merezhkovsky, or Narcissus-like admiringly as Middleton Murry. Shestov,[20] driven by hatred of Utilitarianism and

Mechanism extended his hatred to all intellectual systems. They all seemed to him specious projections of desires, egotistic delusions and falsifications of truth. He was opposed to every kind of abstract formula whether it were Socratic, or Kantian, or positivist. His way of thought was most closely allied to the mysticisms of a Tertullian or a Nietzsche, but he adhered to no one scheme of philosophy. Scornful of Idealism, he strove toward the comprehension of a God who was the embodiment of reality beyond human logic and morality and inapplicable to the ordinary experiences of men. Laws of morality, he thought, were mere substitutes for ancient mythologies, and as false as they. Men believed in Good, Beauty, and Reason, and equated them with God only because they feared the freedom of unbelief. Ideals were the props and fetters of the weak who dared not face the unsystematized reality of experience nor come to grips with the unknowable, one, *un*human reality. They were the bondage of imagined and pragmatic "truth," created for the conduct of human affairs; they were the fundamental illusions on which society operated. Yet nothing was worse than self-delusion; no matter how grandiose the social structure which might be built upon it, the result could not compensate for the falsehood wherein practical necessity masqueraded as truth. His view is the extremity of rebellion against Rationalism and Utilitarian optimism, and the assertion of the ultimate supremacy of individual against social values. And in this assertion, although he considered himself a disillusioned Idealist, Shestov remained an Idealist. Merezhkovsky's elaborate juxtapositions of pagan and Christian virtues, of carnality and spirit, of the God-Man and the Man-God are based on religious more than on metaphysical considerations. They express the characteristic revulsion of an intellectual ascetic who by renouncing the pleasure of the senses thinks he has found his greatest joy in the life of his mind. Middleton Murry's mystic rhetoric carries Idealism to its extremity of Solipsism. Janko Lavrin's analyses are Idealism with a psychoanalytic injection. And Spengler, declaring that between the historian and the poet, both of them interpreters and creators, there is no essential difference, takes Idealism into the realm of history.

What happens to Art when the dominant current of thought progresses from naturalistic Empiricism to Idealism is that it passes from a servile position as a method of explaining objective reality to a more independent role as a presentation of philosophic truth. In this capacity it still lends itself to unfavorable comparison with philosophy, for it is held to be inferior to it as explanation, although in its own limited province of presentation it is supreme; it is esteemed, that is, as a special method of conveying what is already known to be valuable, not as an instrument of discovery. Such is the rationalistic view of Neo-Hegelianism. But once epistomology sets limits to rational knowledge, Art may claim not only a relative independence but complete sovereignty, and even unapproachable power. So for Intuitionism and Mysticism, for which truth is to be sought in realms beyond the reach of Rationalism and may be apprehended and presented but not explained, Art, as a means of discovery and of re-creation, must have a function perforce superior to the merely explanatory one of philosophy. And thus, not only the function but also the nature of Art is changed, for with belief in a supernatural beyond the power of cognition and in an unknown which may also be unknowable, the grandeur of the concrete fact fades in the awe before its hidden meaning. Allusiveness and evocativeness must then be asked of Art rather than clarity and accuracy. The artist, furthermore, becomes more than the passive recipient of knowledge. It is his mind and not the world outside which is the center of reality. No longer therefore need he be self-effacing; on the contrary, he must consciously express himself and explain himself.

These, roughly, are the changes which Art and æsthetic theory underwent in the score of years between 1890 and 1912. They formed the background for all those intellectual ventures—the philosophy of Bergson, the critical doctrines of Anatole France, the dramas of Maeterlinck, the painting of the Impressionists and Expressionists— which proclaimed the right of the individual to respect his own intuitive beliefs as possessing general interest, and suggested the importance of that which lay beyond the grasp of scientific observation. Hardy had already insisted on the reality behind the veil of things, and Arthur Symons, who in a work of primary importance,[21] introduced Symbolism to England, wrote of it as follows:

It is all an attempt to spiritualise literature, to evade the old bondage of exteriority. Description is banished that beautiful things may be evoked, magically; the regular beat of verse is broken in order that words may fly, upon subtler wings. Mystery is no longer feared, as the great mystery in whose midst we are islanded was feared by those to whom that unknown sea was only a great void. We are coming closer to nature, as we seem to shrink from it with something of horror, disdaining to catalogue the trees of the forest. . . . In this revolt against exteriority, against rhetoric, against a materialistic tradition; in this endeavour to disengage the ultimate essence, the soul, of whatever exists and can be realized by the consciousness; in this dutiful waiting upon every symbol by which the soul of things can be made visible; literature, bowed down by so many burdens, may at last attain liberty, and its authentic speech.

In this utterance Arthur Symons voiced the hope for literature in his own day and indicated what was certainly the directing impulse of the movement which, perhaps somewhat vaguely, we call Symbolism, "the swing of the pendulum away from a mechanistic view of nature and from a social conception of man," as another critic put it.[22] But he did not give an adequate explanation of it. For that he came too early, when Symbolism had not yet reached its fuller development in the work of James Joyce, Marcel Proust, and T. S. Eliot. To-day it can be better understood. A love of mystery, we now know, does not characterize the Symbolists. Such love has been imputed to them largely because they have been difficult to understand. But their difficulty depends rather on an intransigent literalness than on an interest in obscurity. They are addicts of a scrupulous honesty. Their purpose is to state accurately their realization of the immensely complex unity implicit in experience. Their view of things is the artistic counterpart of a philosophic trend toward a new synthesis wherein the consciousness of perception and its object are seen as constituting a primary whole. Theirs is the intuitive apprehension that perceiving mind and empirically existing matter are a unit in the *what* and the *that* of awareness. They have been schooled in rigorous introspection; and for that reason, although they have in common with the Romantics, an interest in individual experience, their subjects are not actually the same.

The Romantic dealt with experiences which were characterized by their capacity for generalization; romantic melancholy or romantic love or romantic rebellion were that kind of melancholy, love, and rebellion which were universally understandable. The Romantic's subjectivity served to unite him to the rest of mankind, not to separate him from it. His attitude was fundamentally social. The Symbolist, on the other hand, delves into that kind of experience which differentiates him most completely from his fellow men. He is concerned not with the universal implications of his experience but with its particularization; his work is the extremity of individualism and may lead to incomprehensibility. He is as accurate as the Naturalist in his observation; but his data are the inmost depths of his psyche, not the objective world dispassionately perceived. His care for form is as precise as the Classicist's, but unlike the Classicist he cares nothing for traditional moulds. He is interested in the exact patterning of his own experience which, being unique, must find expressiveness in unique arrangement. Yet, this extremity of individualism may lead to the assertion of the most abstract generalization. Such, for example, is the case with T. S. Eliot who is violently anti-individualist; and whose poetry, up to his most recent dogmatically religious productions, is none the less a sharp delineation of highly original and intimate impressions. His seems to be, but is not actually, a double allegiance to two realities: of the concrete individual event and of the Ideal which is around and beyond it. The fact is that for him immediate, time-bound events are inseparable from eternal existences.

In consonance with this tendency in both philosophy and art to break down the distinction between the *I* that feels and the *thing* which it feels, a new critical approach, taking into account the complexity of the creative process, looks upon the artist's expression, however "Realistic" his theme, as the more or less unconsciously evolved symbol of a unique experience. In this light, all art is seen, therefore, as in different ways and in varying degrees, "subjective"; and the critic's problem comes to be to discover how unacknowledged intellectual predispositions and emotional drives unrecognized by the artist himself take shape in the communicable stuff of art; how the most profoundly individual concerns are transmuted to general interest. Criticism has enlarged its scope and become curious about the ways of art as well as its "duties," and has turned to biography as a basis for its judgments. Thus, within the last ten or fifteen years a new Dostoevsky has been created, a Dostoevsky whose work is "confessional"; who is a Symbolist antidating the Symbolist Movement, whose plots and characters are dramatic metaphors, the concrete images of his own violence externalized and made familiar; or the exponent of a "new Realism" which is a Realism of the passions, not of the observed fact, whose directing impulse is neither scientific curiosity nor philosophic reflection, but consciousness of personal emotion. His amazing knowledge of others, it is implied, begins with knowledge of himself, with introspection and not with observation of things outside himself. His work is like those modern sculptures which are composed of many different materials: wood, glass, wire, and so on, products, of no mere eclecticism but of a strongly centered, pow-

erful and sensitive apprehension emotionally directed and free from
the demands of rationally defined schemes. The diverse elements in
his work: the tradition of religious orthodoxy and philosophic Idealism in which he was brought up, the social movements of his day and
the despotism with which he had come to grips in its least human
manifestations, his concern with æsthetic problems and the effect on
him of the perversities of the late Romantics, his recognition of the
philosophic incompatibility between Idealism and Materialism, of
orthodox Christianity and Socialist ethics, and of the nationalist ideas
of Russia and the West, his comprehension of the psychological bearing of social distinctions, and his knowledge of the artistic aspirations
of his compatriots and of their journalistic ambitions—all these elements, and more, that made up his life, were fused for him, it is now
said, in a profundity of poetic insight which could grasp the complexity of man and understand his susceptibility to the harsh inflic-
tions of a mechanised society, the possibilities in him of intense and
destructive response. His work, therefore, is complex, rich in emotional and intellectual content. And also, in the most exact sense,
organic; it grows from an individual inward root, however far it may
extend to the reaches of a diverse and powerful intelligence. In English fiction it approximates most nearly that of Emily Brontë, for
they were both of them novelists of lyric passion.

As regards the general problem of criticism the present study indicates the obvious: that æsthetic judgment, consciously or unconsciously, and of necessity, is based on the accumulated sum of critical
perceptions at any given time and on the ethical and metaphysical
assumptions of the critic. It tends to the conclusion that objective
judgments of æsthetic value are, except as regards the externals and
trappings of art, practically impossible, art being a form of expression
which in its deeper reaches is not subject to scientific measurement,
and taste, a function too involved in the intricacies of irrelevant habit
and prejudice to be subjected to strict rule of thumb. The Spirit of an
Age, it would seem, the sum total of predilections, that is, by which
within a given time the masses of men are driven, is independently
stamped on every intellectual enterprise, the metaphysician being implicit in the poet, the poet in the metaphysician; and the critic, both
involved and detached, follows and appraises the ways of thought as
they are formulated in philosophy and art. But his appraisal is tied
to the artistic tradition with which he is familiar and is held in the

current itself of the thing he analyzes. Complete detachment for him is impossible.

It is not difficult to see the fluctuations of Dostoevsky's fame as the visible movements of a current of thought. But how far Dostoevsky himself changed this current is not so easy to determine. Walter Neuschäffer, in his dissertation,[23] concluded that the influence of Dostoevsky on the English novel is threefold: on character, on content, and on structure; that the Raskolnikov, the Myshkin, and the Stavrogin "types" have been used by Gissing, Conrad, Hugh Walpole, Somerset Maugham, Ethel Sidgwick, Aldous Huxley, D. H. Lawrence, and Beverley Nichols; that Conrad, Ethel Sidgwick and Hugh Walpole have followed Dostoevsky in constructing plots that evolve from a central psychological problem; that Hugh Walpole and David Garnett have adopted his borderline atmosphere between dream and reality and that, in this direction, D. H. Lawrence went a step farther than they; that Dorothy Richardson and Virginia Woolf have, like Dostoevsky, presented characters who were spirits clad in flesh; that Maugham and Conrad have resembled him in their use of the first-person form, which, however, he grants, may not be wholly attributable to his influence, and that similarly Huxley's introduction of ethical, social, and æsthetic questions into his novels is also *like* but not necessarily *from* Dostoevsky; but that Dorothy Richardson's and Virginia Woolf's treatment of outward events as altered by the experiences of the soul is more clearly attributable to him and especially Virginia Woolf's concept of the relativity of time.

Dostoevsky has been widely read and vastly admired by English novelists. Of that there can be no dispute. And the English novel has greatly changed since the time he became known. But neither admiration nor similarity are sufficient presumptions of influence. The problem of literary influence is more complex than that; it is not expressed in borrowing or conscious imitation merely. Influence is a state of intimate association and response between two imaginations when one of them has grasped and made its own whatever in the other has answered to its need. Within limits, it is an emotional identification of minds which is deeper than consciousness. It involves factors of individual temperament, of philosophic bias and of taste, so that to determine how one author has been influenced by another, one must decide precisely what his need had been, what he thought he found in the other, and how he used his discovery. Merely to point to what he has consciously taken over is not enough. The problem is complicated on the one hand by the element of the unconscious in the matter of an artist's choice and response, and on the other, by the dependence of all artists on the tradition of their art and on the intellectual environment in which they live.

For example, in the case of Stevenson and Dostoevsky I could show, I think, were it not that such a study would take me too far afield, that Stevenson was fundamentally too unlike Dostoevsky both as a man and as a writer to have been more than impressed by him. He could not have been *influenced,* as I understand "influence." The man who remembered, for example, with the smiling commonsense of maturity the childhood impression made on him by a poor hag who had cut her throat, could not have understood Dostoevsky's almost hysterical apprehension of pain. The exquisite author who wrote of her:

She had been tippling; it was but a dingy tragedy; and it seems strange and hard that, after all these years, the poor crazy sinner should be still pilloried on her cart in the scrap-book of my memory,[24]

used his pen for a very different purpose from that of the Russian author. What the relation of this incident indicates is a predominantly social response to personal experience, a conscious feeling of an artist's responsibility to his material and to his audience. It shows a way of thought fundamentally foreign to Dostoevsky. And this profound difference can be seen, I think, in spite of Mr. Knowlton,[25] in a comparison of *Crime and Punishment* and *Markheim.*

That Stevenson had *Crime and Punishment* in mind at the time he wrote *Markheim* is entirely probable. He wrote it in 1884; the French version of *Crime and Punishment,* which was the one he knew, was published in the same year. Both are stories, Mr. Knowlton points out, "beginning with the murder of a pawnbroker and ending, after an experience of crowded mental life, with the self-surrender of the murderer to the police." In both a "criminal is induced to change his course of life by something like moral regeneration." But there, to my mind, the resemblances end; and I remain wholly unconvinced by Mr. Knowlton's "parallels" adduced in proof of "how vividly the mechanical details of *Crime and Punishment* impressed themselves upon Stevenson." These parallels have very little in common beyond the requirements of similar situations. For example:

Le Crime et le Châtiment	*Markheim*
Une mare de sang s'était formée sur le parquet.	This bundle of old clothes and pool of blood began to find eloquent voices.
Son impatience était extrême, il saisit les clefs et se remit à la besogne. Mais ses tentatives pour ouvrir la commode restaient infructueuses, ce qu'il fallait attribuer moins encore au tremblement de ses mains qu'à ses méprises continuelles; il voyait, par exemple, que telle clef n'allait pas à la serrure, et il s'obstinait cependant à l'y faire entrer.	A qualm came over him, a breath of nausea, a sudden weakness of the joints, which he must instantly resist and conquer. (He finds the keys, and after going upstairs tries the lock of a cabinet).

Given the circumstances, Stevenson, it seems to me, could have written what he did without ever having read Dostoevsky; and as for the situation itself, it is trite enough. Points of comparison, of course, there are. But the differences are more profound; they display a thorough incompatibility of taste and of artistic interest.

Does *Markheim,* in effect, produce an impression of "an overwhelming mental existence"? Hardly. The chill of horror in it is drawn neither from the murder nor the mind of the murderer, but from the appearance of the uncanny stranger. Suspense depends on mystery and the supernatural. And for this reason, it produces fear of the naïve ghost-story or fairy-tale variety; the intensity of maddened thought is not there nor the reality of the commonplace in the midst of the extraordinary. There are, to be sure, "seemingly trivial physical impressions of sight, sound, and so on" in both; but with Stevenson these impressions are poetized and dramatized, so that the commonplace takes on the character of unreality and the effect is melodramatic, whereas with Dostoevsky the detail never loses its ordinary aspect and is shockingly real precisely because the mind at the moment, tense with apprehension and unaccustomed horror, could more easily accept and welcome the unreal. Stevenson's interest in stylistic effects stands between him and his subject; his face obtrudes too obviously between the reader and Markheim. Stevenson remains Stevenson, does not identify himself with his hero, and the story remains too plainly a story. Beautiful phrases keep it from grim seriousness. "Time had some score of small voices in that shop" we read directly after the murderer's victim has "tumbled on the floor in a heap"; the murderer hears "a stir of delicate footing," would like "to plunge into a bath of London multitudes, and to reach, on the other side of day, that haven of safety and apparent innocence—his bed," "brute terrors, like the scurrying of rats in a desert attic, filled the more remote chambers of his brain with riot," the dead man is "sunk beneath seas of silence," and so on. Such beautifully wrought phrases intrude on every page, whereas with Dostoevsky the violent act and the concrete detail are made to stand baldly plain, compelling belief in the unreflecting gesture and vision of a distracted mind. Thus in the instant when Raskolnikov has raised the axe to kill Elisaveta, he sees "her lips pitifully distorted, like those of very little children, when they are getting ready to cry"; but he does not reflect, as does Markheim over the dead body, that here was a being "endowed in vain with all those faculties that can make a world a garden of enchantment." All the difference is here between the detached artist concerned with the subtlety and beauty of his effects, and of the thinker tensely absorbed in his theme.

Nor, although his *Mike Fletcher* somehow echoes Dostoevsky, could George Moore with his epigrams and his elaborately polished manner, do more than bite at Dostoevsky's rough fare. Turgenev was the author with whom he could feel kinship, not Dostoevsky.

There have been men of genius who wrote novels [he said], Dostoevsky, for instance, but vapour and tumult do not make tales, and before we can admire them modern life must wring all the Greek out of us. His farrago is wonderful, but I am not won.[26]

That, of course, is but an expression of taste. But what can be said for the following critical ineptitude from Goodwin's *Conversations with George Moore?*[27]

'Dostoevsky' and Mr. Moore paused, as though choosing his words, 'Dostoevsky gives one, why I cannot quite explain, the idea of snow. I think of him as a sculptor in snow, vast, perhaps luminous, but indistinct and brittle. Or if you prefer to think of clay, do so—soft clay which is apt to crumble. You regard it with admiration, but you never fail to ask yourself inwardly how long it will last. You expect, perhaps, to see it crumble before your eyes. The designs are great but there is very little material. Better than the word snow is vapour. We see them all indistinctly as in a mist. There is no gainsaying that they are magnificent silhouettes—magnificent shadows; but when you come to examine them clearly, you find they are no more than shadows. Simplicity is a great virtue; beware of losing vitality. The writer's method is direct carving—and in stone. We should not be asked to look through frosted glass at a lot of phantoms moving vaguely about the lawn. He never lost the capacity to agitate, but he lost, or never had, vitality. . . . I remember reading *The Brothers Karamazov*. Everyone became so very excited. "What is it all about?" I asked. And then it came to such a pass that one man could not meet another over a glass of beer without they must row each other over the origins of Christianity. However, do not misunderstand me. I should think Dostoevsky a much greater man than, let us say, Hall Caine.'

Can it be that Dostoevsky is "too Russian" for the English? Is it true, perhaps, that artists belong so absolutely to their soil that they may not be duplicated or even understood beyond the boundaries of their own land? This is difficult for me to believe; and yet, in spite of all the interest in Dostoevsky and borrowings from him, he has seemed to many to be essentially foreign to the English spirit.

He came to England through intermediate foreign sources. The first article concerning him was an account of his popularity in Germany, the first influential essay about him, was French. The early translations of his novels were done from the French and not the Russian and for a long time the French versions were read in England in preference to the English. And even later, it is striking how little of the critical material came from Englishmen. There have been, of course, Maurice Baring, Edward Garnett, J. A. T. Lloyd, Middleton Murry and E. H. Carr. But against these one must list: the French André Gide; the German Meier-Graefe, Zweig, Bierbaum, Hesse, Thomas Mann; the Danish Brandes; the Spanish Emilia Pardo Bazán; the Polish Waliszewski; the Czech Masaryk; the Serbian Lavrin; the Russian Merezhkovsky, Shestov, Berdyaev; and the Anglicized or Americanized Russians, Kropotkin, Mirsky, Yarmolinsky. And the tone of the English studies has been either aloof or rhapsodic, which would indicate a certain degree of self-consciousness, a feeling of acknowledged or unacknowledged strangeness. There have been, on the one hand, J. A. T. Lloyd and E. H. Carr playing the rôle of interpreters, introducing their countrymen to an interesting foreigner, and on the other, Maurice Baring and J. M. Murry ecstatically and a little too ostentatiously identifying themselves with a strange being.

That Dostoevsky was more typically Russian than other Russian authors has been always considered true, and has been repeated over and over again in English criticism. The latest instance is Walter Duranty's explanation of the recent treason trials in Moscow.[28] Dostoevsky has seemed more strange than either Turgenev or Tolstoy. His novels were first read as documents, so much so indeed that in 1910 Maurice Baring felt it necessary to explain that Dostoevsky's characters were Russian only as Lear was English or Faust, German,

SUMMARY AND DISCUSSION

and even as late as 1927, D. S. Mirsky, that Dostoevsky's Russia was no more the real Russia of Alexander II than *Wuthering Heights* was a correct picture of the West Riding of the early nineteenth century.[29] When from recorder of the Russian people Dostoevsky became the mouthpiece of the Russian "soul," who conveyed more than pictures of time and place, the mere gestures and actions of living, but a special feeling toward life, the Russian feeling, he seemed no more understandable than he had been before. Berdyaev indeed declared this Russian feeling to be forever incomprehensible to the West, for the "Russian soul," he said, which was most particularly Dostoevsky's possession, was unique and untranslatable.

One might ask further, has Dostoevsky been even "popular" in England? For a survey such as the foregoing might give an exaggerated view of the theme's importance. All through it attention has been narrowly focused, and its object appears unique and heightened. Books and journals, combed for comment on Dostoevsky, yield an accumulated mass of documents which appears impressive and leads one to conclude that Dostoevsky has been very well known. Yet, comparison with the fame of other writers, of Zola, for example, or Tolstoy, or Turgenev, would show that relatively speaking Dostoevsky has received little attention. And even the numerous editions and dramatizations of his work are an imperfect indication. The number of volumes sold may be counted more easily than the number read and understood. And it is safe to assume that the "man in the street" does not know Dostoevsky. Both in time and in audience his fame has been concentrated within narrow bounds. Dostoevsky in England, that is, belongs to the "intelligentsia," a very small part of the literate population. But it must, of course, be borne in mind that this small group is not unimportant in the intellectual life of modern societies and that its interests are not wholly foreign to those of the mass. It is a group which being trained to articulateness expresses itself more readily than the mass, but in its expression often voices, whether consciously or unconsciously, whether in agreement or opposition, those aspirations by which inexpressive majorities are more dumbly actuated. It is a kind of filter of the intelligence which transforms the undifferentiated stuff of general belief into a more concentrated, a more durable, and an intellectually more *usable* essence. Dostoevsky has been popular, as it were, by implication.

Over and over again, furthermore, critics have asserted as has been seen, that Dostoevsky has practically transformed the modern English novel. Avrahm Yarmolinsky, for example, does not hesitate to write as follows:

One has only to consider the work of the more important contemporary novelists of the continent and the English-speaking countries to appreciate how compelling his influence has been. For an author so lacking in snobbery, so anxious to reach the common reader, he is to a remarkable degree a writer's writer. There has been some response to his characteristic motifs and problems, but even more to his psychological delvings and discriminations. German expressionism and French *surréalisme* alike have affiliations with his art. One recognizes the debt to him more clearly in the contemporary novelist's emphasis upon the contradictions, the irrational and subconscious elements of the personality formerly neglected or overlooked. His passionate intensity made him careless of the accepted conventions of fiction, and so instrumental in breaking down the formal pattern of the novel. If it is now a freer, more experimental medium, and in its amorphousness, comprehensiveness, variety, and complexity, more closely approximates life, if it no longer draws invidious distinctions between the morbid and the normal, if it traffics in 'idea-feelings'—this is in no small part due to him. The more recent trends in novel writing, as evidenced in the productions of the 'hard-boiled' school and in the novels of mass action, may be accounted testimony to his influence, inasmuch as they are in the nature of a protest against Dostoevsky's concern with spiritual problems and the private perplexities of the individual.[30]

Where the smoke is so thick there must be fire. Yet, it seems to me, the question has not been conclusively answered: what changes would have occurred in English fiction without Dostoevsky? It is a question that requires a more thorough investigation than has yet been made of the trends of the modern English novel and a more searching comparison of Russian and English Realism.

NOTES

CHAPTER I

Page

1. [1] *Poor Folk* 1846, *The House of the Dead* 1861-2, *Crime and Punishment* 1865-6, *The Idiot* 1869
1. [2] It is not surprising, for example to find a chapter on him in *The Twentieth Century Novel* by J. W. Beach.
1. [3] See Kampmann, pp. 15, 16 *et passim*.
1. [4] See Minssen, *Die französische Kritik und Dostojewski.*
1. [5] *Dostoevsky*, p. 323.
1. [6] See, *e.g.*, Lavrin, "Dostoyevsky and Proust," *Slavonic Review*, v. 5, pp. 609-627; Vacquier, "Dostoevsky and Gide," *Sewanee Review*, v. 37, pp. 478-489.
1. [7] See below, pp. 109, 149-152, 177.
1. [8] Neuschäffer, *Dostojewskij's Einfluss auf dem englischen Roman*, 1935.
2. [9] Seidman, *F. M. Dostoevsky v Zapadnoii Literature.*
2. [10] Haarlem, 1924.
2. [11] *Literatura i Marxism*, 1928, v. 5, pp. 95-106.
2. [12] *Dostojewski in Deutschland*, 1931.
2. [13] *Die französische Kritik und Dostojewski*, 1933.
2. [14] *Pechat i Revolutsia*, v. 6, pp. 34-52; *Literatura i Marxism*, 1929, v. 3, pp. 139-176.
2. [15] V. 3, pp. 310-318.
2. [16] See below, pp. 150, 151.
3. [17] *The Westminster Review*, v. 108, p. 215. For a review of *Specimens of the Russian Poets*, see *Monthly Review*, v. 96, pp. 127-139.
3. [18] See, *e.g.*, *Edinburgh Review*, v. 52, pp. 322-325; *Foreign Quarterly Review*, v. 8, pp. 117-139, and v. 30, pp. 242-250; *National Quarterly Review*, v. 9, pp. 43-70.
3. [19] V. 1, pp. 595-631.
3. [20] V. 58, pp. 28-43.
3. [21] But see Hamel, Dr. J., *England and Russia*, translated in 1854.
3. [22] See Leo Wiener, *An Anthology of Russian Literature*, v. 1, pp. ix, x.
3. [23] *National Quarterly Review*, v. 23-4, pp. 347-369.
3. [24] V. 9, p. 120.
3. [25] V. 108, pp. 215-224. The two French works considered were: C. Courrière, *Histoire de la littérature contemporaine en Russie* and A. Rambaud, *La Russie épique.*
5. [26] For the influence of English literature on Russian, see E. J. Simmons, *English Literature and Culture in Russia* (1553-1840).
5. [27] See, *e.g.* a pamphlet by J. W. MacKail, *Russia's Gift to the World.*

CHAPTER II

7. [1] P. 874.
7. [2] V. 37, p. 165.
7. [3] V. 149, pp. 547, 548.
7. [4] V. 19, p. 136.
7. [5] II (1881), p. 893.
8. [6] Longmans Green & Company, Holt.
8. [7] V. 115, p. 582.

Page
8. [8] I (1881), p. 455.
9. [9] V. 19, p. 273. About Ralston, see *Academy*, v. 36, August 10, 1889, pp. 86, 87.
8. [10] V. 130, p. 29.
8. [11] C. E. Turner, "Nicholas Alexeivitch Nekrasoff," v. 36, pp. 499-512.
8. [12] C. E. Turner, *Studies in Russian Literature*, pp. 364-389.
9. [13] *Ibid.*, pp. 371, 372.
9. [14] V. 56, pp. 1484-1486.
9. [15] E. A. Brayley Hodgetts, v. 23, pp. 37, 38.
9. [16] From *Le livre*, v. 21, p. 211.
9. [17] II (1883), pp. 305, 306.
9. [18] *Nineteenth Century*, v. 15, p. 478.
10. [19] V. 28, p. 395.
10. [20] *Crime and Punishment: A Realistic Novel;* published by Vizetelly.
10. [21] Tr. by Frederick Whishaw; published by Vizetelly.
10. [22] Tr. by Nathan Haskell Dole.
10. [23] Tr. and abridged, by Jane Loring Edmunds, 1887: "I have found it necessary to abridge M. de Vogüé's work somewhat, in order to bring it within certain prescribed limits."
10. [24] I (1886), pp. 99, 100. Both *The Athenaeum* and *The Spectator* reviews were of the French version by Victor Dérély, which had come out the same year.
10. [25] V. 59, pp. 937-939.
11. [26] V. 33 (n.s.), p. 421.
11. [27] V. 17, pp. 364, 365.
11. [28] V. 126, p. 298.
11. [29] William Wallace, v. 29, p. 306.
12. [30] V. 63, p. 58.
12. [31] I (1887), p. 281.
12. [32] V. 30, p. 290.
13. [33] V. 62, pp. 272, 766.
13. [34] *Great Masters*, p. 141.
13. [35] *Ibid.*, pp. 203, 204.
13. [36] *Ibid.*, pp. 423-432.
14. [37] *Ibid.*, pp. 433-440.
14. [38] *Ibid.*, p. 204.
14. [39] II (1887), p. 365.
14. [40] V. 17, p. 327.
15. [41] V. 43, pp. 354, 355.
15. [42] See *Encyclopedia Britannica*, 14th. edition, article on Vogüé; also Edmund Gosse, "Melchior de Vogüé," *Contemporary Review*, v. 97, pp. 568-579.
15. [43] D. S. Mirsky, *A History of Russian Literature*, p. 371.
15. [44] V. 43, pp. 312, 313.
16. [45] *Le roman russe*, p. 267.
16. [46] *Ibid.*, p. 237.
16. [47] *Ibid.*, p. 267.
16. [48] *Ibid.*, p. 246.
16. [49] *Ibid.*, p. 215.
16. [50] *Ibid.*, p. 215.
17. [51] *Ibid.*, p. 215.
17. [52] *Ibid.*, p. 255.

Page

17.   [53] Gide, *Dostoievsky,* "D'Après sa Correspondance," p. 4.

17.   [54] *Letters,* v. II, pp. 23, 24.

18.   [55] In 1916 an article on the subject appeared in *Modern Philology*—see below pp. 101, 172-174.

18.   [56] V. 63, p. 70.

18.   [57] Tr. by H. Sutherland Edwards.

18.   [58] Published by Vizetelly.

18.   [59] *The Idiot: A Realistic Novel;* published by Vizetelly.

18.   [60] V. 11, p. 138.

18.   [61] V. 64, p. 457.

19.   [62] I (1887), p. 735.

19.   [63] V. 32, p. 214.

19.   [64] V. 10, p. 199.

19.   [65] I (1887), p. 573.

20.   [66] V. 60, p. 595.

20.   [67] V. 35 (n.s.), p. 297.

20.   [68] V. 63, p. 485.

20.   [69] V. 31, p. 270.

21.   [70] V. 51, p. 422.

21.   [71] II (1887), p. 534.

21.   [72] V. 60, p. 1575.

22.   [73] V. 36 (n.s.), p. 261.

22.   [74] V. 64, p. 563.

22.   [75] V. 128, p. 1056.

23.   [76] V. I, pp. 252-256.

23.   [77] V. 55, pp. 187-198.

25.   [78] To George Alison Armour, *Life and Letters,* p. 216.

25.   [79] V. 60, pp. 199-213.

25.   [80] See below, p. 33.

25.   [81] November 19, 1887.

26.   [82] V. 4, p. 21.

26.   [83] *The Critic,* v. 11, pp. 253-254.

26.   [84] V. 38 (n.s.), p. 74.

26.   [85] V. 66, p. 190.

26.   [86] V. 34, p. 68.

27.   [87] V. 70, pp. 55-73.

27.   [88] N. Tsakni, v. 53, p. 406.

27.   [89] V. 65, p. 740.

28.   [90] Gissing, *Letters to his Family,* October 6, 1888, p. 226.

28.   [91] *Ibid.,* July 31, 1886, p. 183.

28.   [92] See below, p. 41.

28.   [93] V. 8, pp. 465-467.

28.   [94] V. 1, p. 55.

28.   [95] *Modern Novels and Novelists,* pp. 120ff.

CHAPTER III

31.   [1] Pp. 301-336.

31.   [2] See above, p. 10.

32.   [3] V. 64, pp. 696, 697.

32.   [4] V. 37, p. 438.

Page
33.   [5] *Menschen und Werke,* Frankfurt, 1893.
33.   [6] *Literaturnie Harakteristiki,* 1903.
33.   [7] *Lectures on Russian Literature.*
33.   [8] V. 20, p. 415.
33.   [9] V. 52, p. 579.
33.   [10] See above, p. 9.
33.   [11] *The Modern Novelists of Russia.*
33.   [12] *Russia—its People and its Literature,* tr. by Fanny Hale Gardiner.
34.   [13] *Ibid.,* p. 193.
34.   [14] *Ibid.,* pp. 236, 251, 253, 245, 247.
34.   [15] *Modern Novelists of Russia,* p. 77.
34.   [16] *Ibid.,* p. 138.
34.   [17] V. 89, pp. 210-222. The article was signed "J. M." In 1898 it was
reprinted in *The Bookman,* ("The Dawn of the Russian Novel," v. 8, pp.
114-118) over the signature of "Melville Joyce."
34.   [18] V. 91, pp. 243-249.
35.   [19] *The Man of Genius,* pp. 8, 319, 321, 339-341.
35.   [20] *The New Spirit,* pp. 171, 172.
36.   [21] In *Criticism and Fiction.*
36.   [22] *Ibid.,* pp. 128, 129.
36.   [23] Tr. from the Russian by L. Milman.
36.   [24] As a matter of fact, George Moore seems to have been more sure of
his phrase than of his meaning; for he had originally applied this *bon mot*
to Tolstoy and not to Dostoevsky. See *The Fortnightly Review,* "Tur-
gueneff," v. 43 (n.s.), pp. 237-251, February, 1888: "An idea has been im_
provised . . . that he [Turgenev] is more western in form than his illustrious compeers Tolstoi and Dostoieffsky; but it would be hard to point
to a trace of this denaturalisation in his works. Tolstoi I have not read,
but he is only Gaboriau with psychological sauce, and that of an inferior
kind," p. 239.
37.   [25] V. 50 (n.s.), p. 196.
37.   [26] V. 142, p. 355.
37.   [27] V. 46, p. 209.
37.   [28] V. 59, pp. 181, 182.
37.   [29] Vol. 73, pp. 83, 84.
38.   [30] V. 6, pp. 309-312.
38.   [31] V. 144, pp. 539-544.
39.   [32] *Degeneration,* pp. 226, 331, 378, 379.
39.   [33] "Pessimism in the Russian Novel" from the *Nuova Antologia,* v. 22,
pp. 426-430.
39.   [34] V. 8, pp. 4779-4805.
39.   [35] From February 5, 1896-May 5, 1897, published in England two years
later as *Pictures of Russian History and Russian Literature.* About Wolkonsky, see Mirsky, *Contemporary Russian Literature,* pp. 300, 301.
40.   [36] *Pictures of Russian History and Russian Literature,* p. 248.
40.   [37] *Ibid.,* p. 257.
40.   [38] I (1898), 655.
41.   [39] *Charles Dickens: A Critical Study.*
41.   [40] See above, pp. 19, 20.
41.   [41] Gissing, *op. cit.,* pp. 284, 285, 291-294.
41.   [42] *The Forum,* v. 25, p. 758.
42.   [43] "Slavonic Silhouettes," v. 37, pp. 416-426.

Page

42.   [44] *A History of Russian Literature,* Ch. X, pp. 330-403.

42.   [45] V. 84, p. 421.

43.   [46] V. 61 (n.s.), p. 355.

43.   [47] Judah A. Joffe, v. 12, pp. 43-48, 376-378; Waliszewski, pp. 373-376.

43.   [48] V. 80, pp. 419-433.

44.   [49] *Fame and Fiction,* p. 225.

44.   [50] *Crime and Punishment: A Realistic Novel,* W. Scott, 1s.

44.   [51] See below, pp. 49-51.

44.   [52] V. 92, pp. 86, 88.

44.   [53] *A Survey of Russian Literature with Selections,* pp. 212-227.

44.   [54] II (1902), 24.

45.   [55] *Tolstoi as Man and Artist—With an Essay on Dostoievsky.*

45.   [56] *Ibid.,* p. 110.

46.   [57] *Ibid.,* pp. 117, 119, *et passim.*

46.   [58] *Ibid.,* pp. 240-248.

46.   [59] *Ibid.,* pp. 249-251.

46.   [60] *Ibid.,* pp. 251, 252.

47.   [61] *Ibid.,* p. 121.

47.   [62] I (1903), p. 238.

47.   [63] V. 63, p. 685.

48.   [64] V. 64, pp. 14, 15.

48.   [65] *Anthology of Russian Literature,* v. II, pp. 322-339.

48.   [66] V. 29, pp. 623, 624.

49.   [67] *The Puppett Show of Memory,* p. 261.

49.   [68] *Ibid.,* p. 293.

49.   [69] *Letters,* p. 49.

49.   [70] *The Feminine Note in Fiction,* p. 171.

49.   [71] When in 1914 the French dramatic version of *The Brothers Karamazov* by Jean Croué and Jacques Copeau was translated and acted in New York, *Current Opinion* wrote of it, in an elaborately illustrated review ("Dostoevsky in a Drama," v. 64, pp. 179-183), that "as more than one New York critic" had noted, it was "one of the few truly memorable plays presented in New York for several seasons"; that James Huneker had declared it "the most noteworthy play ever created out of a Dostoevsky novel" even though it lacked "the intense Muscovite coloring" of the version "presented twelve or thirteen years ago in New York by the late Paul Orlenev, with the now famous Alla Nazimova as Grushenka."

49.   [72] See *Acad.* 68: 656; *Ath.* 1905, 2: 70; *Critic* 47: 185; *Dial* 39: 19; *Independent* 59: 638; *Lond. Times,* 4: 150; *Nation,* 80: 526; *Sat. Rev.,* 99: 774.

49.   [73] *Ideals and Realities,* pp. 163-170.

49.   [74] *Ibid.,* "He died in 1883," p. 164.

50.   [75] *Ibid.,* p. 169.

51.   [76] V. 71, pp. 202, 203.

52.   [77] Pp. 389, 390.

52.   [78] V. 94, pp. 270-285.

52.   [79] V. 183, pp. 305-307.

53.   [80] I (1908), p. 99.

53.   [81] Tr. by H. Haveloc.

53.   [82] V. 88, p. 630.

53.   [83] V. 75, p. 39.

53.   [84] Chapter 14, pp. 390-416.

Page

54.   [85] V. 2, pp. 215-230, reprinted in *Living Age*, v. 261, pp. 738-748.

54.   [86] V. 211, pp. 180-202.

55.   [87] Chapter 6, pp. 125-262.

55.   [88] V. 7, pp. 25, 26.

55.   [89] V. 104, pp. 629, 630.

55.   [90] I (1910), 339, 340.

55.   [91] V. 76, p. 134.

56.   [92] *Contemporary Review*, v. 97, p. 577.

56.   [93] V. 49, p. 93.

56.   [94] *Letters*, April 24, 1910, p. 177.

56.   [95] *Ibid.*, May 1, 1910, p. 178; May 12, 1910, p. 179.

56.   [96] V. 97, *Literary Supplement*, 32, pp. 1-4.

57.   [97] V. 6 (n.s.), pp. 518, 519.

58.   [98] II (1910), 635, 636.

58.   [99] *Crime and Punishment*, introduction pp. vii-xiii.

59.   [100] *Essays on Russian Novelists*, pp. 130-169.

59.   [101] V. 9, pp. 823-837.

61.   [102] *The Russian People*.

61.   [103] *Ibid.*, pp. 265, 272, 278, 279.

CHAPTER IV

62.   [1] *Literary Supplement*, July 4, pp. 269, 270.

62.   [2] V. 109, pp. 451, 452.

62.   [3] Preface to *The Brothers Karamazov*, Limited Editions Club.

66.   [4] *Literary Supplement*, July 4, p. 269.

66.   [5] *Literary World*, v. 78, p. 277.

68.   [6] *Athenaeum*, I (1912), 613, 614, *Times Literary Supplement, Spectator, Literary World*.

68.   [7] V. 83, p. 448.

68   [8] Of translations other than Constance Garnett's there were *A Christmas Tree and a Wedding* and *An Honest Thief*, prepared by Nevill Forbes for the "Oxford Russian Plain Texts," 1917; and part of *The Journal of an Author*, translated by S. S. Koteliansky and J. Middleton Murry, 1916.

69.   [9] *Independent*, v. 76, p. 177.

69.   [10] *Nation*, v. 13, p. 575; *Athenaeum*, II (1913), 61.

69.   [11] *Spectator*, v. 112, pp. 610, 611.

69.   [12] V. 13, pp. 575, 576.

69.   [13] *New Statesman*, v. 2, p. 796.

69.   [14] I (1914), 89.

70.   [15] V. 14, p. 758.

70.   [16] *Literary World*, v. 81, p. 54.

70.   [17] *Literary Supplement*, March 4, 1915, p. 73.

70.   [18] *Saturday Review*, v. 123, p. 343; See also *Independent*, v. 93, p. 150.

70.   [19] *Literary Supplement*, February 22, 1917, p. 91. *The Gambler, etc.*, was briefly noticed in *Saturday Review*, v. 124, p. 311, and *The Outlook*, v. 117, p. 614.

70.   [20] *Literary Supplement*, October 17, 1918, p. 494; See also *Dial*, v. 65, p. 510.

71.   [21] *Literary Supplement*, October 23, 1919, p. 586.

71.   [22] V. 19, pp. 183-185; See also *Saturday Review*, v. 121, pp. 259, 260.

71.   [23] 1916, p. 187.

Page

71.   [24] V. 117, p. 241.
71.   [25] *Literary Supplement,* March 9, 1916, p. 114.
72.   [26] V. 120, pp. 306, 307.
72.   [27] II (1915), 190.
72.   [28] *Literary Supplement,* September 23, 1915, p. 319.
73.   [29] *Letters,* May 27, 1912, pp. 240, 241.
73.   [30] *Letters,* May 19, 1912, v. 2, p. 237.
74.   [31] *Letters,* April 15, 1914, p. 217.
74.   [32] *Letters,* April 3, 1912, p. 32.
74.   [33] *Letters,* April 13, 1914, p. 219.
74.   [34] *Letters,* June 5, 1914, pp. 199, 200.
75.   [35] *Letters,* p. 241, no date.
75.   [36] *Ibid.,* p. 242, no date.
75.   [37] *Ibid.,* February 1, 1916, pp. 317, 318.
75.   [38] *Ibid.,* February 17, 1916, pp. 329-331.
75.   [39] *Ibid.,* August 28, 1916, pp. 368, 369.
75.   [40] *Ibid.,* December 2, 1916, pp. 387, 388.
75.   [41] *Studies in Classical American Literature,* p. 3.
75.   [42] "Fate and the Younger Generation."
75.   [43] See below, pp. 139, 140.
77.   [44] *Between Two Worlds,* pp. 368, 369, 424.
78.   [45] *Dostoevsky,* p. 28.
79.   [46] *Ibid.,* p. 33.
79.   [47] *Ibid.,* p. 35.
79.   [48] *Between Two Worlds,* p. 213
79.   [49] *Dostoevsky,* p. 36.
80.   [50] *Ibid.,* p. 41.
80.   [51] *Ibid.,* p. 219.
80.   [52] *Ibid.,* pp. 55, 200.
81.   [53] *Ibid.,* pp. 152, 153, 160, 161, 250.
81.   [54] *Ibid.,* pp. 247-249.
82.   [55] *Ibid.,* p. 228.
82.   [56] *Ibid.,* p. 200. Other comments by Murry on Dostoevsky occur in his *The Evolution of an Intellectual,* pp. 42-45, *et passim.*
82.   [57] *Between Two Worlds.*
82.   [58] By D. S. Mirsky, see below, p. 118.
82.   [59] V. 23, p. 287.
82.   [60] 1916, p. 430.
82.   [61] V. 7, pp. 518, 519.
82.   [62] *Literary Supplement,* August 24, 1916, p. 403.
84.   [63] V. 92, pp. 126-137.
84.   [64] Reprinted *Living Age,* v. 289, pp. 436-438. The Encyclopedia to which Seccombe referred must have been the eleventh edition of *The Britannica,* where the article on Dostoevsky is by him.
84.   [65] Charles Gray Shaw, v. 207, pp. 245-256.
85.   [66] V. 38, pp. 94-116.
85.   [67] V. 86, p. 11.
85.   [68] *New Age,* v. 21, p. 254.
85.   [69] *Ibid.,* p. 69.
85.   [70] Paul Vinogradoff, *Quarterly Review,* v. 228, p. 199.
85.   [71] Z. N. Preev, *Fortnightly Review,* v. 107, p. 607.
85.   [72] *New Statesman,* v. 9, pp. 590, 591.

Page

86.   [73] V. 3, pp. 115-118.
86.   [74] *A Guide to Russian Literature,* p. 103.
86.   [75] *Ibid.,* pp. 104-109.
86.   [76] *Dial,* v. 63, pp. 24, 25.
87.   [77] V. 20, pp. 60, 61.
87.   [78] *Letters,* June 15, 1914, p. 169.
88.   [79] *Ibid.,* pp. 170, 171.
88.   [80] *Ibid.,* p. 170.
88.   [81] *Ibid.,* pp. 189, 192.
88.   [82] "Dostoevsky and Tolstoy, and the Younger Choir of Russian Writers," pp. 52-88; an essay on Moussorgsky in the same collection contained references to Dostoevsky.
89.   [83] *Ivory Apes and Peacocks,* pp. 196, 197.
89.   [84] *Letters,* April 17, 1913, p. 120; June 11, 1913, p. 127.
89.   [85] *Landmarks in Russian Literature,* see above, pp. 55-57.
89.   [86] See above, p. 49.
89.   [87] Pp. 157, 160, 161.
89.   [88] Also in 1912 Merezhkovsky's essay on Tolstoy and Dostoevsky came out in a new edition; in 1913 appeared a new translation of Vogüé's *Le roman russe;* and in 1916 a "revised and rewritten" edition of Kropotkin's *Ideals and Realities in Russian Literature.*
89.   [89] V. 113, p. 753.
90.   [90] Lloyd, *A Great Russian Realist,* pp. 16, 30, 32, 38, 39, 114, 115, 173, 174.
91.   [91] *Ibid.,* pp. 132-134, 139, 144, 249-251, 258, 259.
91.   [92] *Ibid.,* pp. 79, 249-251, 258, 259, 286-288.
91.   [93] *Literary Supplement,* July 4.
91.   [94] V. 113, p. 753. Cf. n. 89 above.
92.   [95] V. 11, p. 96.
92.   [96] V. 78, p. 140.
92.   [97] *Fortnightly Review,* v. 114, pp. 854-864.
93.   [98] *Dostoevsky,* p. vi.
93.   [99] *Dostoievsky, his Life and Literary Activity.*
93.   [100] D. S. Mirsky, *Contemporary Russian Literature,* p. 323.
93.   [101] *Athenaeum,* 1916, p. 85.
93.   [102] "Dostoeivsky," p. 226.
93.   [103] *Ibid.,* p. 228.
93.   [104] *Ibid.,* p. 24.
93.   [105] *Ibid.,* pp. 33, 34, 235. For example: "Dostoevsky while denying Epicurism, Materialism, Socialism, and the rest, saw in life chiefly a moral and religious problem, and in its solution—that is to say, in the pursuit of faith in God and of personal self-improvement—the principal task of man on earth. Thus Dostoevsky's view of life was remarkable for its rigour and its own peculiar gloom"; or, "Everything individual, personal, or arbitrary was wrong. . . . He disliked and denounced personal will, all personal striving for happiness and satisfaction."
93.   [106] *Letters,* March 20, 1916, p. 205. Murry's book had not yet appeared. According to *The Spectator* (v. 117, p. 241), the book was "interesting," "short but pleasantly written" with "all the information that ordinary English readers of Dostoevsky" were "likely to need." In *The Athenaeum* (1916, p. 85) it was noticed as "simple" in treatment, but "just and convincing" in its criticism. It was described in *The English Review,* how-

Page

ever (v. 23, p. 94), as "singularly incomplete and uninteresting," "at times . . . irritatingly personal"; and in *The New Age* (v. 18, p. 372) as throwing no new light on Dostoevsky's psychological and intellectual life. Thomas Seccombe in *The New Witness* (reprinted *Living Age*, v. 289, pp. 436-438) wrote that it was "too Russian . . . to please us altogether—too Slavonic, too nebulous, too sketchy"; that one could not "get a good bite at it."

94.   [107] *Letters to his Family and Friends*, tr. Ethel Colburn Mayne.

94.   [108] V. 80, p. 309.

94.   [109] V. 16, pp. 146, 148.

94.   [110] J. C. Squire, v. 4, p. 62.

94.   [111] V. 58, p. 48.

94.   [112] V. 113, pp. 596, 597.

94.   [113] *Literary Supplement*, October 29, 1914, p. 478.

95.   [114] According to E. H. Wilcox in *The Fortnightly Review*, v. 115, pp. 229-239.

95.   [115] *Fyodor Dostoyevsky*, pp. 52ff.

95.   [116] V. 30, pp. 505-507.

95.   [117] *London Mercury*, v. 5, p. 551.

96.   [118] V. 128, p. 115.

96.   [119] V. 18, p. 326.

96.   [120] *Literary Supplement*, January 12, 1922, p. 25. Four years later *The London Mercury*, v. 12, p. 563, reprinted from *The Times* the following notice written by Hugh Walpole:

"Owing to the Russian Revolution, Mlle. Aimée Dostoevski, only surviving member of the Dostoevski family has been left entirely without resources. As Russia did not enter the Copyright Convention, the Dostoevski family has never received a penny from the numerous translations of his works now circulating in Europe and America.

"Some two years ago a small fund was started in Switzerland by various friends and admirers of Mlle. Dostoevsky and administered by a bank in Vevey. By this means she was provided with a small monthly pension—just enough to live on. Unluckily, towards the end of last summer she became seriously ill, and had to be removed to a clinique at Nice, where she was obliged to have special treatment. She is still suffering and weak, and requires great care. The monthly pension had to be doubled, and now by August the fund will be entirely exhausted. The smallest sums contributed to this fund, addressed: 'Dostoevski Fund' c/o Comtoi d'escompte de Genève, Rue du Simplon, Vevey, will be thankfully received and acknowledged.

"There are tens of thousands of people in this country and America who have read *Crime and Punishment*, *The Brothers Karamazoff*, and *The Idiot*, and have found in them not only aesthetic pleasure but spiritual inspiration. There are also publishers, booksellers, papermakers, binders and translators who have made money out of them. Yet, owing to the mere fact that Russia never entered the Berne Convention Dostoevski's heirs are no better off than they would have been had the world completely ignored him."

96.   [121] *The Freeman*, v. 1, pp. 35-39; same, *London Mercury*, v. 1, pp. 428-430.

96.   [122] V. 22, pp. 229-230, 252-254, 272-273, 288-290, 312-314, 327-329, 354-356, 372-374, 389-390, 410-412. They were entitled: "Dostoevsky and

Page

Modern Art," "The Struggle for an Absolute Value," "The Cosmic Mutiny," "The Struggle with the Void (the Riddle of Nikolay Stravrogin)," "The Bankruptcy of 'Superman' (the tragedy of Raskolnikov)," "The 'Two Abysses' (the tragedy of Ivan Karamzov)," "The 'Russian Idea,'" and "Dostoevsky and his Significance."

98. [123] V. 22, pp. 449-451.
98. [124] *Ibid.*, p. 451.
98. [125] *Ibid.*, pp. 465, 466.
98. [126] *Ibid.*, p. 497.
98. [127] *New Age*, v. 23, pp. 7, 8.
98. [128] *Literary Supplement*, December 9, 1920, p. 811.
98. [129] II (1920), 758.
99. [130] V. 32, pp. 557, 558.
99. [131] *Latitudes*, pp. 57-67.
99. [132] Pp. 104-114.
100. [133] G. Katz, v. 180, pp. 627-634.
100. [134] V. 32, pp. 390-407.
100. [135] V. 1, pp. 38-59.
100. [136] *Prophets of Dissent*, pp. 164, 165.
101. [137] V. 66, p. 116.
101. [138] *Literature in a Changing Age*, p. 124.
101. [139] V. 14, pp. 449-454.
101. [140] See above, pp. 17, 18.
101. [141] See also below, pp. 172-174.
101. [142] *A Novelist on Novels*, pp. 119-124.
102. [143] V. 55, pp. 433, 434.
102. [144] *Prophets of Dissent*, p. 164.
102. [145] *The Dial*, v. 58, pp. 5-7.
103. [146] II (1914), 663, 664.
103. [147] It is to this period that Mackail's pamphlet, mentioned above, belongs.
103. [148] V. 118, pp. 419, 420.
103. [149] V. 13, pp. 648-661.
104. [150] See V. 1, p. 197, n. 1.
104. [151] *The Spirit of Russia*, v. 1, pp. vii, xviii.
104. [152] *Ibid.*, v. 2, pp. 467, 565.
105. [153] *Ibid.*, v. 1, pp. 160, 198, 320, 330; v. 2, pp. 59 n., 73, 105, 199, 200, 288, 474.
105. [154] See e.g., *Nation*, v. 25, pp. 650, 652; *Contemporary Review*, v. 116, p. 346.
105. [155] *Contemporary Review*, v. 108, pp. 220-229. Same, *Living Age*, v. 286, pp. 665-672.
106. [156] *London Quarterly Review*, v. 125, pp. 177-188.
106. [157] *Contemporary Review*, v. 113, pp. 695-700.
106. [158] V. 113, pp. 361-368.
107. [159] *Letters*, v. 1, March 13, 1918, p. 154.
107. [160] *Ibid.*, June 3, 1918, p. 190.
107. [161] *Ibid.*, November 4, 1919, pp. 274, 275; see also August 1917, p. 77.
107. [162] II (1919), 1256. Six years later much of this essay was reproduced *verbatim*, without acknowledgment, in an article by C. Williams, "The Ethics of Three Russian Novelists," *International Journal of Ethics*, v. 35, pp. 217-237.

Page

107.   [163] *Letters*, v. 1, November 10, 1919, p. 278.
108.   [104] *Ibid., December* 13, 1919, pp. 313, 314.
108.   [165] V. 116, pp. 1017-1026.
108.   [166] In *A Great Russian Realist*, see above, p. 90.
109.   [167] November 11, 1921, p. 9d.
109.   [168] Nellie B. Bennett, v. 105, pp. 906-916.
109.   [169] Shakhnovski, *A Short History of Russian Literature*, pp. 143-147.
109.   [170] *Quarterly Review*, v. 235, p. 114.
109.   [171] *Dostoievsky—A Study in his Ideology.*
109.   [172] *Le roman anglais de notre temps*, p. 204.
109.   [173] *The Craft of Fiction*, pp. 46, 47, 119, 144, 151.
110.   [174] See *Spectator*, v. 126, pp. 305, 306.

CHAPTER V

111.   [1] *The Life of a Great Sinner* first appeared in *The Criterion* for October 1922, v. 1, pp. 16-33, then in book form together with *Stavrogin's Confession*, with introductory and explanatory notes. Prefatory notices had appeared in *The Times*, January 13, 1922, p. 14d, February 22, p. 11, June 16, p. 16c. See also *The London Mercury*, "Literary Intelligence," v. 7, p. 5. *The Legend of the Grand Inquisitor* was translated by S. S. Koteliansky, published in *The New Age*, October and November 1925, and separately in 1930, with an introduction by D. H. Lawrence. In 1931 *A Gentle Spirit* appeared in a handsome edition; it was very unsympathetically reviewed in *The Times Literary Supplement*, February 4, 1932, p. 72. There was a "de luxe" American edition of *The Brothers Karamazov* (Limited Editions Club) in 1933, revised and introduced by Avrahm Yarmolinsky, with "eighteen portrait illustrations" by Alexander King. A section of "Winter Notes on my Summer Impressions," translated by R. Gill, was published in *The European Quarterly*, v. 1 (1934), 77-87; and a recently discovered sketch, "Vlas," in *The Slavonic Review*, v. 15, pp. 1-13.

111.   [2] *Letters and Reminiscences*, tr. Koteliansky and Murry, 1923. Two of the letters in this collection appeared a month before its publication in *The Criterion*, April 1923, v. 1, pp. 217-226. *New Dostoevsky Letters*, tr. Koteliansky, 1929. *Dostoevsky's Letters to his Wife*, tr. Hill and Mudie, Introduction by D. S. Mirsky, 1930. A letter to Appollinaria Souslova was published in *The Calendar of Modern Letters*, March 1925, v. 1, pp. 44-52. In 1926 some unpublished letters of Dostoevsky, written during 1879-1881 about *The Brothers Karamazov* to N. A. Liubinov, associate editor of *Russky Vestnik*, the journal where the novel was appearing, came out translated and edited by Koteliansky in *The New Criterion*, v. 4, pp. 552-562 and in *The Virginia Quarterly Review*, v. 2, pp. 375-384. *The Contemporary Review*, February 1926, v. 129, pp. 211-216, published Dostoevsky's letter to his brother Michael, written December 22, 1849, "a few hours after his return from the scaffold to the fortress."

111.   [3] *Dostoevsky Portrayed by his Wife*, tr. Koteliansky. *The Diary of Dostoevsky's Wife*, tr. M. Pemberton. By way of introducing the diary *The Nation and Athenaeum* reprinted an incident from it several months before its publication. See "A Practical Joke," v. 38, p. 551.

111.   [4] *New Statesman*, v. 21, pp. 682, 684.

111.   [5] Leonard Woolf in *The Nation and Athenaeum*, v. 46, p. 318.

111.   [6] *New Age*, v. 39, pp. 25, 26.

Page

111.   [7] *Times Literary Supplement,* March 25, 1926, p. 232. See also *The Times,* November 13, 1928, p. 22b.

111.   [8] *Ibid.,* December 20, 1928, pp. 997, 998. See also *Times,* November 13, 1928, p. 22b, *Spectator,* v. 141, pp. 823, 824, *Fortnightly Review,* v. 130, pp. 859, 860, John Freeman, "The Wives of the Russians," *London Mercury,* v. 19, pp. 176-183.

112.   [9] D. S. Mirsky in *London Mercury,* v. 14, p. 542.

112.   [10] *Spectator,* v. 130, pp. 1045, 1046.

112.   [11] V. 134, p. 792.

112.   [12] *Spring Book Supplement,* v. 20, pp. viii, x.

112.   [13] Richard Church, *Spectator,* v. 144, p. 95.

112.   [14] *Nation and Athenaeum,* v. 46, p. 808.

112.   [15] *Saturday Review,* v. 149, p. 170, *London Mercury,* v. 21, p. 378. See also *New Statesman,* v. 34, p. 504.

112.   [16] D. S. Mirsky, Introduction to *Dostoevsky's Letters to his Wife,* p. xii.

112.   [17] *New Age,* v. 44, p. 54.

113.   [18] *Nation and Athenaeum,* v. 44, p. 294, *Ibid.,* v. 46, p. 318. (See note 5 above.)

113.   [19] December 20, 1928. (See note 8 above.)

113.   [20] *Literary Supplement,* November 2, 1922, p. 702.

113.   [21] *Nation and Athenaeum,* v. 32, pp. 357, 358.

113.   [22] *London Mercury,* v. 8, p. 211. See also a review in *The New Age,* v. 32, pp. 78, 79.

113.   [23] V. 1, pp. 44-52.

113.   [24] V. 65, pp. 730-738.

113.   [25] V. 132, pp. 525-533.

113.   [26] *Slavonic Review,* v. 8, pp. 156-163.

114.   [27] *Ibid.,* v. 9, pp. 753, 754.

114.   [28] Clarence A. Manning, *Sewanee Review,* v. 33, pp. 134-148; Anton Florovsky, *Slavonic Review,* v. 9, pp. 411-423.

114.   [29] Arthur McDowall, *London Mercury,* v. 17, pp. 52-61; D. S. Mirsky, *London Mercury,* v. 5, p. 282.

114.   [30] Clarence A. Manning, *Sewanee Review,* v. 30, pp. 286-297; D. S. Mirsky, *Contemporary Review,* v. 122, pp. 205-211.

114.   [31] M. Schwartz, *The Jewish Review,* # 4, 1933, pp. 57-63.

114.   [32] Summarized by Richard Montgomery, *New Age,* v. 40, p. 54.

115.   [33] V. 1, pt. 2, pp. 18-33.

115.   [34] V. 45, pp. 115, 116.

116.   [35] V. 17, pp. 195-207.

116.   [36] *Slavonic Review,* v. 9, pp. 424-431.

116.   [37] V. 4, pp. 12, 13. This poem is reprinted by permission of the author and of Matthew Josephson, assistant editor of *Broom.*

117.   [38] V. 19, p. 466.

117.   [39] Pp. 169ff.

118.   [40] Preface.

119.   [41] *Dostoevsky,* pp. 5, 20, 37, 45, 82, 121, etc.

119.   [42] *Ibid.,* p. 59.

120.   [43] *Ibid.,* pp. 13, 16, 19-27, 35, 88, 119, 193, 210, 255, 257, 259, etc.

120.   [44] *Ibid.,* pp. 75-79, 125-131, 131-135.

120.   [45] *Ibid.,* pp. 188ff., 203ff.

120.   [46] V. 25, p. 310.

120.   [47] Richard Church, v. 147, pp. 548, 549.

Page

120.   [48] Richard Church, v. 2, *Christmas Supplement*, pp. xiv, xvi.

120.   [49] See note 46 above.

120.   [50] October 8, 1931, p. 773.

121.   [51] *Dostoevsky*, pp. 85, 91, 202ff., 19, etc.

121.   [52] *Ibid.*, pp. 5-36.

121.   [53] *Ibid.*, p. 162.

122.   [54] *Ibid.*, pp. 415ff.

122.   [55] *Ibid.*, pp. 60-62, etc.

122.   [56] *Ibid.*, pp. 193, 221, 164, 266, 390, 391.

122.   [57] Carr, *Dostoevsky*, p. 29.

123.   [58] Yarmolinsky, Dostoevsky, p. 49.

123.   [59] *Ibid.*, "Life after Death," pp. 401ff.

123.   [60] *Dead Reckonings in Fiction*, Chapters VI-VII, "The Myth of Abnormality," pp. 129-175. The chapters appeared again, slightly modified, in a new volume on fiction by the same authors in 1934, *Modern Fiction*, pp. 40-64.

124.   [61] V. 35, pp. 108-120, 190-196.

124.   [62] V. 72, pp. 607-618; v. 73, pp. 199-204.

125.   [63] In *Three Masters*, pp. 99-234.

126.   [64] *Dostoievsky—an Interpretation*.

126.   [65] *Ibid.*, p. 8.

127.   [66] *Ibid.*, pp. 39, 48, 49.

127.   [67] *Ibid.*, pp. 21, 61, 133, 135, 68, 26, 161.

128.   [68] *The Decline of the West*, tr. C. F. Atkinson.

128.   [69] *Ibid.*, II, pp. 193-196, 218.

129.   [70] *Ibid.*, p. 295n.

129.   [71] *Dostoevsky—The Man and his Work*.

129.   [72] *Ibid.*, p. 378.

129.   [73] *Ibid.*, pp. 147-206.

129.   [74] *Ibid.*, pp. 288-377.

129.   [75] *Ibid.*, pp. 7, 8.

129.   [76] *Ibid.*, pp. 9, 11-20.

130.   [77] *Ibid.*, pp. 30, 32, 33, 62, *et passim*.

130.   [78] *Nation and Athenaeum*, v. 42, pp. 972, 974.

130.   [79] V. 30, p. 660.

131.   [80] V. 18, p. 214.

131.   [81] *Literary Supplement*, March 22, 1928, p. 211. The book was liked, however, by Alan Porter who thought that despite its often irritating style, jerky, with "small spurts of eloquence" it was "full of enthusiasm and intelligence," indeed, "admirable," in its discussion of the novels. See *Spectator*, v. 140, pp. 385, 386.

131.   [82] *Literary Supplement*, January 26, 1930, p. 530.

131.   [83] V. 153, p. 684.

132.   [84] January 3, 1935, p. 7.

132.   [85] See above, pp. 112, 118.

132.   [86] "The Early Work of Dostoevsky," pp. 220-225; "Dostoevsky (after 1849)," pp. 340-358.

133.   [87] *Russia, a Social History*, p. 271.

134.   [88] Originally the "Clark Lectures which were delivered under the auspices of Trinity College, Cambridge, in the spring of 1927." See pp. 18, 117, 184ff., 192-195, 197-198.

135.   [89] Pp. 243-256.

Page
136.   [90] *Dostoevsky.* Introduction by Arnold Bennett.
136.   [91] *Ibid.,* p. 45.
136.   [92] *Ibid.,* pp. vi-viii.
137.   [93] *Ibid.,* p. 170.
137.   [94] *Ibid.,* pp. 4, 5, 38.
137.   [95] *Ibid.,* p. 115.
137.   [96] *Ibid.,* p. 97.
138.   [97] *Ibid.,* pp. 146, 160, 161.
138.   [98] *Ibid.,* pp. 8-44, 74.
138.   [99] V. 13, pp. 659, 660.
138.   [100] V. 243, p. 199.
138.   [101] *Life and Letters,* August 22, 1926, p. 494.
139.   [102] *Three Essays,* pp. 3-140.
139.   [103] Reviewed in *Times Literary Supplement,* September 11, 1930, p. 712.
A letter from the publishers gives the date of Lawrence's Introduction as
"The latter part of January of this year," *Ibid.,* September 18, 1930, p. 735.
140.   [104] In 1916 some of his essays were translated by S. S. Koteliansky and
Middleton Murry, *Anton Tchehov and other Essays,* published also in
1917 in New York as *Penultimate Words;* and in 1920 a short philosophic
work by him, *All Things Are Possible,* appeared in an English version
by S. S. Koteliansky with a very unappreciative foreword by D. H.
Lawrence.
140.   [105] Published in Berlin 1922, tr. into German 1924.
140.   [106] "The Conquest of the Self-Evident, Dostoievsky's Philosophy," pp.
3-82.
143.   [107] *The Mighty Three,* pp. 191-295. See a review of his work, *Slavonic
Review,* v. 15, p. 232.
143.   [108] Smith and Isotoff, v. 22, #4, pp. 361-391.
143.   [109] *The Structure of the Novel,* pp. 73-80.
144.   [110] *The Twentieth Century Novel,* pp. 94-102; 155-163. Another study
of Dostoevsky's Technique was published in *The University of California Chronicle,* April 1931: Alice McCune, v. 33, pp. 221-230.
145.   [111] V. 5, pp. 609-627. Reprinted in *Studies in European Literature,* pp.
193-222.
145.   [112] V. 37, pp. 478-489; Léon Pierre-Quint, whose study of Gide was
translated into English by Dorothy Richardson in 1934, emphasizes repeatedly Dostoevsky's influence. See *André Gide,* pp. 50, 129, *et passim.*
146.   [113] Translated by Rosalind Ivan.
146.   [114] V. 44, p. 141.
146.   [115] October 16, 1928, p. 14c.
147.   [116] Desmond McCarthy, *New Statesman,* v. 27, pp. 672, 673.
147.   [117] V. 137, p. 342.
147.   [118] August 24, 1926, p. 8.
147.   [119] V. 58, p. 193.
147.   [120] V. 14, p. 644.
147.   [121] V. 43, p. 470.
147.   [122] Desmond McCarthy, see note 116 above.
147.   [123] *Problems of Soviet Literature.*
147.   [124] See, *e.g. Burton Rascoe, Titans of Literature,* pp. 404, 405.
147.   [125] *Problems of Soviet Literature,* pp. 27-69.
148.   [126] *Ibid.,* p. 45.
148.   [127] *Ibid.,* p. 46.

Page

148.   [128] *Ibid.*, p. 47.
149.   [129] *Ibid.*, "Contemporary World Literature and the Tasks of Proletarian Art," p. 152.
149.   [130] V. 117, p. 228.
149.   [131] V. 147, pp. 401-405.
149.   [132] Chapter IX, pp. 47ff.
150.   [133] *Scheherezade or The Future of the Novel*, pp. 51, 54-56, 61, 68.
150.   [134] Pp. 10, 12, 27, 28.
150.   [135] P. 107.
151.   [136] Marrot, *Life and Letters of J. Galsworthy*, August 26, 1932, p. 804.
151.   [137] Translation by Angus Davidson of *La carne, la morte e il diavolo nella letteratura romantica*, pp. 166 n16, 278 n50, 322, 355, 356, 366, 368, 402 n82.
152.   [138] Pp. 23, 24, 94-104. William Chislett, Jr., discussing modern literature, cited Robert Herrick as having changed from an admiration of French models to the Russian, and quoted, in this connection, a comment of his on Mrs. Wharton, that she had "formed her method on the approved tradition of French fiction . . . rather than on the richer if less aesthetically satisfying tradition of English and Russian fiction, of Fielding and Thackeray, of Tolstoy and Dostoevsky," *Moderns and Near-Moderns*, pp. 119, 120.
153.   [139] June 5, 1930, pp. 465, 466.
155.   [140] See also *Times Literary Supplement* review of two studies of Dostoevsky by the Russian scholar Leonid Grossman, February 3, 1931, p. 94.

CHAPTER VI

156.   [1] Schiller, *Literatura i Marxism*, v. 5, p. 95, see above, p. 2.
157.   [2] *Le roman expérimental*, 1887.
158.   [3] *The Scottish Review*, v. 2, pp. 301-334.
158.   [4] *Blackwood's Magazine*, v. 133, p. 423. See also Egerton, "The Scientific Novel and Gustave Flaubert," *The National Review*, v. 1, p. 907.
158.   [5] *Locksley Hall Sixty Years After*.
159.   [6] See, *e.g.*, Tilley, "The New School of Fiction," *National Review*, v. 1, p. 264.
159.   [7] *Atlantic Monthly*, v. 92, pp. 193-210, reprinted in *Notes on Novelists*.
159.   [8] "The Limits of Realism in Fiction," *The Forum*, v. 9, pp. 391-400.
159.   [9] *The Idea of Tragedy*, p. 127.
159.   [10] *The Forum*, v. 2, p. 619.
160.   [11] *Contemporary Review* (May 10, 1910), v. 97, p. 576.
161.   [12] So, Edmund Gosse, *Forum* (June 1890), v. 9, p. 392. "Ten years ago the realistic novel . . . was just beginning to be talked about." See also *Martino, Le roman réaliste sous le Second Empire*.
162.   [13] Whistler's "Ten O'Clock" lecture was delivered in 1885 and published in 1890 in *The Gentle Art of Making Enemies*, Oscar Wilde's "The Decay of Lying" and "The Critic as Artist" came out in 1889 and 1890, *The Yellow Book* and *The Savoy* were published from 1892-1896. The movement has been studied by A. J. Farmer, *Le mouvement esthétique et décadent en Anglettere;* by Louise Rosenblatt, *L'idée de l'art pour l'art dans la littérature anglaise;* by Rose Frances Egan, *The Genesis of the Theory of 'art for art's sake' in Germany and England*.
163.   [14] Brandes, *Friedrich Nietzsche*, p. 103.
163.   [15] To Nietzsche May 23, 1888. *Ibid.*, pp. 86, 87.

163.   [16] *Ibid.*, p. 3n.
164.   [17] *Ibid.*, pp. 104, 105.
Page
164.   [18] The phrase is Thomas Hardy's—*The Early Life of Thomas Hardy,* p. 201.
165.   [19] Edward Garnett, *Academy,* v. 71, pp. 202, 203. See above, p. 51.
165.   [20] About Shestov, see Mirsky, *Contemporary Russian Literature,* pp. 172-175.
167.   [21] *The Symbolist Movement in Literature,* revised ed. 1919, "Introduction," p. 8.
168.   [22] Edmund Wilson, *Axel's Castle,* p. 19.
171.   [23] *Dostojewskij's Einfluss auf den englischen Roman.*
172.   [24] "The Lantern-Bearers" in *Across the Plains.*
172.   [25] "Stevenson and Dostoevski"—see above, p. 101.
174.   [26] *Avowals,* p. 146.
174.   [27] P. 145.
175.   [28] *New York Times,* March 21, 1937.
176.   [29] *A History of Russian Literature,* p. 356.
177.   [30] *Dostoevsky,* p. 403.

BIBLIOGRAPHY

I. BOOKS

Aliotta, Antonio, *The Idealistic Reaction against Science,* tr. by Agnes McCaskill, London, 1914.

Baring, Maurice, *Landmarks in Russian Literature,* London, 1910.

———, *The Mainsprings of Russia,* London, 1914.

———, *The Puppet Show of Memory,* London, 1922.

———, *The Russian People,* London, 1911.

Beach, Joseph Warren, *The Twentieth Century Novel—Studies in Technique,* New York and London, 1932.

Bennett, Arnold, *Books and Persons,* London, 1917.

———, *Fame and Fiction (An Inquiry into Certain Popularities),* London, 1901.

Berdyaev, Nicholas, *Dostoievsky—An Interpretation,* tr. by Donald Attwater, New York, 1934.

Brandes, Georg, *Friedrich Nietzsche,* tr. by A. G. Chater, London, 1914.

———, *Impressions of Russia, tr.* by Samuel C. Eastman, New York, 1889.

Brasol, Boris, *The Mighty Three—(Poushkin, Gogol, Dostoievsky).* Introd. by Prof. Clarence A. Manning, New York, 1934.

Brewster, Dorothy and Burrell, Angus, *Dead Reckonings in Fiction,* New York, 1925.

———, *Modern Fiction,* New York, 1934.

Brückner, A., *A Literary History of Russia,* tr. by H. Haveloc, "The Library of Literary History," London and Leipsic, 1908.

Carr, Edward Hallett, *Dostoevsky, A New Biography,* Preface by D. S. Mirsky, Boston and New York, 1931.

Carruthers, John (pseud.); John Young Thomas Greig, *Scheherezade, or the Future of the English Novel,* "To-day and To-morrow Series," London, 1927.

Chevalley, Abel, *Le roman anglais de notre temps,* Londres, 1921.

Chislett, Wm., Jr., *Moderns and Near Moderns,* New York, 1928.

Clutton-Brock, A., *Essays on Books,* London, 1920.

Conrad, Joseph, *Letters from Joseph Conrad, 1895-1924,* Introd. and notes by Edward Garnett, Indianapolis, 1928.

Courtney, W. L., *The Feminine Note in Fiction,* London, 1904.

———, *The Idea of Tragedy,* London, 1900.

Cowley, Malcolm, *Exile's Return, A Narrative of Ideas*, New York, 1934.

Cunliffe, J. W., *English Literature During the Last Half Century*, New York, 1919.

Dostoyevsky, Aimée, *Fyodor Dostoyevsky, A Study*, London, 1921.

Dupuy, Ernest, *Les Grands maîtres de la littérature russe au dix-neuvième siècle*, Paris, 1886.

———, *The Great Masters of Russian Literature in the Nineteenth Century*, tr. by Nathan Haskell Dole, New York, 1886.

Egan, Maurice Francis, *Modern Novels and Novelists*, New York, 1888.

Ellis, Havelock, *The New Spirit*, London, 1891.

Forster, E. M., *Aspects of the Novel*, New York, 1927.

Galsworthy, John, *Letters from John Galsworthy, 1900-1932*, ed. by Edward Garnett, London and New York, 1934.

George, W. L., *A Novelist on Novels*, London, 1918.

Gide, André, *Dostoievsky*, Paris, 1923.

———, *Dostoevsky*, tr. from the French, Introd. by Arnold Bennett, London, 1925.

Gissing, George, *Charles Dickens, A Critical Study*, New York, 1898.

———, *Letters to George Gissing and Members of his Family*, collected and arranged by Algernon and Ellen Gissing, London, 1927.

Goodwin, Geraint, *Conversations with George Moore*, London, 1929.

Gosse, Edmund, *Life and Letters of the Hon. Evan Charteris, K.C.*, London, 1931.

———, *Questions at Issue*, London, 1893.

Hamel, J., *England and Russia*, London, 1854.

Hapgood, Isabel F., *A Survey of Russian Literature with Selections*, New York, 1902.

Heller, Otto, *Prophets of Dissent: Essays on Maeterlinck, Strindberg, Nietzsche, and Tolstoy*, New York, 1918.

Howells, William Dean, *Criticism and Fiction*, New York, 1892.

Huneker, James Gibbons, *Essays by James Huneker*, Introduction by H. L. Mencken, New York, 1929.

———, *Ivory Apes and Peacocks*, New York, 1915.

———, *Letters of James Gibbons Huneker*, collected and edited by Josephine Huneker, New York, 1922.

Jackson, Holbrook, *The Eighteen Nineties*, London, 1913.

James, Henry, *The Letters of Henry James,* selected and edited by Percy Lubbock, 2 vls., New York, 1920.

————, *Notes on Novelists,* New York, 1914.

Kampmann, Theodorich, *Dostojewski in Deutschland,* Münster in Westfalen, 1931.

Kropotkin, Prince Peter A., *Ideals and Realities in Russian Literature,* London, 1905.

Lavrin, Yanko, *Dostoevsky and his Creation, A psycho-critical study,* London, 1920.

————, *Russian Literature,* "Benn's Sixpenny Library," No. 56, London, 1927.

————, *Studies in European Literature,* New York, 1930.

Lawrence, D. H., *The Letters of D. H. Lawrence,* Introd. by Aldous Huxley, New York, 1932.

————, *Pansies,* New York, 1929.

————, *Studies in Classic American Literature,* New York, 1923.

Lloyd, J. A. T., *A Great Russian Realist, Feodor Dostoieffsky,* New York, 1912.

Lombroso, Cesare, *The Man of Genius,* London, 1891.

Lubbock, Percy, *The Craft of Fiction,* London, 1921.

Lynd, Robert, *Books and Authors,* London, 1922.

Mackail, J. W., *Russia's Gift to the World,* London, etc., 1915.

Mair, G. H., *Modern English Literature,* New York, 1914.

Mann, Thomas, *Three Essays,* tr. from the German by H. T. Lowe-Porter, New York, 1929.

Mansfield, Katherine, *Letters,* ed. by J. M. Murry, London, 1928.

Marrot, Harold Vincent, *The Life and Letters of John Galsworthy,* London, 1935.

Masaryk, Thomas Garrigue, *The Spirit of Russia,* tr. from the German original by Eden and Cedar Paul, London and New York, 1919.

Meier-Graefe, Julius, *Dostoevsky, The Man and his Work,* tr. by H. M. Marks, New York, 1928.

Merejkowski, Dmitri, *Tolstoi as Man and Artist, With an Essay on Dostoievski,* New York and London, 1902.

Minssen, Hanns Friedrich, *Die französische Kritik und Dostojewski,* Hamburg, 1933.

Mirsky, D. S., *Contemporary Russian Literature, 1881-1925,* New York, 1926.

————, *The Intelligentsia of Great Britain,* tr. by Alec Brown, London, 1935.

————, *A History of Russian Literature* (from the Earliest Times to the Death of Dostoyevsky), New York, 1927.

————, *Russia, A Social History*, London, 1931.

Moore, George, *Avowals*, New York, 1926.

————, *Mike Fletcher*, London, 1889.

Muir, Edwin, *Latitudes*, New York, 1924.

————, *The Structure of the Novel*, London, 1928.

————, *Transition*, London, 1926.

Murry, John Middleton, *Between Two Worlds*, New York, 1936.

————, *The Evolution of an Intellectual*, "The Travellers Library," London, 1927.

————, *Fyodor Dostoevsky, A Critical Study*, London, 1916.

Neuschäffer, Walter, *Dostojewskij's Einfluss auf dem englischen Roman*, Heidleberg, 1935.

Nicoll, W. Robertson, *A Bookman's Letters*, New York, 1913.

Nordau, Max, *Degeneration*, New York, 1895.

Olgin, Moissaye J., ed., *A Guide to Russian Literature, 1820-1917*, New York, 1920.

Panin, Ivan, *Lectures on Russian Literature*, New York, 1889.

Pardo-Bazán, Emilia, *Russia—its People and its Literature*, tr. by Fanny Hale Gardiner, Chicago, 1890.

Phelps, William Lyon, *Essays on Russian Novelists*, New York, 1911.

Pierre-Quint, Léon, *André Gide, His Life and His Work*, tr. by Dorothy M. Richardson, New York, 1934.

Praz, Mario, *The Romantic Agony*, tr. by Angus Davidson, London, 1933.

Rascoe, Burton, *Titans of Literature (From Homer to the Present)*, New York and London, 1932.

Romein, Jan M., *Dostojewskij in de Westersche Kritiek*, Haarlem, 1924.

Rose, William and Isaacs, Jacob, *Contemporary Movements in European Literature*, London, 1928.

Saintsbury, George, *Periods of European Literature*, vol. 12, "The Later Nineteenth Century," New York, 1907.

Scott, A. G., ed., *Problems of Soviet Literature*, Reports and Speeches at the First Soviet Writers' Congress, New York, 1934.

Seidman, Moisei, *F. M. Dostoevsky v Zapadnoii Literature*, Odessa, 1911.

Shakhnovski, *A Short History of Russian Literature*, tr. Serge Tomkeyeff, London and New York, 1921.

Shestov, Lev, *Dostoevsky i Nietzsche (Philosophia Tragedii)*, Berlin, 1922.

——, *Dostojewski und Nietzsche, Philosophie der Tragödie*, übers. von R. von Walter, Köln, 1924.

——, *In Job's Balances (On the Sources of the Eternal Truths)*, tr. by Camilla Coventry and C. A. McCartney, London, 1929.

Simmons, Ernest J., *English Literature and Culture in Russia*, Cambridge, 1935.

Soloviev, Eugenii, *Dostoievsky, His Life and Literary Activity*, tr. from the Russian by C. J. Hogarth, London and New York, 1916.

Spengler, Oswald, *The Decline of the West*, tr. Charles Francis Atkinson, New York, 1928.

Starr, Meredith, *The Future of the Novel*, London, 1921.

Stevenson, R. L., *The Letters of Robert Louis Stevenson to his Family and Friends*, ed. Sidney Colvin, New York, 1899.

Symons, Arthur, *The Symbolist Movement in Literature*, London, 1899.

Thorndike, Ashley H., *Literature in a Changing Age*, New York, 1920.

Traill, H. D., *The New Fiction and other Essays on Literary Subjects*, London, 1897.

Turner, Charles Edward, *The Modern Novelists of Russia*, London, 1890.

——, *Studies in Russian Literature*, London, 1882.

Vogüé, Vte. Melchior de, *Le roman russe*, Paris, 1886.

——, *The Russian Novelists*, tr. by Jane Loring Edmunds, Boston, 1887.

Waliszewski, Kuzimierz, *A History of Russian Literature*, New York, 1900.

Warner, Charles Dudley, ed., *Library of the World's Best Literature*, vol. 8, New York, 1896.

Waugh, Arthur, *Tradition and Change*, London, 1919.

Wiener, Leo, *Anthology of Russian Literature*, New York and London, 1903.

Wilson, Edmund, *Axel's Castle*, New York, 1931.

——, *I Thought of Daisy*, New York, 1929.

Wolkonsky, Prince Serge, *Pictures of Russian History and Russian Literature*, London, 1898.

Woolf, Virginia, *The Common Reader*, New York, 1925.

Yarmolinsky, Avrahm, *Dostoevsky, A Life*, New York, 1934.

——, *Dostoievsky, A Study in his Ideology*, New York, 1921.

Zola, Emile, *Le roman expérimental,* Paris, 1887.

Zweig, Stefan, *Three Masters (Balzac, Dickens, Dostoeffsky),* tr. Eden and Cedar Paul, New York, 1930.

II. SIGNED ARTICLES AND REVIEWS

Baring, Maurice, "Tolstoy and Turgeniev," *The Quarterly Review,* CCXI (1909), 180-202.

Bennett, Arnold, Introduction to Gide, *Dostoevsky,* 1925.

———, "Books and Persons," under pseudonym Jacob Tonson. *The New Age,* VI n.s. (1910), 518, 519.

Bennett, Nellie B., "Feodor Dostoievski," *Methodist Review,* CV (1922), 906-916.

Beresford, J. D., "Psycho-analysis and the Novel," *The Freeman,* I (1920), 35-39; also in *London Mercury,* I (1920), 426-434.

Bierbaum, Otto Julius, "Dostoyeffsky and Nietzsche," *The Hibbert Journal,* IX (1911), 823-837.

Blennerhasset, W. L., "The Perennial Friend, A Page out of the Life of Dostoievsky," *Cornhill Magazine,* LXV (1928), 730-738.

Boner, E. G., "Pessimism in the Russian Novel," tr. from the Italian of *Nuova Antologia, The Chautauquan,* XXII (1896), 426.

Bourne, Randolph, "The Immanence of Dostoevsky," *The Dial,* LXIII (1917), 24, 25.

Brinton, Christian, "Slavonic Silhouettes," *The Critic,* XXXVII (1900), 416-426.

Briusov, Valerii, "Continental Literature: Russia," *The Athenæum,* II (1902), 24, 25.

Burchell, S. C., "Dostoieffsky and the Sense of Guilt," *Psychoanalytic Review,* XVII (1930), 195-207.

Burton, R. G., Capt., "An Appreciation of Russian Fictional Literature," *Westminster Review,* CXLIV (1895), 539-544.

Carr, E. H., "Dostoevsky and a Russian Minx," *Fortnightly Review,* CXXXII (1929), 525-533.

———, *Slavonic Review,* IX (1931), 753, 754.

———, "The Philosophy of Dostoevsky," *The Spectator,* CLIII (1934), 684.

———, "Turgenev and Dostoyevsky," *The Slavonic Review,* VIII (1929), 156-163.

———, "Was Dostoevsky an Epileptic?" *The Slavonic Review,* IX (1930), 424-431.

Church, Richard, "Daylight on Dostoevsky," *The New Statesman and Nation,* Supplement, II (1931), xiv, xvi.

————, "Dostoevsky," *The New Age,* XXXIX (1926), 25, 26.

————, "The Warp and Woof of Genius," *The Spectator,* CXLIV (1930), 95.

————, "A Whiff of Sanity," *The Spectator,* CXLVII (1931), 548, 549.

Congreve, R. H., "Readers and Writers," *The New Age,* XVIII (1916), 372.

Dole, Nathan Haskell, "Contemporary Russian Literature," *The Chautauquan,* VIII (1888), 465.

Donlin, George Bernard, "Dostoieffsky," *The Dial,* LVIII (1915), 5-7.

Ellis, Havelock, "The Genius of Russia," *The Contemporary Review,* LXXX (1901), 419-433.

————, "The Supreme Russian," *The New Statesman,* IX (1917), 590.

Flenley, Ralph, "The Novels of Fedor Dostoieffsky," *McGill University Magazine,* XIII (1914), 648-661.

Florovsky, Anton, "Dostoyevsky and the Slavs," *The Slavonic Review,* IX (1930), 411-423.

Forbes, Nevill, "Dostoyevsky," *The Russian Review,* I (1912), 38-59.

Freeman, John, "The Wives of the Russians," *London Mercury,* XIX (1928), 176-183.

————, *London Mercury,* VIII (1923), 211.

————, *London Mercury,* XVIII (1928), 214.

Freud, Siegmund, "Dostoevski and Parricide," tr. by D. F. Taft, *The Realist,* I (1929), 18-33.

Garnett, Edward, "A Literary Causerie: Dostoievsky," *The Academy,* LXXI (1906), 202, 203.

Gates, Barrington, "Fuss and Bother," *Nation and Athenæum,* XLVI (1930), 808.

Gosse, Edmund, "The Limits of Realism in Fiction," *The Forum,* IX (1890), 391-400.

————, "Count Lyof Tolstoi," *The Contemporary Review,* XCIV (1908), 270-285.

————, "Melchior de Vogüé," *The Contemporary Review,* XCVII (1910), 568-579.

Grudin, Louis, "Dostoyevski" (verse), *Broom*, IV (1922), 12, 13.

Heard, John, Jr., "Tourgueneff, Tolstoi, and Dostoyevsky," *The Critic*, XI (1887), 253.

Hesse, Hermann, "The Downfall of Europe—'The Brothers Karamazoff,'" "Thoughts on Dostoevsky's 'Idiot,'" tr. by Stephen Hudson, *The English Review*, XXXV (1922), 108-120, 190-196; also in *The Dial*, LXXII (1922), 607-618; LXXIII (1922), 199-204.

Hewlett, Maurice, *London Mercury*, V (1922), 551.

Hodgetts, E. A. Brayley, *The Academy*, XXXII (1887), 214.

———, *The Academy* XXIII (1883), 37, 38.

Irving, Laurence, Introduction to *Crime and Punishment*, Everyman edition, pages vii-xiii.

Joffe, Judah L., "Russian Literature and its Latest Historian," *The Bookman*, XII (1900), 43-48, 373-376.

Katz, Gershon, "Articulate Russia," *Westminster Review*, CLXXX (1913), 627-634.

Knowlton, Edgar C., "Stevenson and Dostoevski," *Modern Philology*, XIV (1916), 449-454.

Kropotkin, Prince P. A., "The Exile in Siberia," *The Nineteenth Century*, XV (1884), 475.

Lanin, E. B., "Russian Characteristics," *Fortnightly Review*, LII (1889), 410, 574, 722, 854; reprinted, *Living Age*, CLXXXIII.

Lavrin, Janko, "Dostoyevsky and Certain of his Problems," *New Age*, XXII (1918), 229, 230, 252-4, 272-3, 280-290, 312-314, 327-9, 354, 372-4, 389, 390, 410-412, 465; XXIII (1918), 7.

———, "Dostoyevsky and Proust," *The Slavonic Review*, V (1927), 609-627.

Lawrence, D. H., Foreword to Shestov, L., *All Things Are Possible*, tr. by S. S. Koteliansky, New York, 1921.

———, Introduction to *The Grand Inquisitor*, tr. by S. S. Koteliansky, London, 1930.

Lloyd, J. A. T., *Fortnightly Review*, CXXX (1928), 859, 860.

———, "Dostoievsky and Flaubert," *The Fortnightly Review*, CXVI (1921), 1017-1027.

———, "The Russian Novelists of the Nineteenth Century," *The Fortnightly Review*, CXIV (1920), 854-864.

Lomas, John, "Dostoevsky," *MacMillan's Magazine*, LV (1887), 187-198.

Lossky, N., *The Slavonic and East European Review*, XV (1936), 232.

Lucas, F. L., *The Nation and Athenæum*, XXXIII (1923), 158.

Lynd, Robert, "Dostoevsky," *The New Statesman*, VII (1916), 518, 519.

MacCarthy, Desmond, "Drama and Dostoevsky," *The New Statesman*, XXVII (1926), 672, 673.

McCune, Alice, "Dostoyevsky's Technique in Bringing out Character," *University of California Chronicle*, XXXIII (1931), 221-230.

McDowall, Arthur, "The Possessed and Bolshevism," *The London Mercury*, XVII (1928), 52-61.

Maetzu, Ramiro de, "Dostoyevsky the Manichaen," *New Age* XXII (1918), 449-451.

———, "Let Us Be Whole!" *New Age*, XXII (1918), 497.

Maisky, J. M., "The New Soviet Literature," *The Contemporary Review*, CXLVII (1935), 401-405.

Manning, Clarence A., "Dostoyevsky and Modern Russian Literature," *The Sewanee Review*, XXX (1922), 286-297.

———, "Dostoyevsky and Scythism," *The Sewanee Review*, XXXIII (1925), 134-148.

Mansfield, Katherine, "Some Aspects of Dostoevsky," *The Athenæum*, II (1919), 1256.

Marks, Duncan, "The Aunt, the Dog, and the Nose—from the Russian of Dostchekovski," *New Statesman*, XIX (1922), 466.

Marshall, H. P., *The London Mercury*, XIII (1926), 659, 660.

Matthews, Brander, "New Trials for Old Favorites," *The Forum*, XXV (1898), 758.

Meredith, Hugh Owen, "A Philistine on Dostoevsky," *New Statesman*, Spring Bk. Supplement, XX (1923), viii-x.

Mirsky, D. S., "The Literature of Bolshevik Russia," *London Mercury*, V (1922), 276-285.

———, "Russian Literature since 1917," *Contemporary Review*, CXXII (1922), 205.

———, "Dostoevsky," *Nation and Athenæum*, XXXIX (1926), 180-182.

———, *The London Mercury*, XIV (1926), 542.

———, Introduction to *The Letters of Dostoevsky to his Wife*, 1930.

———, Preface to Carr, *Dostoevsky*, 1934.

————, "Dostojevskij in Frankreich und England," *Slavische Rundschau*, III (1931), 310-318.

Montgomery, Neil, "The Man, Dostoyevsky," *New Age*, XLIV (1928), 54.

Montgomery, Richard, "Dr. Adler on Dostoevsky," *New Age*, XL (1926), 54.

————, "Freud, Adler and Dostoevski," *New Age*, XLV (1929), 115, 116.

Moran, Helen, *London Mercury*, XXV (1932), 310.

Morfill, W. R., *The Academy*, XXXVII (1890), 438.

————, "Poor Folk," *The Academy* XLVI (1894), 209.

Muir, Edwin, "A German Estimate of Dostoevsky," *Nation and Athenæum*, XLII (1928), 972, 974.

Murry, J. Middleton, *Nation and Athenæum*, XXX (1921), 505.

————, "The Crisis in Dostoevsky," *Nation and Athenæum*, XXXII (1922), 357, 358.

Oliver, D. E., "Fyodor Michailovitch Dostoevsky," *The Manchester Quarterly*, XXXVIII (1919), 94-116.

Perry, Thomas Sergeant, "Russian Novels," *Scribner's Magazine*, I (1887), 252-256.

Porter, Alan, "Dostoievsky and the Modern World," *The Spectator*, CXL (1928), 385, 386.

————, "Dostoyevsky's Marriage," *The Spectator*, CXLI (1928), 823, 824.

Preev, Zinovy N., "Russia and the Slav Ideal," *Fortnightly Review*, CVII (1917), 606-616.

Preston, Harriet Waters, "The Spell of the Russian Novelists," *The Atlantic Monthly*, LX (1887), 199-213.

Rapoport, Semon, "Dostoevsky," *Contemporary Review*, CXLI (1932), 765-770.

Richmond, Kenneth, "Out of School," *New Age*, XXII (1918), 451.

Riza-Zade, Fatima, "Dostoevsky i Sovremennaya Franzuskaya Literatura," *Petchat i Revolutsia*, VI (1927), 34-52.

————, "Dostoevsky v Zapadnoii Kritike," *Literatura i Marxism*, III (1929), 139-176.

Rudwin, Maximilian J., "The Gloom and Glory of Russian Literature," *The Open Court*, XXXII (1918), 390-407.

Salmon, Arthur L., "A Russian Pietist, Fedor Dostojevski," *Poet Lore*, VI (1894), 309-312.

Schiller, F. P., "Legenda o Dostoevskom v. Zapadno-Evropiéskoii Literaturnoii Kritiké," *Literatura i Marxism*, V (1928), 95-106.

Schwartz, Dr. M., "Dostoievsky and Judaism," *The Jewish Review*, #4 (1933), 57-64.

Seccombe, Thomas, *Living Age*, CCLXXXIX (1916), 436-438.

Sharp, William, *The Academy*, XXX (1886), 290.

———, *The Academy*, XXXI (1887), 270.

———, *The Academy*, XXXIV (1888), 68.

Shaw, Charles, Gray, "Dostoievsky's Mystical Terror," *The North American Review*, CCVII (1918), 246-256.

Shipp, Horace, "The Novel and the Play," *The English Review*, XLIII (1926), 469-470.

Smith, Stephen, and Isotoff, Andrei, "Abnormal from Within: Dostoevsky," *The Psychoanalytic Review*, XXII (1935), #4; also in *University of Oregon Publications*, V. #2 (*Studies in Psychology*, I, Bul. 7), 1935, 361-397.

Squire, J. C., *New Statesman*, IV (1914), 61, 62.

Struve, Gleb, "Literature in Soviet Russia," *Nineteenth Century*, CVII (1935), 228.

Thorn, The Rev. George W., "Dostoevsky as a Religious Teacher," *The Contemporary Review*, CVIII (1915), 220-229.

———, also *Living Age*, CCLXXXVI, 665-672.

———, "Dostoevsky as a Psychologist," *The London Quarterly Review*, XI (1917), 177-188.

———, "Sidelights on the Psychology of the Russian Revolution from Dostoevsky," *The Contemporary Review*, CXIII (1918), 695-700.

Tsakni, M., "Mystical Pessimism in Russia," *Contemporary Review*, LIII (1888), 406.

Turner, C. E., "Nicholas Alexeivitch Nekrasoff," *Fortnightly Review*, XXXVI (1881), 499-512.

Vacquier, Tatiana, "Dostoevsky and Gide," *Sewanee Review*, XXXVII (1929), 478-489.

Vinogradoff, Paul, "Some Elements of the Russian Revolution," *Quarterly Review*, CCVIII (1917), 184-200.

Volynsky, A., "Dostoevsky and Tolstoy," tr. by C. E. Beckhofer, *The New Age*, XX (1916), 60, 61.

Waldman, Milton, *The London Mercury*, XIV (1926), 644.

Waliszewski, K., *The Bookman*, XII (1900), 373-376.

Wallace, William, "New Novels," *The Academy,* XXIX (1886), 306.

West, Rebecca, "Redemption and Dostoevsky," *New Republic,* III (1915), 115-118.

Wilcox, E. H., "Dostoyevski as seen by his Daughter," *Fortnightly Review,* CXV (1921), 229-239.

Wilkinson, Clennell, *London Mercury,* XXI (1930), 378.

Williams, C., "The Ethics of Three Russian Novelists," *International Journal of Ethics,* XXXV (1925), 217-237.

Wilson, H. Schütz, "The Russian Novelist Dostojewsky," *The Academy,* XXVIII (1885), 395.

Woolf, Leonard, "A Fly is Struggling in the Web," *Nation and Athenæum,* XLIV (1928), 294.

———, "The World of Books—Russian Literature," *Nation and Athenæum,* XLVI (1929), 318.

Wright, C. Hagberg, "The Meaning of Russian Literature," *The Quarterly Review,* CCXXXV (1921), 102-120.

———, "The Rebirth of Russia," *Contemporary Review,* CXIII (1918), 361-368.

Yarmolinsky, Avrahm, Introduction to *The Brothers Karamazov,* Limited Editions Club, 1933.

III. UNSIGNED ARTICLES AND REVIEWS

The Academy, IX (1876), 120; XIX (1881), 136; XIX (1881), 273; XXI (1882), 211 [Signed "M. A."]; LXIII (1902), 685; LXIV (1903), 14, 15; LXXXIII (1912), 448; LXXXVI (1914), 11.

American Notes and Queries, I (1888), 55.

The Athenæum, December 25, 1875, p. 874; April 2, 1881, p. 455; December 31, 1881, p. 893; September 8, 1883, pp. 305, 306; January 16, 1886, pp. 99, 100; February 26, 1887, p. 281; April 30, 1887, p. 573; June 4, 1887, p. 735; September 17, 1887, p. 365; October 22, 1887, p. 534; May 21, 1898, p. 655; February 21, 1903, p. 238; January 25, 1908, p. 99; March 19, 1910, p. 339; November 19, 1910, pp. 635, 636; June 1, 1912, pp. 613, 614; July 19, 1913, p. 61; January 17, 1914, p. 89; December 26, 1914, pp. 663, 664; March 6, 1915, p. 211; September 18, 1915, p. 190; February 1916, p. 85; September 1916, p. 430; April 1916, p. 187; August 1916, p. 381; December 3, 1920, p. 758.

Blackwood's Magazine, CXXX (1881), 29; CLXXXIII (1908), 298-307.

The Calendar of Modern Letters, I (1925), 44-52.

The Contemporary Review, Literary Supplement, XXXVII (1880), 165 [Signed "T. S."]; XCVII (1910), 1-4 [Signed "Literatus"]; CXVI (1919), 346, 347; CXXIX (1926), 211, 216.

The Criterion, I (1923), 217.

The Critic, XI (1887), 138.

Current Literature, XLIX (1910), 92-96.

Current Opinion, LV (1913), 433, 434; LVIII (1915), 48, 49; LXIV (1918), 179-183; LXIV (1918), 209, 210; LXVI (1919), 116.

The Dial, LXV (1918), 510.

The Edinburgh Review, LII (1831), 322-325; CCXLI (1925), 405; CCXLIII (1926), 199.

The English Review, XXIII (1916), 94; XXIII (1916), 287; XXXII (1921), 557, 558.

Foreign Quarterly Review, I (1827), 595-631; VIII (1831), 117-139; XXX (1842), 242-250.

The Independent, LXXVI (1913), 177; XCIII (1918), 150.

The Literary World, XXXIII (1886), 421; XXXV (1887), 297; XXXVI (1887), 261; XXXVIII (1888), 74; LI (1894), 196; LXII (1900), 355; LXXV (1909), 39; LXXVI (1910), 134; LXXVIII (1912), 140; LXXVIII (1912), 277; LXXX (1914), 309; LXXXI (1915), 54.

The Literary World (New York), XVII (1886), 327; XVII (1886), 364, 365; XX (1889), 415.

The London Mercury, VII (1922), 5; XII (1925), 563.

The London Quarterly Review, LXX (1888), 55-73.

The London Times, July 10, 1913, p. 294b; November 11, 1921, p. 9d; June 16, 1922, p. 16c; June 13, 1922, p. 14d; February 22, 1922; p. 11; October 25, 1923, p. 11d; April 14, 1925, p. 8d; August 24, 1926, p. 8c; October 16, 1928, p. 14c; November 13, 1928, p. 22b.

The London Times Literary Supplement, July 4, 1912, pp. 269, 270; October 29, 1914, p. 1478; March 4, 1915, p. 73c; September 23, 1915, p. 319c; March 9, 1916, p. 114; August 24, 1916, p. 403; February 22, 1917, p. 91; October 17, 1918, p. 494; October 23, 1919, p. 586; December 9, 1920, p. 811; January 12, 1922, p. 25; November 2, 1922, p. 702; May 17, 1923, p. 336; March 25, 1926, p. 232; March 22, 1928, p. 211; December

20, 1928, pp. 997, 998; October 3, 1929, p. 764; June 5, 1930, p. 456; June 26, 1930, p. 530; September 11, 1930, p. 712; February 3, 1931, p. 94; October 8, 1931, p. 773; February 4, 1932, p. 72; March 2, 1933, p. 148; January 3, 1935, p. 7.

Monthly Review, XCVI (1821), 127-139.

The Nation, XLIII (1886), 312, 313; LXXXVIII (1909), 630; VII (1910), 256; XI (1912), 96; XIII (1913), 575, 576; XIV (1913), 444; XIV (1914), 758; XVI (1914), 146, 148; XIX (1916), 183-5; XXV (1919), 650, 652.

The Nation (New York), XLIII (1886), 354, 355; XLV (1887), 188; LIX (1894), 181.

The Nation and Athenæum, XXXVIII (1926), 551; XLIV (1928), 141.

National Quarterly Review (New York), IX (1864), 43-70; XXIV (1872), 347-369.

The New Age, XXI (1917), 69; XXI (1917), 254; XXXII (1922), 79.

The New Criterion, IV (1926), 552-562; IV (1926), 791, 792.

The New Statesman, II (1914), 796; XVIII (1921), 326; XXI (1923), 682, 683 [Signed "B. H"]; XXX (1928), 660 [Signed "Affable Hawk"]; XXXIV (1930), 504.

The Outlook, LVII (1926), 193; CXVII (1917), 614.

Public Opinion, IV (1887), 21.

Public Opinion (New York), LI (1887), 422.

The Quarterly Review, CXLIX (1880), 518-48.

The Review of Reviews, XXIX (1904), 623.

The Saturday Review, LV (1883), 249, 250; LXII (1886), 272; LXII (1886), 766; LXIII (1887), 70; LXIII (1887), 58; LXIII (1887), 485; LXIV (1887), 457; LXIV (1887), 563; LXV (1888), 740; LXVI (1888), 190; LXIX (1890), 298; XCII (1901), 86, 88; CXIII (1912), 753; CXVIII (1914), 419, 420; CXX (1915), 306, 307; CXXI (1916), 259, 260; CXXIII (1917), 343; CXXIV (1917), 311; CXXXIV (1922), 792; CXXXIX (1925), 592; CXLIX (1930), 170.

The Scottish Review, X (1887), 199.

The Spectator, LVI (1883), 1484; LIX (1886), 937, 939; LX (1887), 595; LX (1887), 1575; LXIV (1890), 696, 697; LXXIII (1894), 83, 84; LXXXIV (1900), 421; CIV (1910), 629, 630; CIX (1912), 451, 452; CXII (1914), 610, 611; CXIII (1914), 596, 597; CXVII (1916), 241; CXXVI (1921), 305,

306; CXXVIII (1922), 115; CXXX (1923), 1045, 1046; CXXXVII (1926), 342.

Temple Bar, LXXXIX (1890), 210-222; XCI (1891), 243-249.

The Westminster Review, CVIII (1877), 215-224; CXV (1881), 582; CXXVI (1886), 298; CXXVIII (1887), 1056; CXLV (1894), 355.

IV. TRANSLATIONS

Dostoevsky's novels were translated by Constance Garnett from 1912-1921, as follows:

> The Brothers Karamazov—1912.
> The Idiot—1913.
> Crime and Punishment—1914.
> The Possessed—1914.
> The House of the Dead—1915.
> The Insulted and Injured—1915.
> A Raw Youth—1916.
> The Eternal Husband, and Other Stories—(includes The Double and A Gentle Spirit)—1917.
> The Gambler and Other Stories—(includes Poor People and The Landlady)—1917.
> White Nights and Other Stories—1918.
> An Honest Thief and Other Stories—1919.
> The Friend of the Family; or, Stepanchikovo and its Inhabitants, and Another Story—(Nyetochka Nyezvanov)—1920.

Other Translations—by Frederick Whishaw:

> Crime and Punishment—1886
> Injury and Insult—1886.
> The Idiot—1887.
> The Friend of the Family and The Gambler—1887
> The Uncle's Dream and The Permanent Husband—1888

> Buried Alive; Ten Years Penal in Siberia—tr. Marie von Thilo —1881
> Prison Life in Siberia—tr. H. Sutherland Edwards—1887
> Poor Folk—tr. Lena Milman—(Preface by George Moore)— 1894

Pages from the Journal of an Author—tr. S. S. Koteliansky and
J. Middleton Murry—1916

A Christmas Tree and a Wedding, and An Honest Thief—tr.
Nevill Forbes—1917

*Stavrogin's Confession and The Plan of the Life of a Great
Sinner*—tr. S. S Koteliansky and Virginia Woolf—1922

The Grand Inquistitor—tr. S. S. Koteliansky—(Introduction by
D. H. Lawrence)—1930

Letters, Diaries, Reminiscences:

Letters to his Family and Friends—tr. Ethel Colburn Mayne—
1914

Letters and Reminiscences—tr. S. S. Koteliansky and J. Middleton Murry—1923.

Letters to his Wife—tr. Elizabeth Hill and Doris Mudie—(Introduction by D. S. Mirsky)—1930.

New Dostoevsky Letters—tr. S. S. Koteliansky—1929.

The Diary of Dostoevsky's Wife—tr. from the German by M.
Pemberton—1928.

Dostoevsky Portrayed by his Wife: The Diary and Reminiscences of Mme. Dostoevsky—tr. S. S. Koteliansky—1926.

INDEX